Prentice Hall

LITERATURE
Timeless Voices, Timeless Themes

Reader's Companion

GOLD LEVEL

Prentice
Hall

Upper Saddle River, New Jersey
Glenview, Illinois
Needham, Massachusetts

ISBN 0-13-062379-2

1 2 3 4 5 6 7 8 9 10   05 04 03 02 01

Acknowledgments

Grateful acknowledgment is made to the following for permission to reprint copyrighted material:

The Estate of Margaret Walker Alexander
"Memory" from *For My People* by Margaret Walker, copyright 1942 Yale University Press.

Susan Bergholz Literary Services
From "A Celebration of Grandfathers." Copyright © 1983 by Rudolfo Anaya. First published in *New Mexico Magazine*, March 1983. All rights reserved.

Brandt & Hochman Literary Agents, Inc.
"The Most Dangerous Game" by Richard Connell. Copyright, 1924 by Richard Connell. Copyright renewed © 1952 by Louise Fox Connell.

Doubleday, a division of Random House, Inc.
"The Machine That Won the War," copyright © 1961 by Mercury Press, Inc., from *Isaac Asimov: The Complete Stories, Vol. I* by Isaac Asimov. "The Gift of the Magi," from *The Complete Works of O. Henry* by O. Henry. Published by Press Publications Company.

Harcourt, Inc.
"A Lincoln Preface," copyright 1953 by Carl Sandburg and renewed 1981 by Margaret Sandburg, Janet Sandburg, and Helga Sandburg Crile.

Rosemary Thurber and The Barbara Hogenson Agency, Inc.
"The Secret Life of Walter Mitty" from *My World—And Welcome To It* copyright © 1942 by James Thurber; copyright renewed © 1971 by James Thurber. All rights reserved.

Houghton Mifflin Company
Excerpt from *Silent Spring* (pp. 1–3) by Rachel Carson. Copyright © 1962 by Rachel L. Carson, renewed 1990 by Roger Christie. All rights reserved.

James R. Hurst
"The Scarlet Ibis" by James Hurst, published in *The Atlantic Monthly*, July 1960. Copyright © 1988 by James Hurst.

International Creative Management, Inc.
"Single Room, Earth View" by Sally Ride, published in the April/May 1986 issue of *Air & Space/Smithsonian Magazine*, published by The Smithsonian Institution.

The Heirs to the Estate of Martin Luther King, Jr. c/o Writer's House
"I Have a Dream" from *The Words of Martin Luther King, Jr.* Copyright 1963 by Martin Luther King, Jr., copyright renewed 1991 by Coretta Scott King.

Andrew MacAndrew
"The Necklace" from *Boule de Suif and Selected Stories* by Guy de Maupassant, translated by Andrew MacAndrew. Translation copyright © 1964 by Andrew MacAndrew.

New American Library, a division of Penguin Putnam, Inc.
From *The Tragedy of Romeo and Juliet* by William Shakespeare, edited by J. A. Bryant, Jr. Published by New American Library, a division of Penguin Putnam, Inc.

The New York Times
"Woman's Work" by Julia Alvarez, published in *The New York Times*, September 5, 1994. Copyright © 1994 by The New York Times Co.

Orchard Books, an imprint of Scholastic, Inc.
"Checkouts" from *A Couple of Kooks and Other Stories About Love* by Cynthia Rylant. Published by Orchard Books, an imprint of Scholastic, Inc. Copyright © 1990 by Cynthia Rylant.

G.P. Putnam's Sons, a division of Penguin Putnam, Inc.
From "Rules of the Game" from *The Joy Luck Club* by Amy Tan, copyright © 1989 by Amy Tan. "Go Deep to the Sewer" from *Childhood* by Bill Cosby. Copyright © 1991 by William H. Cosby, Jr.

University Press of New England
Gary Soto, "The Talk", from *A Summer Life* © 1990 by University Press of New England.

Viking Penguin, a division of Penguin Putnam, Inc.
From *The Road Ahead* by Bill Gates. Copyright © 1995 by William H. Gates III. "Old Man of the Temple", from *Under The Banyan Tree* by R. K. Narayan, copyright © 1985 by R. K. Narayan. "The Interlopers" from *The Complete Short Stories of Saki* by Saki (H. H. Munro). Published by The Viking Press.

Vintage Anchor Publishing
Excerpts from the *Odyssey* by Homer, translated by R. Fitzgerald. Copyright © 1961, 1963 by Robert Fitzgerald and renewed 1989 by Benedict R. C. Fitzgerald.

Note: Every effort has been made to locate the copyright owner of material reprinted in this book. Omissions brought to our attention will be corrected in subsequent editions.

Contents

**Part 1: Selections With Interactive
Reading Support and Practice.** 1

Unit 1: Spine Tinglers
The Cask of Amontillado Edgar Allan Poe. 4
The Most Dangerous Game Richard Connell 12
Casey at the Bat Ernest Lawrence Thayer 32

Unit 2: Challenges and Choices
from **A Lincoln Preface** Carl Sandburg 37
"I Have a Dream" Martin Luther King, Jr. 44
Old Man of the Temple R. K. Narayan 47

Unit 3: Moments of Discovery
Rules of the Game Amy Tan 54
Checkouts Cynthia Rylant 66
The Interlopers Saki (H. H. Munro) 71

Unit 4: The Lighter Side
The Secret Life of Walter Mitty James Thurber 77
Go Deep to the Sewer Bill Cosby 84
Talk Harold Courlander and George Herzog 89

Unit 5: Visions of the Future
from **The Road Ahead** Bill Gates 93
The Machine That Won the War Isaac Asimov 98
from **Silent Spring** Rachel Carson 104

Unit 6: Short Stories
The Gift of the Magi O. Henry 107
The Scarlet Ibis James Hurst 113
The Necklace Guy de Maupassant 125

Unit 7: Nonfiction
Single Room, Earth View Sally Ride 134
On Summer Lorraine Hansberry 140
A Celebration of Grandfathers Rudolfo Anaya 145

Unit 8: Drama

The Tragedy of Romeo and Juliet William Shakespeare 153

Unit 9: Poetry

Memory Margaret Walker 160

Woman's Work Julia Alvarez 162

The Raven Edgar Allan Poe 164

The Seven Ages of Man William Shakespeare 171

Unit 10: The Epic

from the **Odyssey** Homer 174

Part 2: Selection Summaries
With Alternative Reading Strategies **187**

Unit 1: Spine Tinglers

The Cask of Amontillado Edgar Allan Poe 189

The Most Dangerous Game Richard Connell 190

Casey at the Bat Ernest Lawrence Thayer 191

The Birds Daphne du Maurier 192

The Red-headed League Sir Arthur Conan Doyle 193

The Listeners Walter de la Mare 194

Beware: Do Not Read This Poem Ishmael Reed 194

Echo Henriqueta Lisboa, translated by Hélcio Veiga Costa 194

Caucasian Mummies Mystify Chinese Keay Davidson 195

Unit 2: Challenges and Choices

from **A Lincoln Preface** Carl Sandburg 196

"I Have a Dream" Martin Luther King, Jr. 197

from **Rosa Parks: My Story** Rosa Parks with Jim Haskins 197

There Is a Longing Chief Dan George 197

I Hear America Singing Walt Whitman 197

The Golden Kite, the Silver Wind Ray Bradbury 198

The Road Not Taken Robert Frost 199

New Directions Maya Angelou 199

To be of use Marge Piercy 199

Old Man of the Temple R. K. Narayan 200

Perseus Edith Hamilton 201

Slam, Dunk, & Hook Yusef Komunyakaa 202

The Spearthrower Lillian Morrison 202

Shoulders Naomi Shihab Nye 202

Unit 3: Moments of Discovery

Children in the Woods Barry Lopez 203

Rules of the Game Amy Tan 204

Checkouts Cynthia Rylant 205

Fifteen William Stafford 205

Sympathy Paul Laurence Dunbar 206

Caged Bird Maya Angelou 206

We never know how high we are Emily Dickinson 206

from **In My Place** Charlayne Hunter-Gault 206

The Interlopers Saki (H. H. Munro) 207

The Rug Merchant James A. Michener 208

Combing Gladys Cardiff 209

Women Alice Walker 209

maggie and milly and molly and may E. E. Cummings 209

Astonishment Wisława Szymborska 209

Unit 4: The Lighter Side

The Secret Life of Walter Mitty James Thurber 210

The Inspector-General Anton Chekhov, adapted by Michael Frayn . . . 211

Go Deep to the Sewer Bill Cosby 212

Fly Away Ralph Helfer 212

An Entomological Study of Apartment 4A Patricia Volk 213

Macavity: The Mystery Cat T. S. Eliot 214

Problems with Hurricanes Victor Hernández Cruz 214

Jabberwocky Lewis Carroll 214

Talk Harold Courlander and George Herzog 215

One Ordinary Day, With Peanuts Shirley Jackson 216

Unit 5: Visions of the Future

from **The Road Ahead** Bill Gates 217

The Machine That Won the War Isaac Asimov 218

Fire and Ice Robert Frost 219

All Watched Over by Machines of Loving Grace Richard Brautigan . . . 219

"There Will Come Soft Rains" (War Time) Sara Teasdale 219

The Horses Edwin Muir 219

"If I Forget Thee, Oh Earth . . ." Arthur C. Clarke 220

from **Silent Spring** Rachel Carson 220

To the Residents of A.D. 2029 Bryan Woolley 220

Gifts Shu Ting, translated by Donald Finkel 221

Glory and Hope Nelson Mandela 221

Unit 6: Short Stories

The Gift of the Magi O. Henry 222

Sonata for Harp and Bicycle Joan Aiken 223

The Scarlet Ibis James Hurst 224

Blues Ain't No Mockin Bird Toni Cade Bambara 225

Uncle Marcos Isabel Allende 225

The Man to Send Rain Clouds Leslie Marmon Silko 226

The Invalid's Story Mark Twain 226

The Necklace Guy de Maupassant 227

The Harvest Tomás Rivera 227

Unit 7: Nonfiction

Single Room, Earth View Sally Ride 228

The Washwoman Isaac Bashevis Singer 229

On Summer Lorraine Hansberry 229

A Celebration of Grandfathers Rudolfo Anaya 229

from **A White House Diary** Lady Bird Johnson 230

Arthur Ashe Remembered John McPhee 230

Georgia O'Keeffe Joan Didion 230

Understanding Comics Scott McCloud 231

Earhart Redux Alex Chadwick 232

In These Girls, Hope Is a Muscle (Book Review) Steve Gietschier 232

In These Girls, Hope Is a Muscle (Book Jacket) 232

Unit 8: Drama

The Dancers Horton Foote 233

The Tragedy of Romeo and Juliet William Shakespeare

    Act I 234

    Act II 235

    Act III 236

    Act IV 237

    Act V 238

Unit 9: Poetry

I Wandered Lonely as a Cloud William Wordsworth 239

The Eagle Alfred, Lord Tennyson 240

"Hope" is the thing with feathers— Emily Dickinson 240

Dream Deferred Langston Hughes 240

Dreams Langston Hughes 240

Blackberry Eating Galway Kinnell 241

Memory Margaret Walker 241

Woman's Work Julia Alvarez 241

Meciendo ("Rocking") Gabriela Mistral 241

Eulogy for a Hermit Crab Pattiann Rogers 241

Uphill Christina Rossetti 242

Summer Walter Dean Myers 242

Ecclesiastes 3:1–8 The King James Bible 242

The Bells Edgar Allan Poe 242

The Raven Edgar Allan Poe 243

The Seven Ages of Man William Shakespeare 243

On the Grasshopper and the Cricket John Keats 244

Sonnet 30 William Shakespeare 244

Three Haiku Bashō and Chiyojo 244

Hokku Poems Richard Wright 244

Unit 10: The Epic

from the **Odyssey** Homer, translated by Robert Fitzgerald

   Part 1, The Adventures of Odysseus 245

   Part 2, The Return of Odysseus 246

An Ancient Gesture Edna St. Vincent Millay 247

Siren Song Margaret Atwood 247

Prologue and Epilogue *from the* **Odyssey** Derek Walcott 247

Ithaca Constantine Cavafy 247

Part 1

Selections With Interactive Reading Support and Practice

Part 1 is a companion for *Prentice Hall Literature: Timeless Voices, Timeless Themes*. It will guide and support you as you interact with the literature from *Prentice Hall Literature: Timeless Voices, Timeless Themes*.

- Start by looking at the **Prepare to Read** pages for the literature selection in *Prentice Hall Literature: Timeless Voices, Timeless Themes*.

- Review the **Literary Analysis** and **Reading Strategy** skills taught on those **Prepare to Read** pages. You will apply those skills as you use the *Reader's Companion*.

- Look at the art for the selection in *Prentice Hall Literature: Timeless Voices, Timeless Themes*.

- Now go to the **Preview** page in the *Reader's Companion*. Use the written and visual summaries of the selection to direct your reading.

- Then read the selection in the *Reader's Companion*.

- Respond to all the questions as you read. Write in the *Reader's Companion*—really! Circle things that interest you—underline things that puzzle you. Number ideas or events to help you keep track of them. Look for the **Mark the Text** logo for special help with active reading.

- Use the **Reader's Response** and **Thinking About the Skill** questions at the end of each selection to relate your reading to your own life.

Interacting With the Text

As you read, use the information and notes to guide you in interacting with the selection. The examples on these pages show you how to use the notes as a companion when you read. They will guide you in applying reading and literary skills and in thinking about the selections. When you read other texts, you can practice the thinking skills and strategies found here.

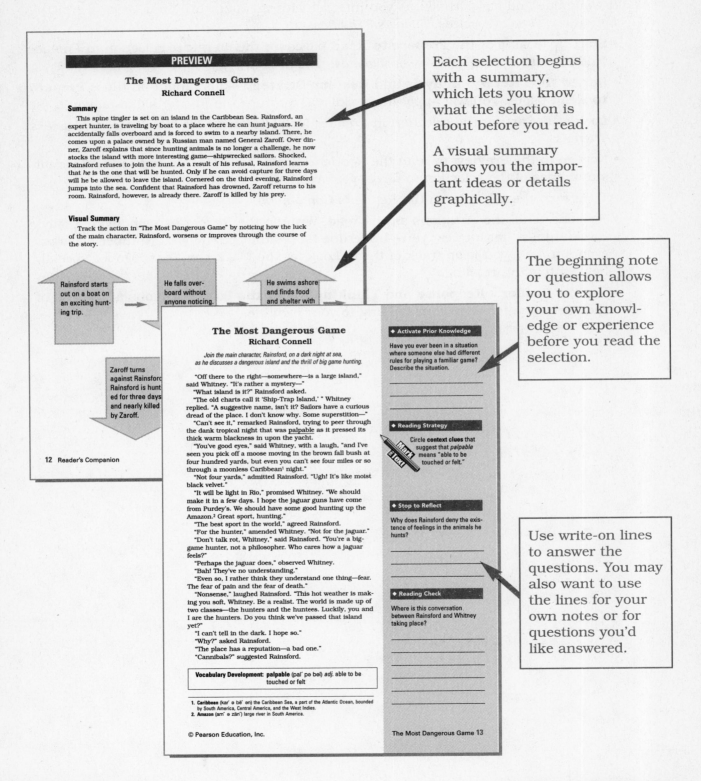

PREVIEW

The Most Dangerous Game
Richard Connell

Summary

This spine tingler is set on an island in the Caribbean Sea. Rainsford, an expert hunter, is traveling by boat to a place where he can hunt jaguars. He accidentally falls overboard and is forced to swim to a nearby island. There, he comes upon a palace owned by a Russian man named General Zaroff. Over dinner, Zaroff explains that since hunting animals is no longer a challenge, he now stocks the island with more interesting game—shipwrecked sailors. Shocked, Rainsford refuses to join the hunt. As a result of his refusal, Rainsford learns that *he* is the one that will be hunted. Only if he can avoid capture for three days will he be allowed to leave the island. Cornered on the third evening, Rainsford jumps into the sea. Confident that Rainsford has drowned, Zaroff returns to his room. Rainsford, however, is already there. Zaroff is killed by his prey.

Visual Summary

Track the action in "The Most Dangerous Game" by noticing how the luck of the main character, Rainsford, worsens or improves through the course of the story.

Rainsford starts out on a boat on an exciting hunting trip.

He falls overboard without anyone noticing.

He swims ashore and finds food and shelter with

Zaroff turns against Rainsford. Rainsford is hunted for three days and nearly killed by Zaroff.

12 Reader's Companion

Each selection begins with a summary, which lets you know what the selection is about before you read.

A visual summary shows you the important ideas or details graphically.

The Most Dangerous Game
Richard Connell

Join the main character, Rainsford, on a dark night at sea, as he discusses a dangerous island and the thrill of big game hunting.

"Off there to the right—somewhere—is a large island," said Whitney. "It's rather a mystery—"

"What island is it?" Rainsford asked.

"The old charts call it 'Ship-Trap Island,' " Whitney replied. "A suggestive name, isn't it? Sailors have a curious dread of the place. I don't know why. Some superstition—"

"Can't see it," remarked Rainsford, trying to peer through the dank tropical night that was <u>palpable</u> as it pressed its thick warm blackness in upon the yacht.

"You've good eyes," said Whitney, with a laugh, "and I've seen you pick off a moose moving in the brown fall bush at four hundred yards, but even you can't see four miles or so through a moonless Caribbean[1] night."

"Not four yards," admitted Rainsford. "Ugh! It's like moist black velvet."

"It will be light in Rio," promised Whitney. "We should make it in a few days. I hope the jaguar guns have come from Purdey's. We should have some good hunting up the Amazon.[2] Great sport, hunting."

"The best sport in the world," agreed Rainsford.

"For the hunter," amended Whitney. "Not for the jaguar."

"Don't talk rot, Whitney," said Rainsford. "You're a big-game hunter, not a philosopher. Who cares how a jaguar feels?"

"Perhaps the jaguar does," observed Whitney.

"Bah! They've no understanding."

"Even so, I rather think they understand one thing—fear. The fear of pain and the fear of death."

"Nonsense," laughed Rainsford. "This hot weather is making you soft, Whitney. Be a realist. The world is made up of two classes—the hunters and the huntees. Luckily, you and I are the hunters. Do you think we've passed that island yet?"

"I can't tell in the dark. I hope so."

"Why?" asked Rainsford.

"The place has a reputation—a bad one."

"Cannibals?" suggested Rainsford.

Vocabulary Development: palpable (pal′ pə bəl) *adj.* able to be touched or felt

1. **Caribbean** (kar′ ə bē′ ən) the Caribbean Sea, a part of the Atlantic Ocean, bounded by South America, Central America, and the West Indies.
2. **Amazon** (am′ ə zän′) large river in South America.

© Pearson Education, Inc.

◆ **Activate Prior Knowledge**

Have you ever been in a situation where someone else had different rules for playing a familiar game? Describe the situation.

_____

_____

_____

◆ **Reading Strategy**

Circle **context clues** that suggest that *palpable* means "able to be touched or felt."

◆ **Stop to Reflect**

Why does Rainsford deny the existence of feelings in the animals he hunts?

_____

_____

_____

◆ **Reading Check**

Where is this conversation between Rainsford and Whitney taking place?

_____

_____

_____

_____

_____

The Most Dangerous Game 13

The beginning note or question allows you to explore your own knowledge or experience before you read the selection.

Use write-on lines to answer the questions. You may also want to use the lines for your own notes or for questions you'd like answered.

knocker, and let it fall. The door opened then, opened as suddenly as if it were on a spring, and Rainsford stood blinking in the river of glaring gold light that poured out. The first thing Rainsford's eyes discerned was the largest man Rainsford had ever seen—a gigantic creature, solidly made and black-bearded to the waist. In his hand the man held a long-barreled revolver, and he was pointing it straight at Rainsford's heart.

Out of the snarl of beard two small eyes regarded Rainsford.

"Don't be alarmed," said Rainsford, with a smile which he hoped was disarming. "I'm no robber. I fell off a yacht. My name is Sanger Rainsford of New York City."

The menacing look in the eyes did not change. The revolver pointed as rigidly as if the giant were a statue. He gave no sign that he understood Rainsford's words, or that he had even heard them. He was dressed in uniform, a black uniform trimmed with gray astrakhan.[6]

"I'm Sanger Rainsford of New York," Rainsford began again. "I fell off a yacht. I am hungry."

The man's only answer was to raise with his thumb the hammer of his revolver. Then Rainsford saw the man's free hand go to his forehead in a military salute, and he saw him click his heels together and stand at attention. Another man was coming down the broad marble steps, an erect, slender man in evening clothes. He advanced to Rainsford and held out his hand.

In a cultivated voice marked by a slight accent that gave it added precision and deliberateness, he said: "It is a very great pleasure and honor to welcome Mr. Sanger Rainsford, the celebrated hunter, to my home."

Automatically Rainsford shook the man's hand.

"I've read your book about hunting snow leopards in Tibet, you see," explained the man. "I am General Zaroff."

Rainsford's first impression was that the man was singularly handsome; his second was that there was an original, almost bizarre quality about the general's face. He was a tall man past middle age, for his hair was a vivid white; but his thick eyebrows and pointed military mustache were as black as the night from which Rainsford had come. His eyes, too, were black and very bright. He had high cheek bones, a sharp-cut nose, a spare, dark face, the face of a man used to giving orders, the face of an aristocrat. Turning to the giant in uniform, the general made a sign. The giant put away his pistol, saluted, withdrew.

"Ivan is an incredibly strong fellow," remarked the general,

Vocabulary Development: bizarre (bi zär´) *adj.* odd in appearance

6. **astrakhan** (as´ tre kan´) *n.* fur made from young lambs.

© Pearson Education, Inc.

◆ Literary Analysis

At first, it seems that Rainsford is saved by his discovery of the château. What ... in the bracketed paragraph that ... page 16 help bring back the feeling of **suspense**? Circle the words and phrases that build suspense.

◆ Reading Check

Disarming has more than one meaning. It can mean "to remove anger or suspicion." It can also mean "to take someone's weapon away." Why is the author's use of the word *disarming* humorous in this passage?

_____
_____
_____
_____
_____

◆ Literary Analysis

How does the appearance of this second gentleman affect the **suspense** in the second bracketed passage?

_____
_____
_____

When you see this symbol, you should underline, circle, or mark the text as indicated.

◆ Rea...

What c... away h...

The M...

---

he went up to his bedroom. He was deliciously tired, he said to himself, as he locked himself in. There was a little moonlight, so, before turning on his light, he went to the window and looked down at the courtyard. He could see the great hounds, and he called: "Better luck another time," to them. Then he switched on the light.

A man, who had been hiding in the curtain of the bed, was standing there.

"Rainsford!" screamed the general. "How in God's name did you get here?"

"Swam," said Rainsford. "I found it quicker than walking through the jungle."

The general sucked in his breath and smiled. "I congratulate you," he said. "You have won the game."

Rainsford did not smile. "I am still a beast at bay," he said, in a low, hoarse voice. "Get ready, General Zaroff."

The general made one of his deepest bows. "I see," he said. "Splendid! One of us is to furnish a repast for the hounds. The other will sleep in this very excellent bed. On guard, Rainsford. . . ."

He had never slept in a better bed, Rainsford decided.

20. **Marcus Aurelius** (ô rē´ lē es) Roman emperor and philosopher (A.D. 121–180).

◆ Literary Analysis

What has happened to the level of suspense by this point in the story?

◆ Reading Check

What is the outcome of the story?

After reading, you can write your thoughts and reactions to the selection.

You can also comment on how certain skills and strategies were helpful to you. Thinking about a skill will help you apply it to other reading situations.

Reader's Response: Were you satisfied with the outcome of this story? Why or why not?

_____
_____
_____
_____

Thinking About the Skill: Did using clues, such as words and ideas, from the surrounding **context** help you understand this story?

_____
_____
_____

© Pearson Education, Inc.

The Most Dangerous Game **31**

The Cask of Amontillado

Edgar Allan Poe

Summary

   This story takes place long ago in Italy. It is carnival season, a time of parties and parades, when people wear costumes and masks. Montresor is a man from an important family. He feels that his friend Fortunato has insulted him. He wants revenge. In fact, his desire for revenge has made him crazy, and he plans a horrible death for Fortunato. But he keeps pretending that he is Fortunato's good friend.

   Fortunato is proud of his knowledge of wine. Montresor uses this to lure Fortunato to the family palace to judge a cask of Amontillado sherry (an elegant Spanish wine). The men descend to caves, where wine is stored and people have been buried. Montresor gets Fortunato drunk. Far into the caves, they come to a small room. Montresor chains Fortunato to the wall. He then begins to brick up the entrance. As the wall rises, Fortunato begs, screams, and finally tries to get Montresor to admit that he is only playing a prank. Montresor ignores Fortunato. As he puts the last stone in place, he hears only the bells jingling on Fortunato's costume.

Visual Summary

Characters	Montresor	Fortunato

Problem	Montresor feels that he has been insulted by Fortunato.

Events	1. Montresor meets Fortunato and mentions the cask of Amontillado. 2. Fortunato goes with Montresor to Montresor's palace. They descend winding stairways and wander through caves filled with wine bottles and bones. 3. Montresor acts as if he is Fortunato's friend, getting Fortunato drunk as he leads him deeper into the caves. 4. Montresor chains Fortunato in a small room far into the caves. He then walls up the room, as Fortunato screams and begs for mercy.

Conclusion	Montresor notes that it has been fifty years since these events occurred.

The Cask of Amontillado[1]
Edgar Allan Poe

The festival of Carnival serves as the setting for the opening scene of Poe's story. It is such a wild, chaotic celebration that two people disappearing into underground caves would not be noticed. That is why it is the perfect backdrop for murder.

The thousand injuries of Fortunato (Fōrt ōō nä′ tō) I had borne as I best could, but when he ventured upon insult I vowed revenge. You, who so well know the nature of my soul, will not suppose, however, that I gave utterance to a threat. At *length* I would be avenged; this was a point definitely settled—but the very definitiveness with which it was resolved precluded the idea of risk. I must not only punish but punish with impunity.[2] A wrong is unredressed when retribution overtakes its redresser. It is equally unredressed when the avenger fails to make himself felt as such to him who has done the wrong.

It must be understood that neither by word nor deed had I given Fortunato cause to doubt my good will. I continued, as was my wont, to smile in his face, and he did not perceive that my smile *now* was at the thought of his immolation.[3]

He had a weak point—this Fortunato—although in other regards he was a man to be respected and even feared. He prided himself on his connoisseurship[4] in wine. Few Italians have the true virtuoso[5] spirit. For the most part their enthusiasm is adopted to suit the time and opportunity, to practice imposture upon the British and Austrian millionaires. In painting and gemmary, Fortunato like his countrymen, was a quack, but in the matter of old wines he was sincere. In this respect I did not differ from him materially; I was skillful in the Italian vintages myself, and bought largely whenever I could.

Vocabulary Development: **be avenged** (ə venjed′) *v.* have taken revenge for a wrong that was committed
precluded (prē klōōd′ id) *v.* prevented; made impossible in advance
retribution (re trə byōō′ shən) *n.* payback; punishment for a misdeed or reward for a good deed

---

1. **Amontillado** (ə män′ tē yä dō) *n.* pale, dry sherry.
2. **impunity** (im pyōō′ nə tē′) *n.* freedom from consequences.
3. **immolation** (im′ ə lā′ shən) *n.* destruction.
4. **connoisseurship** (kän′ ə sɘr′ ship) *n.* expert judgment.
5. **virtuoso** (vɘr′ chōō ō′ sō) *adj.* masterly skill in a particular field.

◆ Activate Prior Knowledge

The narrator in this story feels that he has been insulted. In your experience, what is an effective way to deal with an insult?

_____

_____

_____

◆ Reading Strategy

Break down the underlined sentence by circling phrases that seem important to the action of the story. Then, explain the decision the narrator has made.

_____

_____

_____

_____

_____

_____

_____

_____

_____

_____

_____

_____

_____

◆ Literary Analysis

Mood is the emotion or feeling that an author creates through his or her writing. In the bracketed passage, Poe describes a mood of celebration. Identify specific details that set this mood and underline them in the text.

◆ Reading Check

Why does Montresor state in the underlined sentence that Fortunato is "luckily met?"

_____

_____

_____

◆ Stop to Reflect

What does Montresor accomplish by praising Luchesi as a good judge of wine?

_____

_____

_____

_____

_____

◆ Reading Strategy

Break down the sentence that is bracketed by circling the main events. Then, list the events that occur in the sentence.

_____

_____

_____

_____

_____

It was about dusk, one evening during the supreme madness of the carnival season, that I encountered my friend. He accosted me with excessive warmth, for he had been drinking much. The man wore motley.[6] He had on a tight-fitting parti-striped dress, and his head was surmounted by the conical cap and bells. I was so pleased to see him that I thought I should never have done wringing his hand.

I said to him, "My dear Fortunato, you are luckily met. How remarkably well you are looking today. But I have received a pipe[7] of what passes for Amontillado, and I have my doubts."

"How?" said he. "Amontillado? A pipe? Impossible! And in the middle of the carnival!"

"I have my doubts," I replied: "and I was silly enough to pay the full Amontillado price without consulting you in the matter. You were not to be found, and I was fearful of losing a bargain."

"Amontillado!"

"I have my doubts."

"Amontillado!"

"And I must satisfy them."

"Amontillado!"

"As you are engaged, I am on my way to Luchesi (Lōō kā´zē). If any one has a critical turn it is he. He will tell me—"

"Luchesi cannot tell Amontillado from sherry."

"And yet some fools will have it that his taste is a match for your own."

"Come, let us go."

"Whither?"

"To your vaults."

"My friend, no; I will not impose upon your good nature. I perceive you have an engagement. Luchesi—"

"I have no engagement—come."

"My friend, no. It is not the engagement, but the severe cold with which I perceive you are afflicted. The vaults are insufferably damp. They are encrusted with niter."

"Let us go, nevertheless. The cold is merely nothing. Amontillado! You have been imposed upon. And as for Luchesi, he cannot distinguish sherry from Amontillado."

Thus speaking, Fortunato possessed himself of my arm; and putting on a mask of black silk and drawing a *roquelaure*[8] closely about my person, I suffered him to hurry me to my palazzo.[9]

Vocabulary Development: accosted (ə kôst id) *v.* greeted, especially in a forward or aggressive way
afflicted (ə flikt´ id) *v.* suffering or sickened

---

6. **motley** (mät´ lē) *n.* a clown's multicolored costume.
7. **pipe** (pīp) *n.* large barrel, holding approximately 126 gallons.
8. ***roquelaure*** (räk´ ə lôr) *n.* knee-length cloak.
9. **palazzo** (pə lä´ tsō) Italian word for palace.

There were no attendants at home; they had <u>absconded</u> to make merry in honor of the time. I had told them that I should not return until the morning, and had given them <u>explicit</u> orders not to stir from the house. These orders were sufficient, I well knew, to insure their immediate disappearance, one and all, as soon as my back was turned.

I took from their sconces two flambeaux,[10] and giving one to Fortunato, bowed him through several suites of rooms to the archway that led into the vaults. I passed down a long and winding staircase, requesting him to be cautious as he followed. We came at length to the foot of the descent, and stood together upon the damp ground of the catacombs[11] of the Montresors (Mōn´ tre zôrz).

The gait of my friend was unsteady, and the bells upon his cap jingled as he strode.

"The pipe," he said.

"It is farther on," said I; "but observe the white webwork which gleams from these cavern walls."

He turned towards me, and looked into my eyes with two filmy orbs that distilled the rheum of intoxication.

"Niter?" he asked, at length.

"Niter," I replied. "How long have you had that cough?"

"Ugh! ugh! ugh!—ugh! ugh! ugh!—ugh! ugh! ugh!—ugh! ugh! ugh!—ugh! ugh! ugh!"

My poor friend found it impossible to reply for many minutes.

"It is nothing," he said, at last.

"Come," I said, with decision, "we will go back; your health is precious. You are rich, respected, admired, beloved; you are happy, as once I was. You are a man to be missed. For me it is no matter. We will go back; you will be ill, and I cannot be responsible. Besides, there is Luchesi—"

"Enough," he said; "the cough is a mere nothing; it will not kill me. I shall not die of a cough."

"True—true," I replied; "and, indeed, I had no intention of alarming you unnecessarily—but you should use all proper caution. A draft of this Medoc will defend us from the damps."

Here I knocked off the neck of a bottle which I drew from a long row of its fellows that lay upon the mold.

"Drink," I said, presenting him the wine.

He raised it to his lips with a leer. He paused and nodded to me familiarly, while his bells jingled.

> **Vocabulary Development: absconded** (ab skänd ed) *v.* went away hastily
> **explicit** (eks plis´ it) *adj.* clearly stated

---

10. **took from their sconces two flambeaux** took two torches from where they hung on the wall.
11. **catacombs** underground burial chambers.

◆ Literary Analysis

 In the bracketed paragraph, underline the details that create a **mood** of eerie suspense.

◆ Reading Check

Why does Fortunato continue to follow Montresor deeper underground if he feels ill?

_____

_____

_____

◆ Reading Check

If Fortunato has already been drinking, why does Montresor want him to drink more?

_____

_____

_____

_____

_____

_____

_____

_____

Obviously, Montresor is not really worried about Fortunato's health. Why do you think he keeps acting as if he thinks Fortunato should go back?

_____

_____

_____

_____

_____

What is Montresor hiding under the folds of his cloak?

_____

_____

_____

"I drink," he said "to the buried that repose around us."

"And I to your long life."

He again took my arm, and we proceeded.

"These vaults," he said, "are extensive."

"The Montresors," I replied, "were a great and numerous family."

"I forget your arms."

"A huge human foot d'or, in a field azure; the foot crushes a serpent rampant whose fangs are imbedded in the heel."

"And the motto?"

Nemo me impune lacessit.[12]

"Good!" he said.

The wine sparkled in his eyes and the bells jingled. My own fancy grew warm with the Medoc. We had passed through long walls of piled skeletons, with casks and puncheons[13] intermingling, into the inmost recesses of the catacombs. I paused again, and this time I made bold to seize Fortunato by an arm above the elbow.

"The niter!" I said; "see, it increases. It hangs like moss upon the vaults. We are below the river's bed. The drops of moisture trickle among the bones. Come, we will go back ere it is too late. Your cough—"

"It is nothing," he said; "let us go on. But first, another draft of the Medoc."

I broke and reached him a flagon of De Grâve. He emptied it at a breath. His eyes flashed with a fierce light. He laughed and threw the bottle upwards with a gesticulation I did not understand.

I looked at him in surprise. He repeated the movement—a grotesque one.

"You do not comprehend?" he said.

"Not I," I replied.

"Then you are not of the brotherhood."

"How?"

"You are not of the masons."[14]

"Yes, yes," I said; "yes, yes."

"You? Impossible! A mason?"

"A mason," I replied.

"A sign," he said, "a sign."

"It is this," I answered, producing from beneath the folds of my *roquelaure* a trowel.

Vocabulary Development: gesticulation (jes tik´ yoo lā´ shən) *n.* gesture or movement
trowel (trow´ əl) *n.* pointed tool used for digging or spreading mortar

---

12. *Nemo me impune lacessit* Latin for "No one attacks me with impunity."
13. **puncheons** (pun´ chənz) *n.* large barrels.
14. **masons** the Freemasons, an international secret society.

"You jest," he exclaimed, recoiling a few paces. "But let us proceed to the Amontillado."

"Be it so," I said, replacing the tool beneath the cloak and again offering him my arm. He leaned upon it heavily. We continued our route in search of the Amontillado. We passed through a range of low arches, descended, passed on, and descending again, arrived at a deep crypt, in which the foulness of the air caused our flambeaux rather to glow than flame.

At the most remote end of the crypt there appeared another less spacious. Its walls had been lined with human remains, piled to the vault overhead, in the fashion of the great catacombs of Paris. Three sides of this interior crypt were still ornamented in this manner. From the fourth side the bones had been thrown down, and lay promiscuously upon the earth, forming at one point a mound of some size. Within the wall thus exposed by the displacing of the bones, we perceived a still interior crypt or recess, in depth about four feet, in width three, in height six or seven. It seemed to have been constructed for no especial use within itself, but formed merely the interval between two of the colossal supports of the roof of the catacombs, and was backed by one of their circumscribing walls of solid granite.

It was in vain that Fortunato, uplifting his dull torch, endeavored to pry into the depth of the recess. Its termination the feeble light did not enable us to see.

"Proceed," I said: "herein is the Amontillado. As for Luchesi—"

"He is an ignoramus," interrupted my friend, as he stepped unsteadily forward, while I followed immediately at his heels. In an instant he had reached the extremity of the niche, and finding his progress arrested by the rock, stood stupidly bewildered. A moment more and I had fettered him to the granite. In its surface were two iron staples, distant from each other about two feet, horizontally. From one of these depended a short chain, from the other a padlock. Throwing the links about his waist, it was but the work of a few seconds to secure it. He was too much astounded to resist. Withdrawing the key I stepped back from the recess.

"Pass your hand," I said, "over the wall; you cannot help feeling the niter. Indeed, it is *very* damp. Once more let me *implore* you to return. No? Then I must positively leave you. But I must first render you all the little attentions in my power."

"The Amontillado!" ejaculated my friend, not yet recovered from his astonishment.

Vocabulary Development: recoiling (ri koil´ iŋ) *v.* staggering back
termination (tʉr mə nā´ shən) *n.* end

Reading Strategy

Break down the sentence that is underlined by circling the portion that describes the route the two men traveled. Draw a rough diagram of their route in the space provided.

Literary Analysis

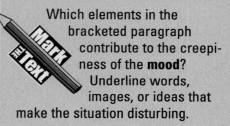

Which elements in the bracketed paragraph contribute to the creepiness of the **mood**? Underline words, images, or ideas that make the situation disturbing.

Reading Check

What has Montresor just done to Fortunato?

_____

_____

_____

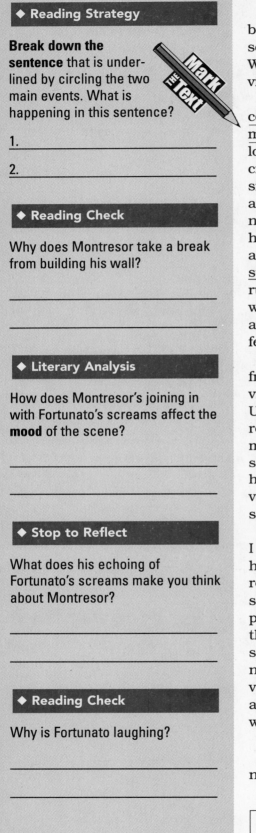

◆ **Reading Strategy**

Break down the sentence that is underlined by circling the two main events. What is happening in this sentence?

1. _____

2. _____

◆ **Reading Check**

Why does Montresor take a break from building his wall?

_____

_____

◆ **Literary Analysis**

How does Montresor's joining in with Fortunato's screams affect the **mood** of the scene?

_____

_____

◆ **Stop to Reflect**

What does his echoing of Fortunato's screams make you think about Montresor?

_____

_____

◆ **Reading Check**

Why is Fortunato laughing?

_____

_____

"True," I replied; "the Amontillado."

As I said these words I busied myself among the pile of bones of which I have before spoken. Throwing them aside, I soon uncovered a quantity of building stone and mortar. With these materials and with the aid of my trowel, I began vigorously to wall up the entrance of the niche.

I had scarcely laid the first tier of the masonry when I discovered that the intoxication of Fortunato had in a great measure worn off. The earliest indication I had of this was a low moaning cry from the depth of the recess. It was *not* the cry of a drunken man. There was then a long and obstinate silence. I laid the second tier, and the third, and the fourth; and then I heard the furious vibrations of the chain. The noise lasted for several minutes, during which, that I might hearken to it with the more satisfaction, I ceased my labors and sat down upon the bones. When at last the clanking subsided, I resumed the trowel, and finished without interruption the fifth, the sixth, and the seventh tier. The wall was now nearly upon a level with my breast. I again paused, and holding the flambeaux over the masonwork, threw a few feeble rays upon the figure within.

A succession of loud and shrill screams, bursting suddenly from the throat of the chained form, seemed to thrust me violently back. For a brief moment I hesitated, I trembled. Unsheathing my rapier, I began to grope with it about the recess; but the thought of an instant reassured me. I placed my hand upon the solid fabric of the catacombs, and felt satisfied. I reapproached the wall; I replied to the yells of him who clamored. I reechoed, I aided, I surpassed them in volume and in strength. I did this, and the clamorer grew still.

It was now midnight, and my task was drawing to a close. I had completed the eighth, the ninth, and the tenth tier. I had finished a portion of the last and the eleventh; there remained but a single stone to be fitted and plastered in. I struggled with its weight; I placed it partially in its destined position. But now there came from out the niche a low laugh that erected the hairs upon my head. It was succeeded by a sad voice, which I had difficulty in recognizing as that of the noble Fortunato. The voice said—"Ha! ha! ha!—he! he! he!—a very good joke, indeed—an excellent jest. We will have many a rich laugh about it at the palazzo—he! he! he!—over our wine—he! he! he!"

"The Amontillado!" I said.

"He! he! he!—he! he! he!—yes, the Amontillado. But is it not getting late? Will not they be awaiting us at the palazzo,

---

Vocabulary Development: subsided (səb sīd´ id) *v.* settled down; became less active or intense

the Lady Fortunato and the rest? Let us be gone."

"Yes," I said, "let us be gone."

"For the love of God, Montresor!"

"Yes," I said, "for the love of God!"

But to these words I hearkened in vain for a reply. I grew impatient. I called aloud—

"Fortunato!"

No answer. I called again—

"Fortunato!"

No answer still. I thrust a torch through the remaining aperture and let it fall within. There came forth in return only a jingling of the bells. My heart grew sick; it was the dampness of the catacombs that made it so. I hastened to make an end of my labor. I forced the last stone into its position; I plastered it up. Against the new masonry I reerected the old rampart of bones. For the half of a century no mortal has disturbed them. *In pace requiescat!* [15]

---

15. *In pace requiescat* Latin for "May he rest in peace!"

♦ **Reading Check**

We learn in the last sentence that Montresor has been telling an old story. How long has it been since he murdered Fortunato?

_____

_____

_____

Reader's Response: How might you have reacted if you were in Fortunato's position?

_____

_____

_____

Thinking About the Skill: What does breaking down long sentences enable you to do?

_____

_____

_____

_____

The Most Dangerous Game

Richard Connell

Summary

This spine tingler is set on an island in the Caribbean Sea. Rainsford, an expert hunter, is traveling by boat to a place where he can hunt jaguars. He accidentally falls overboard and is forced to swim to a nearby island. There, he comes upon a palace owned by a Russian man named General Zaroff. Over dinner, Zaroff explains that since hunting animals is no longer a challenge, he now stocks the island with more interesting game—shipwrecked sailors. Shocked, Rainsford refuses to join the hunt. As a result of his refusal, Rainsford learns that *he* is the one that will be hunted. Only if he can avoid capture for three days will he be allowed to leave the island. Cornered on the third evening, Rainsford jumps into the sea. Confident that Rainsford has drowned, Zaroff returns to his room. Rainsford, however, is already there. Zaroff is killed by his prey.

Visual Summary

Track the action in "The Most Dangerous Game" by noticing how the luck of the main character, Rainsford, worsens or improves through the course of the story.

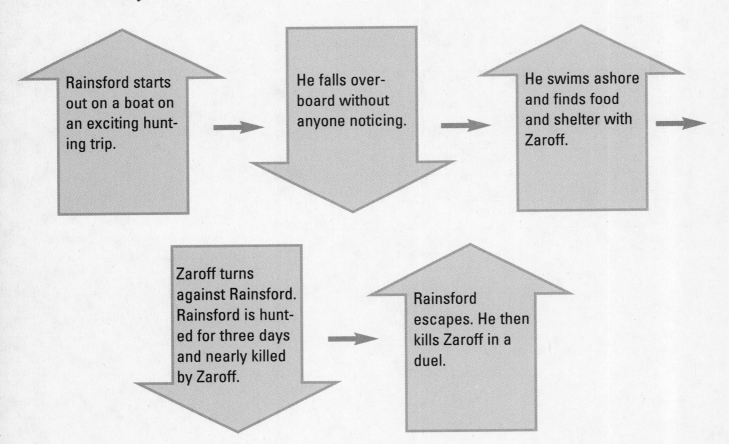

Rainsford starts out on a boat on an exciting hunting trip.

He falls overboard without anyone noticing.

He swims ashore and finds food and shelter with Zaroff.

Zaroff turns against Rainsford. Rainsford is hunted for three days and nearly killed by Zaroff.

Rainsford escapes. He then kills Zaroff in a duel.

The Most Dangerous Game
Richard Connell

*Join the main character, Rainsford, on a dark night at sea,
as he discusses a dangerous island and the thrill of big game hunting.*

"Off there to the right—somewhere—is a large island," said Whitney. "It's rather a mystery—"

"What island is it?" Rainsford asked.

"The old charts call it 'Ship-Trap Island,' " Whitney replied. "A suggestive name, isn't it? Sailors have a curious dread of the place. I don't know why. Some superstition—"

"Can't see it," remarked Rainsford, trying to peer through the dank tropical night that was <u>palpable</u> as it pressed its thick warm blackness in upon the yacht.

"You've good eyes," said Whitney, with a laugh, "and I've seen you pick off a moose moving in the brown fall bush at four hundred yards, but even you can't see four miles or so through a moonless Caribbean[1] night."

"Not four yards," admitted Rainsford. "Ugh! It's like moist black velvet."

"It will be light in Rio," promised Whitney. "We should make it in a few days. I hope the jaguar guns have come from Purdey's. We should have some good hunting up the Amazon.[2] Great sport, hunting."

"The best sport in the world," agreed Rainsford.

"For the hunter," amended Whitney. "Not for the jaguar."

"Don't talk rot, Whitney," said Rainsford. "You're a big-game hunter, not a philosopher. Who cares how a jaguar feels?"

"Perhaps the jaguar does," observed Whitney.

"Bah! They've no understanding."

"Even so, I rather think they understand one thing—fear. The fear of pain and the fear of death."

"Nonsense," laughed Rainsford. "This hot weather is making you soft, Whitney. Be a realist. The world is made up of two classes—the hunters and the huntees. Luckily, you and I are the hunters. Do you think we've passed that island yet?"

"I can't tell in the dark. I hope so."

"Why?" asked Rainsford.

"The place has a reputation—a bad one."

"Cannibals?" suggested Rainsford.

Vocabulary Development: palpable (pal′ pə bəl) *adj.* able to be touched or felt

---

1. **Caribbean** (kar′ ə bē′ ən) the Caribbean Sea, a part of the Atlantic Ocean, bounded by South America, Central America, and the West Indies.
2. **Amazon** (am′ ə zän′) large river in South America.

◆ **Activate Prior Knowledge**

Have you ever been in a situation where someone else had different rules for playing a familiar game? Describe the situation.

_____

_____

_____

◆ **Reading Strategy**

Circle **context clues** that suggest that *palpable* means "able to be touched or felt."

◆ **Stop to Reflect**

Why does Rainsford deny the existence of feelings in the animals he hunts?

_____

_____

_____

◆ **Reading Check**

Where is this conversation between Rainsford and Whitney taking place?

_____

_____

_____

_____

_____

_____

Circle the words and phrases in the bracketed conversation between Whitney and Rainsford that create a mood of **suspense.** Then, make a list below.

_____

_____

_____

_____

◆ **Reading Strategy**

Which **context clues** in the under-lined sentence tell you that to "taint" is to spread something negative?

_____

_____

_____

◆ **Literary Analysis**

Why do you think the author describes Rainsford's drowsiness so soon after he has built **suspense** in the story?

_____

_____

◆ **Reading Check**

What is the sound that startles Rainsford out of his drowsiness?

_____

_____

"Hardly. Even cannibals wouldn't live in such a God-forsaken place. But it's gotten into sailor lore, somehow. Didn't you notice that the crew's nerves seemed a bit jumpy today?"

"They were a bit strange, now you mention it. Even Captain Nielsen—"

"Yes, even that tough-minded old Swede, who'd go up to the devil himself and ask him for a light. Those fishy blue eyes held a look I never saw there before. All I could get out of him was: 'This place has an evil name among sea-faring men, sir.' Then he said to me, very gravely: 'Don't you feel anything?'—as if the air about us was actually poisonous. Now, you mustn't laugh when I tell you this—I did feel something like a sudden chill.

"There was no breeze. The sea was as flat as a plate-glass window. We were drawing near the island then. What I felt was a—a mental chill; a sort of sudden dread."

"Pure imagination," said Rainsford. "One superstitious sailor can taint the whole ship's company with his fear."

"Maybe. But sometimes I think sailors have an extra sense that tells them when they are in danger. Sometimes I think evil is a tangible thing—with wave lengths, just as sound and light have. An evil place can, so to speak, broadcast vibrations of evil. Anyhow, I'm glad we're getting out of this zone. Well, I think I'll turn in now, Rainsford."

"I'm not sleepy," said Rainsford. "I'm going to smoke another pipe on the after deck."

"Good night, then, Rainsford. See you at breakfast."

"Right. Good night, Whitney."

There was no sound in the night as Rainsford sat there, but the muffled throb of the engine that drove the yacht swiftly through the darkness, and the swish and ripple of the wash of the propeller.

Rainsford, reclining in a steamer chair, <u>indolently</u> puffed on his favorite brier. The sensuous drowsiness of the night was on him. "It's so dark," he thought, "that I could sleep without closing my eyes; the night would be my eyelids—"

An abrupt sound startled him. Off to the right he heard it, and his ears, expert in such matters, could not be mistaken. Again he heard the sound, and again. Somewhere, off in the blackness, someone had fired a gun three times.

Rainsford sprang up and moved quickly to the rail, mysti-fied. He strained his eyes in the direction from which the reports had come, but it was like trying to see through a blanket. He leaped upon the rail and balanced himself there, to get greater elevation; his pipe, striking a rope, was

---

Vocabulary Development: indolently (in´ də lənt lē) *adv.* lazily; idly

knocked from his mouth. He lunged for it; a short, hoarse cry came from his lips as he realized he had reached too far and had lost his balance. The cry was pinched off short as the blood-warm waters of the Caribbean Sea closed over his head.

He struggled up to the surface and tried to cry out, but the wash from the speeding yacht slapped him in the face and the salt water in his open mouth made him gag and strangle. Desperately he struck out with strong strokes after the receding lights of the yacht, but he stopped before he had swum fifty feet. A certain cool-headedness had come to him; it was not the first time he had been in a tight place. There was a chance that his cries could be heard by someone aboard the yacht, but that chance was slender, and grew more slender as the yacht raced on. He wrestled himself out of his clothes, and shouted with all his power. The lights of the yacht became faint and ever-vanishing fireflies; then they were blotted out entirely by the night.

Rainsford remembered the shots. They had come from the right, and doggedly he swam in that direction, swimming with slow, deliberate strokes, conserving his strength. For a seemingly endless time he fought the sea. He began to count his strokes; he could do possibly a hundred more and then—

Rainsford heard a sound. It came out of the darkness, a high screaming sound, the sound of an animal in an extremity of anguish and terror.

He did not recognize the animal that made the sound; he did not try to; with fresh vitality he swam toward the sound. He heard it again; then it was cut short by another noise, crisp, staccato.

"Pistol shot," muttered Rainsford, swimming on.

Ten minutes of determined effort brought another sound to his ears—the most welcome he had ever heard—the muttering and growling of the sea breaking on a rocky shore. He was almost on the rocks before he saw them; on a night less calm he would have been shattered against them. With his remaining strength he dragged himself from the swirling waters. Jagged crags appeared to jut into the opaqueness, he forced himself upward, hand over hand. Gasping, his hands raw, he reached a flat place at the top. Dense jungle came down to the very edge of the cliffs. What perils that tangle of trees and underbrush might hold for him did not concern Rainsford just then. All he knew was that he was safe from his enemy, the sea, and that utter weariness was on him. He flung himself down at the jungle edge and tumbled headlong into the deepest sleep of his life.

When he opened his eyes he knew from the position of the sun that it was late in the afternoon. Sleep had given him new vigor; a sharp hunger was picking at him. He looked

◆ Reading Check

What does the first bracketed passage tell you about the way Rainsford reacts to bad situations?

_____

_____

_____

_____

_____

◆ Reading Strategy

The underlined words in the second bracketed passage are **context clues** that can help you determine the meaning of *anguish*. Write its meaning here.

_____

_____

_____

◆ Reading Check

What were the dangers that Rainsford faced before he was able to pull himself on shore?

_____

_____

_____

_____

"Where there are pistol shots, there are men. Where there are men, there is food," he thought. But what kind of men, he wondered, in so forbidding a place? An unbroken front of snarled and ragged jungle fringed the shore.

He saw no sign of a trail through the closely knit web of weeds and trees; it was easier to go along the shore, and Rainsford floundered along by the water. Not far from where he had landed, he stopped.

Some wounded thing, by the evidence a large animal, had thrashed about in the underbrush; the jungle weeds were crushed down and the moss was lacerated; one patch of weeds was stained crimson. A small, glittering object not far away caught Rainsford's eye and he picked it up. It was an empty cartridge.

"A twenty-two," he remarked. "That's odd. It must have been a fairly large animal too. The hunter had his nerve with him to tackle it with a light gun. It's clear that the brute put up a fight. I suppose the first three shots I heard was when the hunter flushed his quarry³ and wounded it. The last shot was when he trailed it here and finished it."

He examined the ground closely and found what he had hoped to find—the print of hunting boots. They pointed along the cliff in the direction he had been going. Eagerly he hurried along, now slipping on a rotten log or a loose stone, but making headway; night was beginning to settle down on the island.

Bleak darkness was blacking out the sea and jungle when Rainsford sighted the lights. He came upon them as he turned a crook in the coast line, and his first thought was that he had come upon a village, for there were many lights. But as he forged along he saw to his great astonishment that all the lights were in one enormous building—a lofty structure with pointed towers plunging upward into the gloom. His eyes made out the shadowy outlines of a palatial château;⁴ it was set on a high bluff, and on three sides of it cliffs dived down to where the sea licked greedy lips in the shadows.

"Mirage," thought Rainsford. But it was no mirage, he found, when he opened the tall spiked iron gate. The stone steps were real enough; the massive door with a leering gargoyle⁵ for a knocker was real enough; yet about it all hung an air of unreality.

He lifted the knocker, and it creaked up stiffly, as if it had never before been used. He let it fall, and it startled him with its booming loudness. He thought he heard steps within; the door remained closed. Again Rainsford lifted the heavy

◆ Reading Strategy

A cartridge is the casing for a bullet. How could you use this knowledge as a **context clue** that might help you determine what a *twenty-two* is?

_____

_____

_____

◆ Reading Check

What did Rainsford see that astonished him?

_____

_____

◆ Reading Strategy

How does the repeated phrase "was real enough" help you to understand what a *mirage* is in the first bracketed paragraph?

_____

_____

_____

---

3. **flushed his quarry** (kwôr′ ē) drove his prey into the open.
4. **palatial château** (pə lā′ shəl sha tō′) a mansion as luxurious as a palace.
5. **gargoyle** (gär′ goil) *n.* strange and distorted animal form projecting from a building.

knocker, and let it fall. The door opened then, opened as suddenly as if it were on a spring, and Rainsford stood blinking in the river of glaring gold light that poured out. The first thing Rainsford's eyes discerned was the largest man Rainsford had ever seen—a gigantic creature, solidly made and black-bearded to the waist. In his hand the man held a long-barreled revolver, and he was pointing it straight at Rainsford's heart.

Out of the snarl of beard two small eyes regarded Rainsford.

"Don't be alarmed," said Rainsford, with a smile which he hoped was <u>disarming</u>. "I'm no robber. I fell off a yacht. My name is Sanger Rainsford of New York City."

The menacing look in the eyes did not change. The revolver pointed as rigidly as if the giant were a statue. He gave no sign that he understood Rainsford's words, or that he had even heard them. He was dressed in uniform, a black uniform trimmed with gray astrakhan.[6]

"I'm Sanger Rainsford of New York," Rainsford began again. "I fell off a yacht. I am hungry."

The man's only answer was to raise with his thumb the hammer of his revolver. Then Rainsford saw the man's free hand go to his forehead in a military salute, and he saw him click his heels together and stand at attention. Another man was coming down the broad marble steps, an erect, slender man in evening clothes. He advanced to Rainsford and held out his hand.

In a cultivated voice marked by a slight accent that gave it added precision and deliberateness, he said: "It is a very great pleasure and honor to welcome Mr. Sanger Rainsford, the celebrated hunter, to my home."

Automatically Rainsford shook the man's hand.

"I've read your book about hunting snow leopards in Tibet, you see," explained the man. "I am General Zaroff."

Rainsford's first impression was that the man was singularly handsome; his second was that there was an original, almost <u>bizarre</u> quality about the general's face. He was a tall man past middle age, for his hair was a vivid white; but his thick eyebrows and pointed military mustache were as black as the night from which Rainsford had come. His eyes, too, were black and very bright. He had high cheek bones, a sharp-cut nose, a spare, dark face, the face of a man used to giving orders, the face of an aristocrat. Turning to the giant in uniform, the general made a sign. The giant put away his pistol, saluted, withdrew.

"Ivan is an incredibly strong fellow," remarked the general,

Vocabulary Development: bizarre (bi zär´) *adj.* odd in appearance

---

6. **astrakhan** (as´ trə kan´) *n.* fur made from young lambs.

◆ **Literary Analysis**

Mark the Text

At first, it seems that Rainsford is saved by his discovery of the château. What details in the bracketed paragraph that starts on page 16 help bring back the feeling of **suspense**? Circle the words and phrases that build suspense.

◆ **Reading Check**

Disarming has more than one meaning. It can mean "to remove anger or suspicion." It can also mean "to take someone's weapon away." Why is the author's use of the word *disarming* humorous in this passage?

_____

_____

_____

◆ **Literary Analysis**

How does the appearance of this second gentleman affect the **suspense** in the second bracketed passage?

_____

_____

_____

◆ **Reading Check**

What causes the giant man to put away his gun?

_____

_____

What is your impression of the general? In your answer, indicate the details or dialogue that contribute to your impression.

_____

_____

_____

_____

_____

What do you think is the meaning of *amenities*? Circle the **context clues** that help you determine its meaning.

_____

_____

_____

_____

"but he has the misfortune to be deaf and dumb. A simple fellow, but, I'm afraid, like all his race, a bit of a savage."

"Is he Russian?"

"He is a Cossack,"[7] said the general, and his smile showed red lips and pointed teeth. "So am I."

"Come," he said, "we shouldn't be chatting here. We can talk later. Now you want clothes, food, rest. You shall have them. This is a most restful spot."

Ivan had reappeared, and the general spoke to him with lips that moved but gave forth no sound.

"Follow Ivan, if you please, Mr. Rainsford," said the general. "I was about to have my dinner when you came. I'll wait for you. You'll find that my clothes will fit you, I think."

It was to a huge, beam-ceilinged bedroom with a canopied bed big enough for six men that Rainsford followed the silent giant. Ivan laid out an evening suit, and Rainsford, as he put it on, noticed that it came from a London tailor who ordinarily cut and sewed for none below the rank of duke.

The dining room to which Ivan conducted him was in many ways remarkable. There was a medieval magnificence about it; it suggested a baronial hall of feudal times with its oaken panels, its high ceiling, its vast refectory table where twoscore men could sit down to eat. About the hall were the mounted heads of many animals—lions, tigers, elephants, moose, bears; larger or more perfect specimens Rainsford had never seen. At the great table the general was sitting, alone.

"You'll have a cocktail, Mr. Rainsford," he suggested. The cocktail was surpassingly good; and, Rainsford noted, the table appointments were of the finest—the linen, the crystal, the silver, the china.

They were eating *borsch*, the rich, red soup with whipped cream so dear to Russian palates. Half apologetically General Zaroff said: "We do our best to preserve the amenities of civilization here. Please forgive any lapses. We are well off the beaten track, you know. Do you think the champagne has suffered from its long ocean trip?"

"Not in the least," declared Rainsford. He was finding the general a most thoughtful and affable host, a true cosmopolite.[8] But there was one small trait of the general's that made Rainsford uncomfortable. Whenever he looked up from his plate he found the general studying him, appraising him narrowly.

"Perhaps," said General Zaroff, "you were surprised that I recognized your name. You see, I read all books on hunting published in English, French, and Russian. I have but one

---

7. **Cossack** (käs´ ak) member of a people from southern Russia, famous for their fierceness.
8. **cosmopolite** (käz mäp´ ə lĭt´) *n.* person at home in all parts of the world.

passion in my life, Mr. Rainsford, and it is the hunt."

"You have some wonderful heads here," said Rainsford as he ate a particularly well cooked filet mignon. "That Cape buffalo is the largest I ever saw."

"Oh, that fellow. Yes, he was a monster."

"Did he charge you?"

"Hurled me against a tree," said the general. "Fractured my skull. But I got the brute."

"I've always thought," said Rainsford, "that the Cape buffalo is the most dangerous of all big game."

For a moment the general did not reply; he was smiling his curious red-lipped smile. Then he said slowly: "No. You are wrong, sir. The Cape buffalo is not the most dangerous big game." He sipped his wine. "Here in my preserve on this island," he said in the same slow tone, "I hunt more dangerous game."

Rainsford expressed his surprise. "Is there big game on this island?"

The general nodded. "The biggest."

"Really?"

"Oh, it isn't here naturally, of course. I have to stock the island."

"What have you imported, general?" Rainsford asked. "Tigers?"

The general smiled. "No," he said. "Hunting tigers ceased to interest me some years ago. I exhausted their possibilities, you see. No thrill left in tigers, no real danger. I live for danger, Mr. Rainsford."

The general took from his pocket a gold cigarette case and offered his guest a long black cigarette with a silver tip; it was perfumed and gave off a smell like incense.

"We will have some capital hunting, you and I," said the general. "I shall be most glad to have your society."

"But what game—" began Rainsford.

"I'll tell you," said the general. "You will be amused, I know. I think I may say, in all modesty, that I have done a rare thing. I have invented a new sensation. May I pour you another glass of port, Mr. Rainsford?"

"Thank you, general."

The general filled both glasses, and said: "God makes some men poets. Some He makes kings, some beggars. Me He made a hunter. My hand was made for the trigger, my father said. He was a very rich man with a quarter of a million acres in the Crimea,[9] and he was an ardent sportsman. When I was only five years old he gave me a little gun, specially made in Moscow for me, to shoot sparrows with. When I shot some of his prize turkeys with it, he did not punish me; he complimented me on my marksmanship. I killed my

---

9. **Crimea** (krī mē´ ə) region in southwestern Russia on the Black Sea.

◆ **Stop to Reflect**

Zaroff killed the Cape buffalo in spite of his fractured skull. What does that tell you about his character?

_____

_____

_____

_____

◆ **Literary Analysis**

How does the general's secretive behavior increase the sense of **suspense**?

_____

_____

_____

_____

◆ **Reading Check**

What do we learn about the general that explains his confident attitude and interest in hunting?

_____

_____

_____

Read the footnote on *debacle* at the bottom of the page. Use it as a clue to help you determine the meaning of the word *imprudent*. Write what you think it means here.

_____

_____

_____

_____

Has your impression of Zaroff changed since you met him on page 17? Explain.

_____

_____

_____

_____

Why is the general bored with hunting ordinary animals?

_____

_____

_____

_____

_____

_____

first bear in the Caucasus[10] when I was ten. My whole life has been one prolonged hunt. I went into the army—it was expected of noblemen's sons—and for a time commanded a division of Cossack cavalry, but my real interest was always the hunt. I have hunted every kind of game in every land. It would be impossible for me to tell you how many animals I have killed."

The general puffed at his cigarette.

"After the debacle[11] in Russia I left the country, for it was <u>imprudent</u> for an officer of the Czar to stay there. Many noble Russians lost everything. I, luckily, had invested heavily in American securities, so I shall never have to open a tea room in Monte Carlo or drive a taxi in Paris. Naturally, I continued to hunt—grizzlies in your Rockies, crocodiles in the Ganges, rhinoceroses in East Africa. It was in Africa that the Cape buffalo hit me and laid me up for six months. As soon as I recovered I started for the Amazon to hunt jaguars, for I had heard they were unusually cunning. They weren't." The Cossack sighed. "They were no match at all for a hunter with his wits about him, and a high-powered rifle. I was bitterly disappointed. I was lying in my tent with a splitting headache one night when a terrible thought pushed its way into my mind. Hunting was beginning to bore me! And hunting, remember, had been my life. I have heard that in America business men often go to pieces when they give up the business that has been their life."

"Yes, that's so," said Rainsford.

The general smiled. "I had no wish to go to pieces," he said. "I must do something. Now, mine is an analytical mind, Mr. Rainsford. Doubtless that is why I enjoy the problems of the chase."

"No doubt, General Zaroff."

"So," continued the general, "I asked myself why the hunt no longer fascinated me. You are much younger than I am, Mr. Rainsford, and have not hunted as much, but you perhaps can guess the answer."

"What was it?"

"Simply this: hunting had ceased to be what you call 'a sporting proposition.' It had become too easy. I always got my quarry. Always. There is no greater bore than perfection."

The general lit a fresh cigarette.

"No animal had a chance with me any more. That is no boast; it is a mathematical certainty. The animal had nothing but his legs and his instinct. Instinct is no match for reason. When I thought of this it was a tragic moment for

---

10. **Caucasus** (kô′ kə səs) mountain range in southern Russia.
11. **debacle** (di bäk′ əl) *n.* bad defeat—Zaroff is referring to the Russian Revolution of 1917, a defeat for upper-class Russians like himself.

me, I can tell you."

Rainsford leaned across the table, absorbed in what his host was saying.

"It came to me as an inspiration what I must do," the general went on.

"And that was?"

The general smiled the quiet smile of one who has faced an obstacle and surmounted it with success. "I had to invent a new animal to hunt," he said.

"A new animal? You're joking."

"Not at all," said the general. "I never joke about hunting. I needed a new animal. I found one. So I bought this island, built this house, and here I do my hunting. The island is perfect for my purpose—there are jungles with a maze of trails in them, hills, swamps—"

"But the animal, General Zaroff?"

"Oh," said the general, "it supplies me with the most exciting hunting in the world. No other hunting compares with it for an instant. Every day I hunt, and I never grow bored now, for I have a quarry with which I can match my wits."

Rainsford's bewilderment showed in his face.

"I wanted the ideal animal to hunt," explained the general. "So I said: 'What are the attributes of an ideal quarry?' And the answer was, of course: 'It must have courage, cunning, and, above all, it must be able to reason.' "

"But no animal can reason," objected Rainsford.

"My dear fellow," said the general, "there is one that can."

"But you can't mean—" gasped Rainsford.

"And why not?"

"I can't believe you are serious, General Zaroff. This is a grisly joke."

"Why should I not be serious? I am speaking of hunting."

"Hunting? General Zaroff, what you speak of is murder."

The general laughed with entire good nature. He regarded Rainsford quizzically. "I refuse to believe that so modern and civilized a young man as you seem to be harbors romantic ideas about the value of human life. Surely your experiences in the war—"

"Did not make me condone cold-blooded murder," finished Rainsford stiffly.

Laughter shook the general. "How extraordinarily droll you are!" he said. "One does not expect nowadays to find a young man of the educated class, even in America, with such a naive, and, if I may say so, mid-Victorian point of view.[12] It's like finding a snuff-box in a limousine. Ah, well, doubtless

---

Vocabulary Development: naive (nä ēv´) *adj.* unsophisticated

---

12. **mid-Victorian point of view** a point of view emphasizing proper behavior and associated with the time of Queen Victoria of England (1819–1901).

◆ **Literary Analysis**

The general is intentionally building the **suspense** here. Can you predict what the animal is? If you have not guessed, pay close attention as you read the rest of the page. Circle the sentence at the point that you figure out what the animal is.

_____

_____

◆ **Reading Check**

To what is Rainsford referring when he uses the underlined phrase "This is a grisly joke"?

_____

_____

◆ **Reading Strategy**

What do you think is the meaning of *condone*? Underline the **context clues** that help you determine its meaning.

_____

_____

What does he mean when Rainsford says "I'm a hunter, not a murderer"?

_____

_____

_____

Do you agree with Zaroff's philosophy as it is expressed in the bracketed paragraph? Explain.

_____

_____

_____

_____

_____

What **context clues** in the first underlined sentence help you determine what Zaroff means by "Providence"? Circle the clues, then write the meaning of the word *Providence* here.

_____

_____

_____

What trick does the general use to bring ships to the island?

_____

_____

_____

_____

_____

you had Puritan ancestors. So many Americans appear to have had. I'll wager you'll forget your notions when you go hunting with me. You've a genuine new thrill in store for you, Mr. Rainsford."

"Thank you, I'm a hunter, not a murderer."

"Dear me," said the general, quite unruffled, "again that unpleasant word. But I think I can show you that your scruples are quite ill founded."

"Yes?"

"Life is for the strong, to be lived by the strong, and, if need be, taken by the strong. The weak of the world were put here to give the strong pleasure. I am strong. Why should I not use my gift? If I wish to hunt, why should I not? I hunt the scum of the earth—sailors from tramp ships—lascars,[13] blacks, Chinese, whites, mongrels—a thoroughbred horse or hound is worth more than a score of them."

"But they are men," said Rainsford hotly.

"Precisely," said the general. "That is why I use them. It gives me pleasure. They can reason, after a fashion. So they are dangerous."

"But where do you get them?"

The general's left eyelid fluttered down in a wink. "This island is called Ship-Trap," he answered. "Sometimes an angry god of the high seas sends them to me. Sometimes, when Providence is not so kind, I help Providence a bit. Come to the window with me."

Rainsford went to the window and looked out toward the sea.

"Watch! Out there!" exclaimed the general, pointing into the night. Rainsford's eyes saw only blackness, and then, as the general pressed a button, far out to sea Rainsford saw the flash of lights.

The general chuckled. "They indicate a channel," he said, "where there's none: giant rocks with razor edges crouch like a sea monster with wide-open jaws. They can crush a ship as easily as I crush this nut." He dropped a walnut on the hardwood floor and brought his heel grinding down on it. "Oh, yes," he said, casually, as if in answer to a question, "I have electricity. We try to be civilized here."

"Civilized? And you shoot down men?"

A trace of anger was in the general's black eyes, but it was there for but a second, and he said, in his most pleasant manner: "Dear me, what a righteous young man you are! I assure you I do not do the thing you suggest. That would

---

Vocabulary Development: scruples (scrōō´ pəlz) *n.* misgivings about something one feels is wrong

---

13. **lascars** (las´ kərz) *n.* Oriental sailors, especially natives of India.

be barbarous. I treat these visitors with every considera- tion. They get plenty of good food and exercise. They get into splendid physical condition. You shall see for yourself tomorrow."

"What do you mean?"

"We'll visit my training school," smiled the general. "It's in the cellar. I have about a dozen pupils down there now. They're from the Spanish bark San Lucar that had the bad luck to go on the rocks out there. A very inferior lot, I regret to say. Poor specimens and more accustomed to the deck than to the jungle."

He raised his hand, and Ivan, who served as waiter, brought thick Turkish coffee. Rainsford, with an effort, held his tongue in check.

"It's a game, you see," pursued the general blandly. "I sug- gest to one of them that we go hunting. I give him a supply of food and an excellent hunting knife. I give him three hours' start. I am to follow, armed only with a pistol of the smallest caliber and range. If my quarry eludes me for three whole days, he wins the game. If I find him"—the general smiled—"he loses."

"Suppose he refuses to be hunted?"

"Oh," said the general, "I give him his option, of course. He need not play the game if he doesn't wish to. If he does not wish to hunt, I turn him over to Ivan. Ivan once had the honor of serving as official knouter[14] to the Great White Czar, and he has his own ideas of sport. Invariably, Mr. Rainsford, invariably they choose the hunt."

"And if they win?"

The smile on the general's face widened. "To date I have not lost," he said.

Then he added, hastily: "I don't wish you to think me a braggart, Mr. Rainsford. Many of them afford only the most elementary sort of problem. Occasionally I strike a tartar.[15] One almost did win. I eventually had to use the dogs."

"The dogs?"

"This way, please. I'll show you."

The general steered Rainsford to a window. The lights from the windows sent a flickering illumination that made grotesque patterns on the courtyard below, and Rainsford could see moving about there a dozen or so huge black

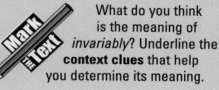

Vocabulary Development: blandly (bland´ lē) *adv.* in a mild and soothing manner
grotesque (grō tesk´) *adj.* having a strange, bizarre design

---

14. **knouter** (nout´ ər) *n.* someone who beats criminals with a leather whip, or knout.
15. **tartar** (tär´ tər) *n.* stubborn, violent person.

shapes; as they turned toward him, their eyes glittered greenly.

"A rather good lot, I think," observed the general. "They are let out at seven every night. If anyone should try to get into my house—or out of it—something extremely regrettable would occur to him." He hummed a snatch of song from the Folies Bergère.[16]

"And now," said the general, "I want to show you my new collection of heads. Will you come with me to the library?"

"I hope," said Rainsford, "that you will excuse me tonight, General Zaroff. I'm really not feeling at all well."

"Ah, indeed?" the general inquired solicitously. "Well, I suppose that's only natural, after your long swim. You need a good, restful night's sleep. Tomorrow you'll feel like a new man, I'll wager. Then we'll hunt, eh? I've one rather promising prospect—"

Rainsford was hurrying from the room.

"Sorry you can't go with me tonight," called the general. "I expect rather fair sport—a big, strong black. He looks resourceful—Well good night, Mr. Rainsford; I hope you have a good night's rest."

The bed was good, and the pajamas of the softest silk, and he was tired in every fiber of his being, but nevertheless Rainsford could not quiet his brain with the opiate of sleep. He lay, eyes wide open. Once he thought he heard stealthy steps in the corridor outside his room. He sought to throw open the door; it would not open. He went to the window and looked out. His room was high up in one of the towers. The lights of the château were out now, and it was dark and silent, but there was a fragment of sallow moon, and by its wan light he could see, dimly, the courtyard; there, weaving in and out in the pattern of shadow, were black, noiseless forms; the hounds heard him at the window and looked up, expectantly, with their green eyes. Rainsford went back to the bed and lay down. By many methods he tried to put himself to sleep. He had achieved a doze when, just as morning began to come, he heard, far off in the jungle, the faint report of a pistol.

General Zaroff did not appear until luncheon. He was dressed faultlessly in the tweeds of a country squire. He was solicitous about the state of Rainsford's health.

"As for me," sighed the general, "I do not feel so well. I am worried, Mr. Rainsford. Last night I detected traces of my old complaint."

To Rainsford's questioning glance the general said: "Ennui. Boredom."

Then, taking a second helping of crêpes suzette, the gen-

---

16. **Folies Bergère** (fô lē ber zhār´) musical theater in Paris.

◆ Stop to Reflect

What kind of heads are likely to be in Zaroff's "new collection" in the library?

_____

_____

◆ Literary Analysis

Underline the details that build **suspense** in the bracketed passage.

◆ Reading Check

Why is General Zaroff not feeling well this morning?

_____

_____

eral explained: "The hunting was not good last night. The fellow lost his head. He made a straight trail that offered no problems at all. That's the trouble with these sailors; they have dull brains to begin with, and they do not know how to get about in the woods. They do excessively stupid and obvious things. It's most annoying. Will you have another glass of Chablis, Mr. Rainsford?"

"General," said Rainsford firmly, "I wish to leave this island at once."

The general raised his thickets of eyebrows; he seemed hurt. "But, my dear fellow," the general protested, "you've only just come. You've had no hunting—"

"I wish to go today," said Rainsford. He saw the dead black eyes of the general on him, studying him. General Zaroff's face suddenly brightened.

He filled Rainsford's glass with venerable Chablis from a dusty bottle.

"Tonight," said the general, "we will hunt—you and I."

Rainsford shook his head. "No, general," he said. "I will not hunt."

The general shrugged his shoulders and delicately ate a hothouse grape. "As you wish, my friend," he said. "The choice rests entirely with you. But may I not venture to suggest that you will find my idea of sport more diverting than Ivan's?"

He nodded toward the corner to where the giant stood, scowling, his thick arms crossed on his hogshead of chest.

"You don't mean—" cried Rainsford.

"My dear fellow," said the general, "have I not told you I always mean what I say about hunting? This is really an inspiration. I drink to a foeman worthy of my steel—at last."

The general raised his glass, but Rainsford sat staring at him.

"You'll find this game worth playing," the general said enthusiastically. "Your brain against mine. Your woodcraft against mine. Your strength and stamina against mine. Outdoor chess! And the stake is not without value, eh?"

"And if I win—" began Rainsford huskily.

"I'll cheerfully acknowledge myself defeated if I do not find you by midnight of the third day," said General Zaroff. "My sloop will place you on the mainland near a town."

The general read what Rainsford was thinking.

"Oh, you can trust me," said the Cossack. "I will give you my word as a gentleman and a sportsman. Of course you, in turn, must agree to say nothing of your visit here."

"I'll agree to nothing of the kind," said Rainsford.

"Oh," said the general, "in that case—But why discuss that now? Three days hence we can discuss it over a bottle of Veuve Cliquot, unless—"

The general sipped his wine.

Why do you think Zaroff gives
Rainsford so much advice if Zaroff
wants to hunt and kill him?

_____

_____

_____

How does Zaroff's use of the
French phrase "Au revoir" ("Until
we meet again") heighten the
sense of suspense?

_____

_____

_____

_____

Why does Rainsford decide to
change his strategy?

_____

_____

_____

_____

Then a businesslike air animated him. "Ivan," he said to Rainsford, "will supply you with hunting clothes, food, a knife. I suggest you wear moccasins; they leave a poorer trail. I suggest too that you avoid the big swamp in the southeast corner of the island. We call it Death Swamp. There's quicksand there. One foolish fellow tried it. The deplorable part of it was that Lazarus followed him. You can imagine my feelings, Mr. Rainsford. I loved Lazarus; he was the finest hound in my pack. Well, I must beg you to excuse me now. I always take a siesta after lunch. You'll hardly have time for a nap, I fear. You'll want to start, no doubt. I shall not follow till dusk. Hunting at night is so much more exciting than by day, don't you think? Au revoir,[17] Mr. Rainsford, au revoir."

General Zaroff, with a deep, courtly bow, strolled from the room.

From another door came Ivan. Under one arm he carried khaki hunting clothes, a haversack of food, a leather sheath containing a long-bladed hunting knife; his right hand rested on a cocked revolver thrust in the crimson sash about his waist. . . .

Rainsford had fought his way through the bush for two hours. "I must keep my nerve. I must keep my nerve," he said through tight teeth.

He had not been entirely clear-headed when the château gates snapped shut behind him.

His whole idea at first was to put distance between himself and General Zaroff, and, to this end, he had plunged along, spurred on by the sharp rowels of something very like panic. Now he had got a grip on himself, had stopped, and was taking stock of himself and the situation.

He saw that straight flight was <u>futile</u>; inevitably it would bring him face to face with the sea. He was in a picture with a frame of water, and his operations, clearly, must take place within that frame.

"I'll give him a trail to follow," muttered Rainsford, and he struck off from the rude paths he had been following into the trackless wilderness. He executed a series of intricate loops; he doubled on his trail again and again, recalling all the lore of the fox hunt, and all the dodges of the fox. Night found him leg-weary, with his hands and face lashed by the branches, on a thickly wooded ridge. He knew it would be insane to blunder on through the dark, even if he had the strength. His need for rest was imperative and he thought: "I

Vocabulary Development: futile (fyo͞ot´ əl) *adj.* useless; hopeless

---

17. **Au revoir** (ō´ rə vwär´) French for "until we meet again."

have played the fox, now I must play the cat of the fable." A big tree with a thick trunk and outspread branches was nearby, and, taking care to leave not the slightest mark, he climbed up into the crotch, and stretching out on one of the broad limbs, after a fashion, rested. Rest brought him new confidence and almost a feeling of security. Even so zealous a hunter as General Zaroff could not trace him there, he told himself; only the devil himself could follow that complicated trail through the jungle after dark. But, perhaps, the general was a devil—

An apprehensive night crawled slowly by like a wounded snake, and sleep did not visit Rainsford, although the silence of a dead world was on the jungle. Toward morning when a dingy gray was varnishing the sky, the cry of some startled bird focused Rainsford's attention in that direction. Something was coming through the bush, coming slowly, carefully, coming by the same winding way Rainsford had come. He flattened himself down on the limb, and through a screen of leaves almost as thick as tapestry, he watched. The thing that was approaching was a man.

It was General Zaroff. He made his way along with his eyes fixed in utmost concentration on the ground before him. He paused, almost beneath the tree, dropped to his knees and studied the ground. Rainsford's impulse was to hurl himself down like a panther, but he saw the general's right hand held something metallic—a small automatic pistol.

The hunter shook his head several times, as if he were puzzled. Then he straightened up and took from his case one of his black cigarettes; its pungent incense-like smoke floated up to Rainsford's nostrils.

Rainsford held his breath. The general's eyes had left the ground and were traveling inch by inch up the tree. Rainsford froze there, every muscle tensed for a spring. But the sharp eyes of the hunter stopped before they reached the limb where Rainsford lay; a smile spread over his brown face. Very deliberately he blew a smoke ring into the air; then he turned his back on the tree and walked carelessly away, back along the trail he had come. The swish of the underbrush against his hunting boots grew fainter and fainter.

The pent-up air burst hotly from Rainsford's lungs. His first thought made him feel sick and numb. The general could follow a trail through the woods at night; he could follow an extremely difficult trail; he must have uncanny powers; only by the merest chance had the Cossack failed to see his quarry.

Rainsford's second thought was even more terrible. It sent a shudder of cold horror through his whole being. Why had the general smiled? Why had he turned back?

◆ **Reading Strategy**

Context clues are found not only in nearby words, but also in a story's ideas. What do you know about Zaroff's character that might be a clue to the meaning of the word *zealous*? Give your definition of the word *zealous*. Then explain what helped you determine its meaning.

_____

_____

_____

_____

◆ **Literary Analysis**

How does the detailed description of Zaroff's actions create suspense in the bracketed section? Mark the words or phrases that you feel build **suspense** most effectively.

_____

_____

◆ **Reading Check**

In the underlined sentence, why is Rainsford tensed up, ready to spring?

_____

_____

_____

_____

_____

_____

_____

_____

_____

_____

◆ Reading Strategy

Explain, based on the **context**, what
a "Malay mancatcher" is.

_____

_____

◆ Literary Analysis

What impact does each of
Rainsford's narrow escapes have
on you as a reader?

_____

_____

Rainsford did not want to believe what his reason told him was true, but the truth was as evident as the sun that had by now pushed through the morning mists. The general was playing with him! The general was saving him for another day's sport! The Cossack was the cat; he was the mouse. Then it was that Rainsford knew the full meaning of terror.

"I will not lose my nerve. I will not."

He slid down from the tree, and struck off again into the woods. His face was set and he forced the machinery of his mind to function. Three hundred yards from his hiding place he stopped where a huge dead tree leaned precariously on a smaller, living one. Throwing off his sack of food, Rainsford took his knife from its sheath and began to work with all his energy.

The job was finished at last, and he threw himself down behind a fallen log a hundred feet away. He did not have to wait long. The cat was coming again to play with the mouse.

Following the trail with the sureness of a bloodhound, came General Zaroff. Nothing escaped those searching black eyes, no crushed blade of grass, no bent twig, no mark, no matter how faint, in the moss. So intent was the Cossack on his stalking that he was upon the thing Rainsford had made before he saw it. His foot touched the protruding bough that was the trigger. Even as he touched it, the general sensed his danger and leaped back with the agility of an ape. But he was not quite quick enough; the dead tree, delicately adjusted to rest on the cut living one, crashed down and struck the general a glancing blow on the shoulder as it fell; but for his alertness, he must have been smashed beneath it. He staggered, but he did not fall; nor did he drop his revolver. He stood there, rubbing his injured shoulder, and Rainsford, with fear again gripping his heart, heard the general's mocking laugh ring through the jungle.

"Rainsford," called the general, "if you are within the sound of my voice, as I suppose you are, let me congratulate you. Not many men know how to make a Malay mancatcher. Luckily, for me, I too have hunted in Malacca. You are proving interesting, Mr. Rainsford. I am going now to have my wound dressed; it's only a slight one. But I shall be back. I shall be back."

When the general, nursing his bruised shoulder, had gone, Rainsford took up his flight again. It was flight now, a desperate, hopeless flight, that carried him on for some hours. Dusk came, then darkness, and still he pressed on. The ground grew softer under his moccasins; the vegetation grew ranker, denser; insects bit him savagely. Then, as he stepped forward, his foot sank into the ooze. He tried to wrench it back, but the muck sucked viciously at his foot as if it were a giant leech. With a violent effort, he tore his foot loose. He knew where he was now. Death Swamp and its quicksand.

His hands were tight closed as if his nerve were something tangible that some one in the darkness was trying to tear from his grip. The softness of the earth had given him an idea. He stepped back from the quicksand a dozen feet or so, and, like some huge prehistoric beaver, he began to dig.

Rainsford had dug himself in in France[18] when a second's delay meant death. That had been a placid pastime compared to his digging now. The pit grew deeper; when it was above his shoulders, he climbed out and from some hard saplings cut stakes and sharpened them to a fine point. These stakes he planted in the bottom of the pit with the points sticking up. With flying fingers he wove a rough carpet of weeds and branches and with it he covered the mouth of the pit. Then, wet with sweat and aching with tiredness, he crouched behind the stump of a lightning-charred tree.

He knew his pursuer was coming; he heard the padding sound of feet on the soft earth, and the night breeze brought him the perfume of the general's cigarette. It seemed to Rainsford that the general was coming with unusual swiftness; he was not feeling his way along, foot by foot. Rainsford, crouching there, could not see the general, nor could he see the pit. He lived a year in a minute. Then he felt an impulse to cry aloud with joy, for he heard the sharp crackle of the breaking branches as the cover of the pit gave way; he heard the sharp scream of pain as the pointed stakes found their mark. He leaped up from his place of concealment. Then he cowered back. Three feet from the pit a man was standing, with an electric torch in his hand.

"You've done well, Rainsford," the voice of the general called. "Your Burmese tiger pit has claimed one of my best dogs. Again you score. I think, Mr. Rainsford, I'll see what you can do against my whole pack. I'm going home for a rest now. Thank you for a most amusing evening."

At daybreak Rainsford, lying near the swamp, was awakened by a sound that made him know that he had new things to learn about fear. It was a distant sound, faint and wavering, but he knew it. It was the baying of a pack of hounds.

Rainsford knew he could do one of two things. He could stay where he was and wait. That was suicide. He could flee. That was postponing the inevitable. For a moment he stood there, thinking. An idea that held a wild chance came to him, and, tightening his belt, he headed away from the swamp.

The baying of the hounds drew nearer, then still nearer, nearer, ever nearer. On a ridge Rainsford climbed a tree.

18. **dug himself in in France** had dug a foxhole to protect himself during World War I.

© Pearson Education, Inc.

What gives Rainsford the idea to dig a trap?

_____

_____

_____

◆ Stop to Reflect

Reread the underlined sentence. How do you think Rainsford feels after his efforts?

_____

_____

_____

_____

◆ Literary Analysis

How do Zaroff's unemotional speeches after each incident contribute to the **suspense**?

_____

_____

_____

_____

_____

◆ Reading Strategy

The two words *bay* and *baying* are closely related but have different meanings.

What is an animal at bay?

_____

Which **context clues** led you to your definition?

_____

What is the baying of hounds?

_____

What context clues helped you determine the meaning?

_____

◆ Reading Check

Circle the clues that tell you Zaroff's state of mind after he has driven Rainsford into the sea.

Down a watercourse, not a quarter of a mile away, he could see the bush moving. Straining his eyes, he saw the lean figure of General Zaroff; just ahead of him Rainsford made out another figure whose wide shoulders surged through the tall jungle weeds; it was the giant Ivan, and he seemed pulled forward by some unseen force; Rainsford knew that Ivan must be holding the pack in leash.

They would be on him any minute now. His mind worked frantically. He thought of a native trick he had learned in Uganda. He slid down the tree. He caught hold of a springy young sapling and to it he fastened his hunting knife, with the blade pointing down the trail; with a bit of wild grapevine he tied back the sapling. Then he ran for his life. The hounds raised their voices as they hit the fresh scent. Rainsford knew now how an animal at <u>bay</u> feels.

He had to stop to get his breath. The <u>baying</u> of the hounds stopped abruptly, and Rainsford's heart stopped too. They must have reached the knife.

He shinnied excitedly up a tree and looked back. His pursuers had stopped. But the hope that was in Rainsford's brain when he climbed died, for he saw in the shallow valley that General Zaroff was still on his feet. But Ivan was not. The knife, driven by the recoil of the springing tree, had not wholly failed.

"Nerve, nerve, nerve!" he panted, as he dashed along. A blue gap showed between the trees dead ahead. Ever nearer drew the hounds. Rainsford forced himself on toward that gap. He reached it. It was the shore of the sea. Across a cove he could see the gloomy gray stone of the château. Twenty feet below him the sea rumbled and hissed. Rainsford hesitated. He heard the hounds. Then he leaped far out into the sea. . . .

When the general and his pack reached the place by the sea, the Cossack stopped. For some minutes he stood regarding the blue-green expanse of water. He shrugged his shoulders. Then he sat down, took a drink of brandy from a silver flask, lit a perfumed cigarette, and hummed a bit from Madame Butterfly.[19]

General Zaroff had an exceedingly good dinner in his great paneled dining hall that evening. With it he had a bottle of Pol Roger and half a bottle of Chambertin. Two slight annoyances kept him from perfect enjoyment. One was the thought that it would be difficult to replace Ivan; the other was that his quarry had escaped him; of course the American hadn't played the game—so thought the general as he tasted his after-dinner liqueur. In his library he read, to soothe himself, from the works of Marcus Aurelius.[20] At ten

---

19. **Madame Butterfly** an opera by Giacomo Puccini.

he went up to his bedroom. He was deliciously tired, he said to himself, as he locked himself in. There was a little moonlight, so, before turning on his light, he went to the window and looked down at the courtyard. He could see the great hounds, and he called: "Better luck another time," to them. Then he switched on the light.

A man, who had been hiding in the curtain of the bed, was standing there.

"Rainsford!" screamed the general. "How in God's name did you get here?"

"Swam," said Rainsford. "I found it quicker than walking through the jungle."

The general sucked in his breath and smiled. "I congratulate you," he said. "You have won the game."

Rainsford did not smile. "I am still a beast at bay," he said, in a low, hoarse voice. "Get ready, General Zaroff."

The general made one of his deepest bows. "I see," he said. "Splendid! One of us is to furnish a repast for the hounds. The other will sleep in this very excellent bed. On guard, Rainsford. . . ."

He had never slept in a better bed, Rainsford decided.

---

20. **Marcus Aurelius** (ô rē′ lē əs) Roman emperor and philosopher (A.D. 121–180).

© Pearson Education, Inc.

◆ Literary Analysis

What has happened to the level of suspense by this point in the story?

_____

_____

_____

_____

◆ Reading Check

What is the outcome of the story?

_____

_____

_____

Reader's Response: Were you satisfied with the outcome of this story? Why or why not?

_____

_____

_____

_____

Thinking About the Skill: Did using clues, such as words and ideas, from the surrounding **context** help you understand this story?

_____

_____

_____

_____

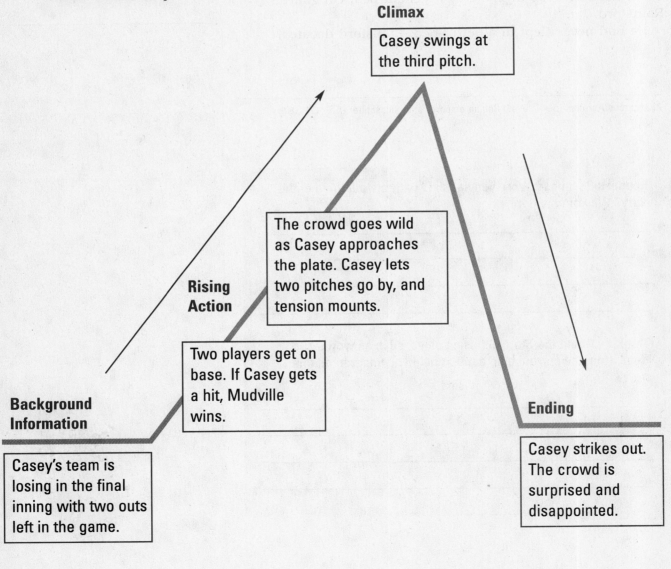

Casey at the Bat
Ernest Lawrence Thayer

Summary

As the poem opens, a baseball game is entering its ninth inning. The score is four to two, and the Mudville baseball team seems sure to lose. Two men are out; then two batters get on base. That brings star player Casey up to bat as the crowd cheers. A cocky Casey entertains the fans and sneers at the pitcher. Casey lets the first two pitches go by. The fans object to the umpire calling them strikes, but Casey signals to the crowd that he does not object, and they become quiet. At the third pitch, Casey finally makes a mighty swing—and strikes out.

Visual Summary

Climax
Casey swings at the third pitch.

Rising Action

The crowd goes wild as Casey approaches the plate. Casey lets two pitches go by, and tension mounts.

Two players get on base. If Casey gets a hit, Mudville wins.

Background Information

Casey's team is losing in the final inning with two outs left in the game.

Ending

Casey strikes out. The crowd is surprised and disappointed.

Casey at the Bat
Ernest Lawrence Thayer

There is a moment in many sports contests when the spectators hold their breath in anticipation. In Thayer's poem, the entire baseball game is on the line when we join the action in the final inning.

It looked extremely rocky for the Mudville nine
    that day;
The score stood two to four, with but an inning left
    to play.
So, when Cooney died at second, and Burrows did
    the same,
    A <u>pallor</u> <u>wreathed</u> the features of the patrons of the
    game.

5 A straggling few got up to go, leaving there the rest,
    With that hope which springs eternal within the
    human breast.
    For they thought: "If only Casey would get a whack
    at that,"
    They'd put even money now, with Casey at
    the bat.

    But Flynn preceded Casey, and likewise so did Blake,
10 And the former was a pudd'n, and the latter was a
    fake.
    So on that stricken multitude a deathlike silence sat;
    For there seemed but little chance of Casey's getting
    to the bat.

    But Flynn let drive a "single," to the wonderment of all.
    And the much-despised Blakey "tore the cover off
    the ball."
15 And when the dust had lifted, and they saw what
    had occurred,
    There was Blakey safe at second, and Flynn a-huggin'
    third.

Vocabulary Development: pallor (paľ ər) *n.* paleness
                               wreathed (rēthd) *v.* curled around

---

◆ **Activate Prior Knowledge**

Think of a high pressure situation in which you were expected to perform well. How do you think the added pressure affected your ability to perform?

_____

_____

_____

_____

_____

◆ **Reading Strategy**

Underline the main events in lines 1–8. Then, briefly retell in your own words what happened.

_____

_____

_____

_____

_____

_____

◆ **Reading Check**

What has happened that might give Mudville fans some hope of victory?

_____

_____

_____

_____

_____

The **climax** is the high point of the story. Usually, an author builds suspense up until the climax, then a major event occurs. Can you guess what the climax will be in "Casey at the Bat"?

_____

_____

Summarize, in your own words, what has happened up to this point.

_____

_____

_____

_____

_____

_____

_____

_____

Then from the gladdened multitude went up a joyous
   yell—
It rumbled in the mountaintops, it rattled in the dell;[1]
It struck upon the hillside and rebounded on the flat;
20 For Casey, mighty Casey, was advancing to the bat.

There was ease in Casey's manner as he stepped into
   his place,
There was pride in Casey's bearing and a smile on
   Casey's face;
And when responding to the cheers he lightly doffed[2]
   his hat,
No stranger in the crowd could doubt 'twas Casey at
   the bat.

25 Ten thousand eyes were on him as he rubbed his
   hands with dirt,
Five thousand tongues applauded when he wiped them
   on his shirt;
Then when the <u>writhing</u> pitcher ground the ball into
   his hip,
Defiance glanced in Casey's eye, a sneer curled
   Casey's lip.

And now the leather-covered sphere came hurtling
   through the air,
30 And Casey stood a-watching it in haughty grandeur
   there.
Close by the sturdy batsman the ball unheeded sped;
"That ain't my style," said Casey. "Strike one," the
   umpire said.

Vocabulary Development: writhing (rīth´iŋ) *v.* twisting; turning

---

1. **dell** (del) *n.* small, secluded valley.
2. **doffed** (däft) *v.* lifted, took off.

From the benches, black with people, there went up a
    muffled roar,
Like the beating of the storm waves on the stern and
    distant shore.
35 "Kill him! kill the umpire!" shouted someone on the
    stand;
And it's likely they'd have killed him had not
    Casey raised his hand.

With a smile of Christian charity great Casey's visage[3]
    shone;
He stilled the rising <u>tumult</u>, he made the game go on;
He signaled to the pitcher, and once more the spheroid
    flew;
40 But Casey still ignored it, and the umpire said,
    "Strike two."

"Fraud!" cried the maddened thousands, and the echo
    answered "Fraud!"
But one scornful look from Casey and the audience
    was awed;
They saw his face grow stern and cold, they saw his
    muscles strain,
And they knew that Casey wouldn't let the ball go
    by again.

45 The sneer is gone from Casey's lips, his teeth are
    clenched in hate.
He pounds with cruel vengeance his bat upon
    the plate:
And now the pitcher holds the ball, and now he
    lets it go,
And now the air is shattered by the force of Casey's
    blow.

Vocabulary Development: tumult (tōō´ məlt) *n.* noisy commotion

---

3. **visage** (viz´ ij) *n.* face.

◆ **Reading Check**

What are the reactions of Casey and the crowd to the umpire's decision to call a strike?

The crowd's reaction:

_____

_____

Casey's reaction:

_____

_____

Are they similar or different?

_____

_____

◆ **Reading Strategy**

You do not need to include every event in a summary—only events that are important to the action. If you were to summarize the main events in the bracketed stanza, which events would you choose?

_____

_____

_____

_____

◆ **Literary Analysis**

Circle the line in which the **climax,** or high point, of the story occurs. How did you know which line to choose?

_____

_____

Who lost the baseball game?

_____

_____

_____

_____

_____

Oh, somewhere in this favored land the sun is
    shining bright,
50 The band is playing somewhere, and somewhere
    hearts are light:
And somewhere men are laughing, and somewhere
    children shout,
But there is no joy in Mudville: Mighty Casey has
    struck out.

Reader's Response: An **anticlimax** occurs when you feel suddenly disappointed by the outcome of the climax. Was the ending of this story an anticlimax? Explain why or why not.

_____

_____

_____

Thinking About the Skill: How did summarizing help you understand the poem?

_____

_____

_____

from A Lincoln Preface

Carl Sandburg

Summary

This selection is a profile of the sixteenth U.S. president, Abraham Lincoln. Carl Sandburg, the profile's author, begins by describing Lincoln's assassination. Next, he describes Lincoln's role in the Civil War. Sandburg shows how Lincoln stubbornly supported the cause of the Union despite tremendous loss of life and property. In the final section, Sandburg explores the conflicting sides of Lincoln's personality. He tells stories that show how Lincoln could be cunning and ill-tempered. But he also shows Lincoln as a man who was often humorous, patient, and generous. In his essay, Sandburg crafts a portrait of a complex man who was determined to save the Union at any cost.

Visual Summary

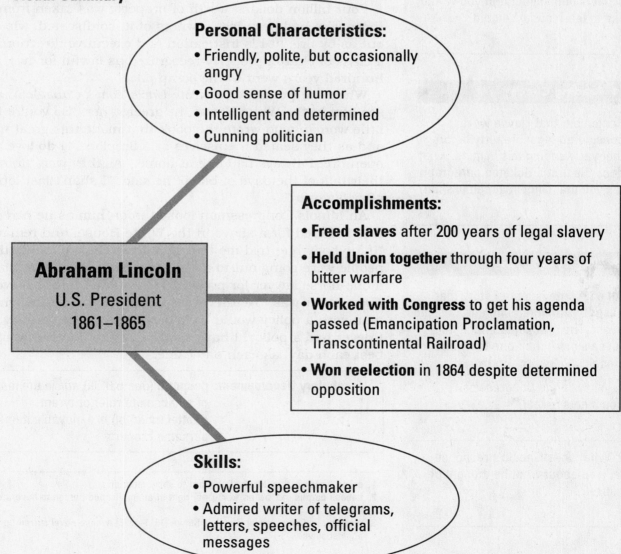

Personal Characteristics:
- Friendly, polite, but occasionally angry
- Good sense of humor
- Intelligent and determined
- Cunning politician

Abraham Lincoln
U.S. President
1861–1865

Accomplishments:
- **Freed slaves** after 200 years of legal slavery
- **Held Union together** through four years of bitter warfare
- **Worked with Congress** to get his agenda passed (Emancipation Proclamation, Transcontinental Railroad)
- **Won reelection** in 1864 despite determined opposition

Skills:
- Powerful speechmaker
- Admired writer of telegrams, letters, speeches, official messages

_____

_____

Before you read further, **establish your purpose for reading.** Read this selection with the **purpose** of learning more about Abraham Lincoln. What is one aspect that you would like to learn about Lincoln?

_____

_____

Remember that slaves were considered legal property before the war. Keeping this in mind, what does the first bracketed paragraph tell you that Lincoln accomplished?

_____

_____

An **anecdote** is a brief story that describes an interesting or amusing event. The bracketed anecdote reveals more than one thing about Lincoln.

1. What do the Congressman's comments reveal?

_____

_____

2. What does Lincoln's response tell you about what he thought of himself?

_____

_____

from A Lincoln Preface
Carl Sandburg

This selection is taken from the preface to Carl Sandburg's six-volume biography of Abraham Lincoln.

In the time of the April lilacs in the year 1865, a man in the City of Washington, D.C., trusted a guard to watch at a door, and the guard was careless, left the door, and the man was shot, lingered a night, passed away, was laid in a box, and carried north and west a thousand miles; bells sobbed; cities wore crepe;[1] people stood with hats off as the railroad burial car came past at midnight, dawn or noon.

During the four years of time before he gave up the ghost, this man was clothed with despotic power, commanding the most powerful armies till then assembled in modern warfare, enforcing drafts of soldiers, abolishing the right of habeas corpus,[2] directing politically and spiritually the wild, massive forces loosed in civil war.

Four billion dollars' worth of property was taken from those who had been legal owners of it, confiscated, wiped out as by fire, at his instigation and executive direction; a class of chattel property recognized as lawful for two hundred years went to the scrap pile.

When the woman who wrote *Uncle Tom's Cabin*[3] came to see him in the White House, he greeted her, "So you're the little woman who wrote the book that made this great war," and as they seated themselves at a fireplace, "I do love an open fire: I always had one at home." As they were finishing their talk of the days of blood, he said, "I shan't last long after it's over."

An Illinois Congressman looked in on him as he had his face lathered for a shave in the White House, and remarked, "If anybody had told me that in a great crisis like this the people were going out to a little one-horse town and pick out a one-horse lawyer for president, I wouldn't have believed it." The answer was, "Neither would I. But it was a time when a man with a policy would have been fatal to the country. I never had a policy. I have simply tried to do what seemed best each day, as each day came."

Vocabulary Development: despotic (des pät´ ik) *adj.* in the manner of an absolute ruler or tyrant
chattel (chat´ əl) *n.* a movable item of personal property

---

1. **crepe** (krāp) *n.* thin, black cloth worn to show mourning.
2. **habeas corpus** (hā bē əs kor´ pəs) right of an imprisoned person to have a court hearing.
3. **woman . . . *Cabin*** Harriet Beecher Stowe (1811–1896), whose novel stirred up opinion against slavery.

"I don't intend precisely to throw the Constitution overboard, but I will stick it in a hole if I can," he told a Cabinet officer. The enemy was violating the Constitution to destroy the Union, he argued, and therefore, "I will violate the Constitution, if necessary, to save the Union." He instructed a messenger to the Secretary of the Treasury, "Tell him not to bother himself about the Constitution. Say that I have that sacred instrument here at the White House, and I am guarding it with great care."

When he was renominated, it was by the device of seating delegates from Tennessee, which gave enough added votes to seat favorable delegates from Kentucky, Missouri, Louisiana, Arkansas, and from one county in Florida. Until late in that campaign of 1864, he expected to lose the November election; military victories brought the tide his way; the vote was 2,200,000 for him and 1,800,000 against him. Among those who bitterly fought him politically, and accused him of blunders or crimes, were Franklin Pierce, a former president of the United States; Horatio Seymour, the Governor of New York; Samuel F. B. Morse, inventor of the telegraph; Cyrus H. McCormick, inventor of the farm reaper; General George B. McClellan, a Democrat who had commanded the Army of the Potomac; and the *Chicago Times*, a daily newspaper. In all its essential propositions the Southern Confederacy had the moral support of powerful, respectable elements throughout the North, probably more than a million votes believing in the justice of the cause of the South as compared with the North.

While propagandas raged, and the war winds howled, he sat in the White House, the Stubborn Man of History, writing that the Mississippi was one river and could not belong to two countries, that the plans for railroad connection from coast to coast must be pushed through and the Union Pacific[4] realized.

His life, mind and heart ran in contrasts. When his white kid gloves broke into tatters while shaking hands at a White House reception, he remarked, "This looks like a general bustification." When he talked with an Ohio friend one day during the 1864 campaign, he mentioned one public man, and murmured, "He's a thistle! I don't see why God lets him live." Of a devious Senator, he said, "He's too crooked to lie still!" And of a New York editor, "In early life in the West, we used to make our shoes last a great while with much mending, and sometimes, when far gone, we found the leather so rotten the stitches would not hold. Greeley is so rotten that nothing can be done with him. He is not truthful; the stitches all tear out." As he sat in the telegraph office of the War

---

4. **Union Pacific** railroad chartered by Congress in 1862 to form part of a transcontinental system.

◆ Literary Analysis

What does the **anecdote** about the Constitution reveal about Lincoln's goals and methods?

_____

_____

_____

_____

_____

◆ Reading Strategy

Lincoln seemed to be fighting an uphill battle in the election of 1864. Circle the forces listed in the bracketed paragraph that were working against his reelection.

◆ Reading Check

Judging from his remark, what did Lincoln think of Horace Greeley?

_____

_____

_____

Sandburg admires Lincoln's leadership during the Civil War. What do you think makes a wartime leader successful?

_____

_____

_____

Remember that you are reading for the **purpose** of learning new information. What new information do you learn in the first bracketed paragraph?

_____

_____

_____

To what is the author referring when he mentions the "mixed shame and blame of the immense wrongs of two crashing civilizations"?

_____

_____

What do the **anecdotes** in the second bracketed paragraph reveal about Lincoln and the times in which he lived?

_____

_____

_____

_____

_____

Department, reading cipher dispatches, and came to the words, Hosanna and Husband, he would chuckle, "Jeffy D.,"[5] and at the words, Hunter and Happy, "Bobby Lee."[6]

While the luck of war wavered and broke and came again, as generals failed and campaigns were lost, he held enough forces of the Union together to raise new armies and supply them, until generals were found who made war as victorious war has always been made, with terror, frightfulness, destruction, and valor and sacrifice past words of man to tell.

A slouching, gray-headed poet,[7] haunting the hospitals at Washington, characterized him as "the grandest figure on the crowded canvas of the drama of the nineteenth century— a Hoosier Michael Angelo."[8]

His own speeches, letters, telegrams and official messages during that war form the most significant and enduring document from any one man on why the war began, why it went on, and the dangers beyond its end. He mentioned "the politicians," over and again "the politicians," with scorn and blame. As the platoons filed before him at a review of an army corps, he asked, "What is to become of these boys when the war is over?"

He was a chosen spokesman: yet there were times he was silent; nothing but silence could at those times have fitted a chosen spokesman; in the mixed shame and blame of the immense wrongs of two crashing civilizations, with nothing to say, he said nothing, slept not at all, and wept at those times in a way that made weeping appropriate, decent, majestic.

His hat was shot off as he rode alone one night in Washington; a son he loved died as he watched at the bed; his wife was accused of betraying information to the enemy, until denials from him were necessary; his best companion was a fine-hearted and brilliant son with a deformed palate and an impediment of speech; when a Pennsylvania Congressman told him the enemy had declared they would break into the city and hang him to a lamppost, he said he had considered "the violent preliminaries" to such a scene; on his left thumb was a scar where an ax had nearly chopped the thumb off when he was a boy; over one eye was a scar where he had been hit with a club in the hands of a man trying to steal the cargo off a Mississippi River flatboat;

Vocabulary Development: cipher (sī´ fər) *adj.* code
slouching (slouch´ iŋ) *adj.* drooping

---

5. **"Jeffy D."** Jefferson Davis (1808–1889), president of the Confederacy.
6. **"Bobby Lee"** Robert E. Lee (1807–1870), commander in chief of the Confederate army.
7. **slouching . . . poet** Walt Whitman (1819–1892).
8. **Michael Angelo** Michelangelo (mik´ əl an´ jə lō), a famous Italian artist (1475–1564).

he threw a cashiered[9] officer out of his room in the White House, crying, "I can bear censure, but not insult. I never wish to see your face again."

As he shook hands with the correspondent of the London *Times,* he drawled, "Well, I guess the London *Times* is about the greatest power on earth—unless perhaps it is the Mississippi River." He rebuked with anger a woman who got on her knees to thank him for a pardon that saved her son from being shot at sunrise; and when an Iowa woman said she had journeyed out of her way to Washington just for a look at him, he grinned, "Well, in the matter of looking at one another, I have altogether the advantage."

He asked his Cabinet to vote on the high military command, and after the vote, told them the appointment had already been made; one Cabinet officer, who had been governor of Ohio, came away personally baffled and frustrated from an interview, to exclaim, to a private secretary, "That man is the most cunning person I ever saw in my life"; an Illinois lawyer who had been sent on errands carrying his political secrets, said, "He is a trimmer[10] and such a trimmer as the world has never seen."

He manipulated the admission of Nevada as a state in the Union, when her votes were needed for the Emancipation Proclamation,[11] saying, "It is easier to admit Nevada than to raise another million of soldiers." At the same time he went to the office of a former New York editor, who had become Assistant Secretary of War, and said the votes of three congressmen were wanted for the required three-quarters of votes in the House of Representatives, advising, "There are three that you can deal with better than anybody else . . . . Whatever promise you make to those men, I will perform it." And in the same week, he said to a Massachusetts politician that two votes were lacking, and, "Those two votes must be procured. I leave it to you to determine how it shall be done; but remember that I am President of the United States and clothed with immense power, and I expect you to procure those votes." And while he was thus employing every last resource and device of practical politics to constitutionally abolish slavery, the abolitionist[12] Henry Ward Beecher attacked him with javelins of scorn and detestation in a series of editorials that brought from him the single comment, "Is thy servant a dog?"

Vocabulary Development: censure (sen´ shər) *n.* strong disapproval

---

9. **cashiered** (ka shird´) *adj.* dishonorably discharged.
10. **trimmer** (trim´ ər) *n.* person who changes his opinion to suit the circumstances.
11. **Emancipation Proclamation** document issued by President Lincoln freeing the slaves in all territories still at war with the Union.
12. **abolitionist** (ab´ ə lish´ ən ist) *n.* person in favor of doing away with slavery in the United States.

◆ **Literary Analysis**

Sandburg presents a variety of different **anecdotes** about Lincoln in the first bracketed paragraph. Two anecdotes show a good-natured Lincoln; one shows an angry Lincoln. What is Sandburg attempting to demonstrate by presenting Lincoln in different moods?

_____

_____

_____

◆ **Stop to Reflect**

How do the events described in the second bracketed paragraph differ from the usual notion of "Honest Abe"?

_____

_____

_____

◆ **Reading Check**

What steps does Lincoln take to make sure the Emancipation Proclamation is passed?

_____

_____

_____

_____

_____

Why does Lincoln write a thank-you letter to the King of Siam?

_____

_____

_____

_____

_____

When the King of Siam sent him a costly sword of exquisite embellishment, and two elephant tusks, along with letters and a photograph of the King, he acknowledged the gifts in a manner as lavish as the Orientals. Addressing the King of Siam as "Great and Good Friend," he wrote thanks for each of the gifts, including "also two elephant's tusks of length and magnitude, such as indicate they could have belonged only to an animal which was a native of Siam." After further thanks for the tokens received, he closed the letter to the King of Siam with strange grace and humor, saying, "I appreciate most highly your Majesty's tender of good offices in forwarding to this Government a stock from which a supply of elephants might be raised on our soil. . . . our political jurisdiction, however, does not reach a latitude so low as to favor the multiplication of the elephant, and steam on land as well as water has been our best agent of transportation . . . Meantime, wishing for your Majesty a long and happy life, and, for the generous and emulous people of Siam, the highest possible prosperity, I commend both to the blessing of Almighty God."

He sent hundreds of telegrams, "Suspend death sentence" or "Suspend execution" of So-and-So, who was to be shot at sunrise. The telegrams varied oddly at times, as in one, "If Thomas Samplogh, of the First Delaware Regiment, has been sentenced to death, and is not yet executed, suspend and report the case to me." And another, "Is it Lieut. Samuel B. Davis whose death sentence is commuted? If not done, let it be done."

◆ Stop to Reflect

Why would President Lincoln pay such close attention to the sentences of men who have been condemned to death?

_____

_____

_____

While the war drums beat, he liked best of all the stories told of him, one of two Quakeresses[13] heard talking in a railway car. "I think that Jefferson will succeed." "Why does thee think so?" "Because Jefferson is a praying man." "And so is Abraham a praying man." "Yes, but the Lord will think Abraham is joking."

An Indiana man at the White House heard him say, "Voorhees, don't it seem strange to you that I, who could never so much as cut off the head of a chicken, should be elected, or selected, into the midst of all this blood?"

◆ Literary Analysis

What does the bracketed **anecdote** reveal about how Lincoln must have felt about the war?

_____

_____

_____

A party of American citizens, standing in the ruins of the Forum in Rome, Italy, heard there the news of the first assassination of the first American dictator, and took it as a sign of the growing up and the aging of the civilization on the North American continent. Far out in Coles County, Illinois, a beautiful, <u>gaunt</u> old woman in a log cabin said, "I knowed he'd never come back."

Vocabulary Development: gaunt (gônt) *adj.* thin and bony

---

13. **Quakeresses** (kwāk´ ər es əz) *n.* female members of the religious group known as the Society of Friends, or Quakers.

Of men taking too fat profits out of the war, he said, "Where the carcass is there will the eagles be gathered together."

An enemy general, Longstreet, after the war, declared him to have been "the one matchless man in forty millions of people," while one of his private secretaries, Hay, declared his life to have been the most perfect in its relationships and adjustments since that of Christ.

Between the days in which he crawled as a baby on the dirt floor of a Kentucky cabin, and the time when he gave his final breath in Washington, he packed a rich life with work, thought, laughter, tears, hate, love.

With vast reservoirs of the comic and the <u>droll</u>, and notwithstanding a mastery of mirth and nonsense, he delivered a volume of addresses and letters of terrible and serious appeal, with import beyond his own day, shot through here and there with far, thin ironics, with paragraphs having raillery[14] of the quality of the Book of Job,[15] and echoes as subtle as the whispers of wind in prairie grass.

Perhaps no human clay pot has held more laughter and tears.

The facts and myths of his life are to be an American possession, shared widely over the world, for thousands of years, as the tradition of Knute or Alfred, Lao-tse or Diogenes, Pericles or Caesar,[16] are kept. This because he was not only a genius in the science of neighborly human relationships and an artist in the personal handling of life from day to day, but a strange friend and a friendly stranger to all forms of life that he met.

He lived fifty-six years of which fifty-two were lived in the West—the prairie years.

Vocabulary Development: droll (drōl) *adj.* comic and amusing in an odd way

---

14. **raillery** (rāl´ ər ē) *n.* good-natured teasing.
15. **Book of Job** (jōb) book of the Old Testament in which a man named Job is tested by God.
16. **Knute** (kno͞ot) **or Alfred, Lao-tse** (lou´ dzu´) **or Diogenes** (dī äj´ ə nēz), **Pericles** (per´ ə klēz) **or Caesar** (sē´ zər) well-known thinkers and leaders from different eras and places.

Reader's Response: Compare your prior knowledge of Abraham Lincoln with what you know now. How did your impression of President Lincoln change as a result of reading Sandburg's essay?

_____

_____

◆ Stop to Reflect

What kind of person do you have to be to have your enemies describe you with respect?

_____

_____

_____

◆ Reading Strategy

Circle the words that Sandburg uses to describe Lincoln's writing and speeches. What information do these words convey about Lincoln's talent as a writer?

_____

_____

_____

◆ Reading Check

Why does Sandburg think that Lincoln has generated so much attention over the years?

_____

_____

_____

_____

_____

"I Have a Dream"
Martin Luther King, Jr.

Summary

   In this famous speech, Dr. Martin Luther King, Jr., presents his vision of what America would be like if racism and inequality did not exist. He quotes from the Declaration of Independence and the Bible in order to illustrate his idea of freedom. King begins the speech by identifying what he wants to see happen. This is done in a series of word pictures, all of which begin with the phrase "I have a dream." Then he states that it is through faith that these changes can occur. He closes with an encouragement to all who are listening to "let freedom ring" throughout the country.

Visual Summary

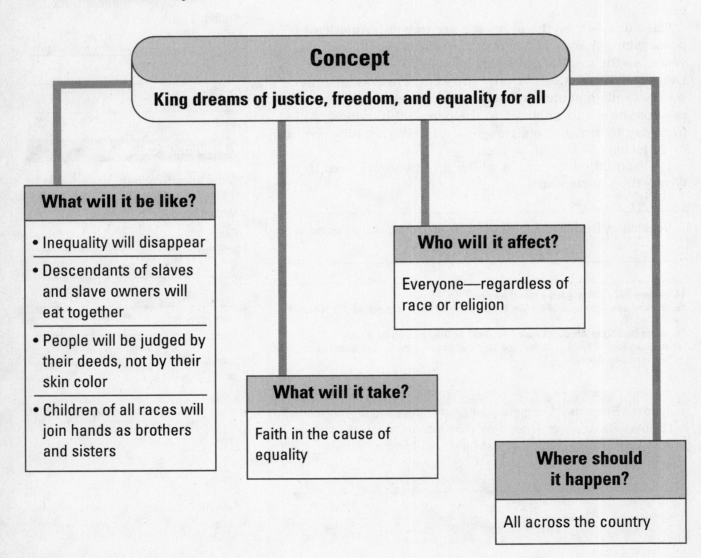

Concept

King dreams of justice, freedom, and equality for all

What will it be like?

- Inequality will disappear
- Descendants of slaves and slave owners will eat together
- People will be judged by their deeds, not by their skin color
- Children of all races will join hands as brothers and sisters

Who will it affect?

Everyone—regardless of race or religion

What will it take?

Faith in the cause of equality

Where should it happen?

All across the country

"I Have a Dream"
Martin Luther King, Jr.

Martin Luther King, Jr., was an important leader of the civil rights movement—a movement that fought racial inequality. He delivered his "I Have a Dream" speech in August 1963 at the March on Washington for Jobs and Freedom. He spoke from the steps of the Lincoln Memorial in front of 250,000 people.

. . . I say to you today, my friends, that in spite of the difficulties and frustrations of the moment I still have a dream. It is a dream deeply rooted in the American dream.

I have a dream that one day this nation will rise up and live out the true meaning of its creed: "We hold these truths to be self-evident; that all men are created equal."

I have a dream that one day on the red hills of Georgia the sons of former slaves and the sons of former slaveowners will be able to sit down together at the table of brotherhood.

I have a dream that one day even the state of Mississippi, a desert state sweltering with the heat of injustice and oppression, will be transformed into an oasis of freedom and justice.

I have a dream that my four little children will one day live in a nation where they will not be judged by the color of their skin but by the content of their character.

I have a dream today.

I have a dream that one day the state of Alabama, whose governor's lips are presently dripping with the words of interposition and nullification,[1] will be transformed into a situation where little black boys and black girls will be able to join hands with little white boys and white girls and walk together as sisters and brothers.

I have a dream today.

I have a dream that one day every valley shall be exalted, every hill and mountain shall be made low, the rough places will be made plains, and the crooked places will be made straight, and the glory of the Lord shall be revealed, and all flesh shall see it together.[2]

Vocabulary Development: creed (krēd) *n.* statement of belief
oppression (ə presh′ ən) *n.* keeping others down by the unjust use of power
oasis (ō ā′ sis) *n.* fertile place in the desert
exalted (eg zôlt′ əd) *v.* lifted up

---

1. **interposition** (in′ tər pə zish′ ən) **and nullification** (nul′ ə fi kā′ shən) controversial belief that a state can reject federal laws considered to be violations of state law. In this case, the governor was arguing that federal civil rights laws did not apply to Alabama.
2. **every valley . . . all flesh shall see it together** refers to a biblical passage (Isaiah 40: 4–5).

◆ **Activate Prior Knowledge**

Think of what you already know about Martin Luther King, Jr. Why do we honor this civil rights leader with a national holiday every year?

_____

_____

◆ **Reading Strategy**

To **respond** means to react. As you read King's statements, think about the emotions you feel and what his ideas mean to you. What emotional response do you have to the dream that King expresses in the first bracketed paragraph?

_____

_____

_____

◆ **Reading Check**

Read the second bracketed paragraph and footnote #1 below. What transformation, or change, does King hope will take place in Alabama?

_____

_____

_____

_____

An author's **tone** is the way he or she says something. A tone can be serious, lighthearted, inspirational, or depressing. How would you describe King's tone in the first bracketed paragraph? Circle details on which you base your answer.

_____

_____

Speakers often make appeals to patriotism during a speech. How does King's appeal to America's ideals affect your **response** in the second bracketed paragraph?

_____

_____

_____

_____

_____

Why do you think King chose to end his speech with the image of joining hands and singing a spiritual?

_____

_____

_____

_____

_____

This is our hope. This is the faith with which I return to the South. With this faith we will be able to transform the jangling discords of our nation into a beautiful symphony of brotherhood. With this faith we will be able to work together, to pray together, to struggle together, to go to jail together, to stand up for freedom together, knowing that we will be free one day.

This will be the day when all of God's children will be able to sing with new meaning "My country 'tis of thee, sweet land of liberty, of thee I sing. Land where my fathers died, land of the pilgrim's pride, from every mountainside, let freedom ring."

And if America is to be a great nation this must become true. So let freedom ring from the prodigious hilltops of New Hampshire. Let freedom ring from the mighty mountains of New York. Let freedom ring from the heightening Alleghenies of Pennsylvania!

Let freedom ring from the snowcapped Rockies of Colorado!

Let freedom ring from the curvaceous peaks of California!

But not only that: let freedom ring from Stone Mountain of Georgia!

Let freedom ring from every hill and molehill of Mississippi. From every mountainside, let freedom ring.

When we let freedom ring, when we let it ring from every village and every hamlet, from every state and every city, we will be able to speed up that day when all of God's children, black men and white men, Jews and Gentiles, Protestants and Catholics, will be able to join hands and sing in the words of that old Negro spiritual, "Free at last! Free at last! Thank God almighty, we are free at last!"

Vocabulary Development: prodigious (prə dij´ əs) *adj.* wonderful; of great size
hamlet (ham´ lit) *n.* very small village

Reader's Response: What do you imagine it would have been like to have been in King's audience in 1963?

_____

_____

_____

_____

Old Man of the Temple

R. K. Narayan

Summary

This work of fantasy is set in India. As the story opens, the narrator, called The Talkative Man, is explaining events that happened "some years ago." He and his driver were driving down a lonely country road at night. Doss, the driver, suddenly swerved the car, shouting at an old man. The narrator, however, saw no one. Doss claimed to have seen an old man come out the door of the nearby temple. The narrator is confused, because the temple is in ruins. Doss passes out. When Doss wakes up, he speaks in the voice of an old man. He claims to be Krishna Battar, the builder of the temple. The narrator tells Battar that he is dead and that he should join his deceased wife, Seetha. Battar thinks about his dead wife, then sees her coming. He falls to the ground. When Doss awakens, he is his old self. The narrator learns that strange knocking has disturbed village residents and animals for years. After this incident, however, the knocking stops and the animals are no longer afraid.

Visual Summary

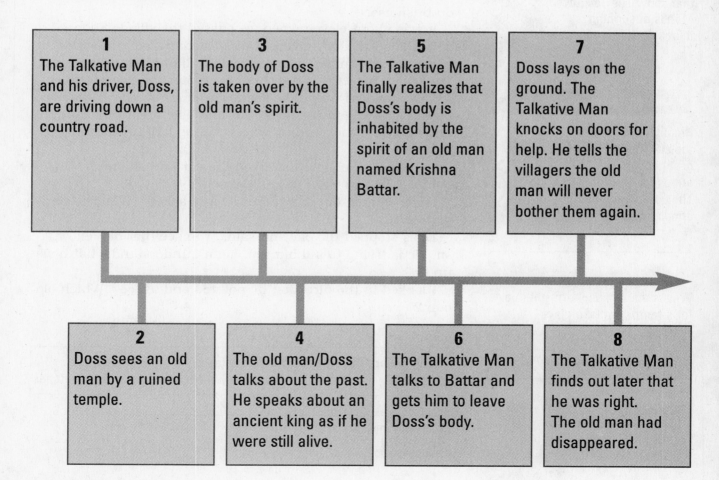

1
The Talkative Man and his driver, Doss, are driving down a country road.

3
The body of Doss is taken over by the old man's spirit.

5
The Talkative Man finally realizes that Doss's body is inhabited by the spirit of an old man named Krishna Battar.

7
Doss lays on the ground. The Talkative Man knocks on doors for help. He tells the villagers the old man will never bother them again.

2
Doss sees an old man by a ruined temple.

4
The old man/Doss talks about the past. He speaks about an ancient king as if he were still alive.

6
The Talkative Man talks to Battar and gets him to leave Doss's body.

8
The Talkative Man finds out later that he was right. The old man had disappeared.

Old Man of the Temple
R. K. Narayan

Indian villages are often located far from cities and connected by dirt roads to the rest of the country. The narrator begins his story by describing a strange taxi ride near a remote Indian village.

The Talkative Man said:

It was some years ago that this happened. I don't know if you can make anything of it. If you do, I shall be glad to hear what you have to say; but personally I don't understand it at all. It has always mystified me. Perhaps the driver was drunk; perhaps he wasn't.

I had engaged a taxi for going to Kumbum, which, as you may already know, is fifty miles from Malgudi.[1] I went there one morning and it was past nine in the evening when I finished my business and started back for the town. Doss,[2] the driver, was a young fellow of about twenty-five. He had often brought his car for me and I liked him. He was a well-behaved, obedient fellow, with a capacity to sit and wait at the wheel, which is really a rare quality in a taxi driver. He drove the car smoothly, seldom swore at passers-by, and exhibited perfect judgment, good sense, and sobriety; and so I preferred him to any other driver whenever I had to go out on business.

It was about eleven when we passed the village Koopal,[3] which is on the way down. It was the dark half of the month and the surrounding country was swallowed up in the night. The village street was deserted. Everyone had gone to sleep; hardly any light was to be seen. The stars overhead sparkled brightly. Sitting in the back seat and listening to the continuous noise of the running wheels, I was half lulled into a drowse.

All of a sudden Doss swerved the car and shouted: "You old fool! Do you want to kill yourself?"

I was shaken out of my drowse and asked: "What is the matter?"

Doss stopped the car and said, "You see that old fellow, sir. He is trying to kill himself. I can't understand what he is up to."

I looked in the direction he pointed and asked, "Which old man?"

Vocabulary Development: sobriety (sə brī′ ə tē) *n.* moderation, especially in the use of alcoholic beverages

---

1. **Malgudi** (mäl gōō′ dē) fictional city about which Narayan often writes.
2. **Doss** (däs)
3. **Koopal** (kōō päl′)

"There, there. He is coming towards us again. As soon as I saw him open that temple door and come out I had a feeling, somehow, that I must keep an eye on him."

I took out my torch, got down, and walked about, but could see no one. There was an old temple on the roadside. It was utterly in ruins; most portions of it were mere mounds of old brick; the walls were <u>awry</u>; the doors were shut to the main doorway, and brambles and thickets grew over and covered them. It was difficult to guess with the aid of the torch alone what temple it was and to what period it belonged.

"The doors are shut and sealed and don't look as if they had been opened for centuries now," I cried.

"No, sir," Doss said coming nearer. "I saw the old man open the doors and come out. He is standing there; shall we ask him to open them again if you want to go in and see?"

I said to Doss, "Let us be going. We are wasting our time here."

We went back to the car. Doss sat in his seat, pressed the self-starter, and asked without turning his head, "Are you permitting this fellow to come with us, sir? He says he will get down at the next milestone."

"Which fellow?" I asked.

Doss indicated the space next to him.

"What is the matter with you, Doss? Have you had a drop of drink or something?"

"I have never tasted any drink in my life. sir," he said, and added, "Get down, old boy. Master says he can't take you."

"Are you talking to yourself?"

"After all, I think we needn't care for these unknown fellows on the road," he said.

"Doss," I pleaded. "Do you feel confident you can drive? If you feel dizzy don't drive."

"Thank you, sir," said Doss. "I would rather not start the car now. I am feeling a little out of sorts." I looked at him anxiously. He closed his eyes, his breathing became heavy and noisy, and gradually his head sank.

"Doss, Doss," I cried desperately. I got down, walked to the front seat, opened the door, and shook him vigorously. He opened his eyes, assumed a hunched-up position, and rubbed his eyes with his hands, which trembled like an old man's.

"Do you feel better?" I asked.

"Better! Better! Hi! Hi!" he said in a thin, piping voice.

"What has happened to your voice? You sound like someone else," I said.

Vocabulary Development: awry (ə rī´) *adj.* not straight

◆ **Reading Strategy**

The narrator's and Doss's impressions of the temple are quite different.

What is the narrator's impression?

_____

_____

What is Doss's impression?

_____

_____

◆ **Stop to Reflect**

How would you react if you were in a car with a driver who saw imaginary people?

_____

_____

_____

_____

_____

◆ **Reading Check**

What has happened to Doss?

_____

_____

_____

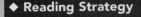

_____

_____

The conversation in the second bracketed passage blends reality and fantasy. Identify which elements are real and which are fantasy by circling phrases and marking "R" or "F" in the text.

Why does Doss fail to recognize his own name in the underlined passage?

_____

_____

Why do you think that the narrator and Doss are having so much trouble understanding each other?

_____

_____

_____

"Nothing. My voice is as good as it was. When a man is eighty he is bound to feel a few changes coming on."

"You aren't eighty, surely," I said.

"Not a day less," he said. "Is nobody going to move this vehicle? If not, there is no sense in sitting here all day. I will get down and go back to my temple."

"I don't know how to drive," I said. "And unless you do it, I don't see how it can move."

"Me!" exclaimed Doss. "These new chariots! God knows what they are drawn by, I never understand, though I could handle a pair of bullocks[4] in my time. May I ask a question?"

"Go on," I said.

"Where is everybody?"

"Who?"

"Lots of people I knew are not to be seen at all. All sorts of new fellows everywhere, and nobody seems to care. Not a soul comes near the temple. All sorts of people go about but not one who cares to stop and talk. Why doesn't the king ever come this way? He used to go this way at least once a year before."

"Which king?" I asked.

"Let me go, you idiot," said Doss, edging towards the door on which I was leaning. "You don't seem to know anything." He pushed me aside, and got down from the car. He stooped as if he had a big hump on his back, and hobbled along towards the temple. I followed him, hardly knowing what to do. He turned and snarled at me: "Go away, leave me alone. I have had enough of you."

"What has come over you, Doss?" I asked.

"Who is Doss, anyway? Doss, Doss, Doss. What an absurd name! Call me by my name or leave me alone. Don't follow me calling 'Doss, Doss.' "

"What is your name?" I asked.

"Krishna Battar,[5] and if you mention my name people will know for a hundred miles around. I built a temple where there was only a cactus field before. I dug the earth, burnt every brick, and put them one upon another, all single-handed. And on the day the temple held up its tower over the surrounding country, what a crowd gathered! The king sent his chief minister . . ."

"Who was the king?"

"Where do you come from?" he asked.

"I belong to these parts certainly, but as far as I know there has been only a collector at the head of the district. I have never heard of any king."

"Hi! Hi! Hi!" he cackled, and his voice rang through the gloomy silent village. "Fancy never knowing the king! He will behead you if he hears it."

---

4. **bullocks** (bŏŏl´ əks) *n.* oxen; steer.
5. **Krishna Battar** (krish´ nə bə tar´)

"What is his name?" I asked.

This tickled him so much that he sat down on the ground, literally unable to stand the joke any more. He laughed and coughed uncontrollably.

"I am sorry to admit," I said, "that my parents have brought me up in such utter ignorance of worldly affairs that I don't know even my king. But won't you enlighten me? What is his name?"

"Vishnu Varma,[6] the emperor of emperors . . ."

I cast my mind up and down the range of my historical knowledge but there was no one by that name. Perhaps a local chief of pre-British days, I thought.

"What a king! He often visited my temple or sent his minister for the Annual Festival of the temple. But now nobody cares."

"People are becoming less godly nowadays," I said. There was silence for a moment. An idea occurred to me, I can't say why. "Listen to me," I said. "You ought not to be here any more."

"What do you mean?" he asked, drawing himself up, proudly.

"Don't feel hurt; I say you shouldn't be here any more because you are dead."

"Dead! Dead!" he said. "Don't talk nonsense. How can I be dead when you see me before you now? If I am dead how can I be saying this and that?"

"I don't know all that," I said. I argued and pointed out that according to his own story he was more than five hundred years old, and didn't he know that man's longevity was only a hundred? He constantly interrupted me, but considered deeply what I said.

He said: "It is like this . . . I was coming through the jungle one night after visiting my sister in the next village. I had on me some money and gold ornaments. A gang of robbers set upon me. I gave them as good a fight as any man could, but they were too many for me. They beat me down and knifed me; they took away all that I had on me and left thinking they had killed me. But soon I got up and tried to follow them. They were gone. And I returned to the temple and have been here since . . ."

I told him, "Krishna Battar, you are dead, absolutely dead. You must try and go away from here."

Vocabulary Development: literally (lit′ ər əl ē) *adv.* actually; in fact
longevity (län jev′ ə tē) *n.* the length or duration of a life

---

6. **Vishnu Varma** (vish′ nōō vär′ mə)

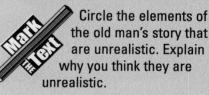

◆ **Reading Check**

Why is the narrator so preoccupied with the time of death of Krishna Battar's wife?

_____

_____

_____

◆ **Reading Strategy**

How does the narrator take advantage of Krishna Battar's confusion between what happened in the past and what is now occurring?

_____

_____

_____

◆ **Reading Check**

Circle the clues in the bracketed paragraphs that tell you that Doss has reentered the world of reality. How would you explain the narrator's success at bringing Doss back?

_____

_____

_____

"What is to happen to the temple?" he asked.

"Others will look after it."

"Where am I to go? Where am I to go?"

"Have you no one who cares for you?" I asked.

"None except my wife. I loved her very much."

"You can go to her."

"Oh, no. She died four years ago . . ."

Four years! It was very puzzling. "Do you say four years back from now?" I asked.

"Yes, four years ago from now." He was clearly without any sense of time.

So I asked, "Was she alive when you were attacked by thieves?"

"Certainly not. If she had been alive she would never have allowed me to go through the jungle after nightfall. She took very good care of me."

"See here," I said. "It is <u>imperative</u> you should go away from here. If she comes and calls you, will you go?"

"How can she when I tell you that she is dead?"

I thought for a moment. Presently I found myself saying, "Think of her, and only of her, for a while and see what happens. What was her name?"

"Seetha,[7] a wonderful girl . . ."

"Come on, think of her." He remained in deep thought for a while. He suddenly screamed, "Seetha is coming! Am I dreaming or what? I will go with her . . ." He stood up, very erect; he appeared to have lost all the humps and twists he had on his body. He drew himself up, made a dash forward, and fell down in a heap.

Doss lay on the rough ground. The only sign of life in him was his faint breathing. I shook him and called him. He would not open his eyes. I walked across and knocked on the door of the first cottage. I banged on the door violently.

Someone moaned inside, "Ah, it is come!"

Someone else whispered, "You just cover your ears and sleep. It will knock for a while and go away." I banged on the door and shouted who I was and where I came from.

I walked back to the car and sounded the horn. Then the door opened, and a whole family crowded out with lamps. "We thought it was the usual knocking and we wouldn't have opened if you hadn't spoken."

"When was this knocking first heard?" I asked.

"We can't say," said one. "The first time I heard it was when my grandfather was living; he used to say he had even seen it once or twice. It doesn't harm anyone, as far as I

Vocabulary Development: imperative (im per´ ə tiv) *adj.* absolutely necessary; urgent

---

7. **Seetha** (sē´ thə)

know. The only thing it does is bother the bullock carts passing the temple and knock on the doors at night . . ."

I said as a <u>venture</u>, "It is unlikely you will be troubled any more."

It proved correct. When I passed that way again months later I was told that the bullocks passing the temple after dusk never shied now and no knocking on the doors was heard at nights. So I felt that the old fellow had really gone away with his good wife.

Vocabulary Development: venture (ven´ chər) *n.* chance

Reader's Response: Some readers enjoy a story built around fantasy; others do not. Did you enjoy the way this story blended fantasy with reality? Explain.

_____

_____

Thinking About the Skill: How did recognizing elements of fantasy help you understand this selection?

_____

_____

Why does the narrator believe that the villagers will no longer be troubled?

_____

_____

_____

◆ Literary Analysis

What element of fantasy can be found in the closing paragraph?

_____

_____

_____

_____

Rules of the Game
Amy Tan

Summary

   This story is set in San Francisco's Chinatown. Waverly Jong, the main character, is a nine-year-old girl with Chinese parents. When her brother Vincent gets a used chess set, Waverly becomes fascinated with the game. She challenges her brothers, the men at the park, and finally tournament players, eventually beating them all. At the end of the story, Waverly is frustrated with her mother's tendency to "show her off" to complete strangers. She feels her mother does not understand her, and runs away after an argument with her mother. When Waverly returns home two hours later, her mother refuses to talk with her. It is clear that Waverly and her mother have different perspectives because of their difference in age and where they were born.

Visual Summary

Main Characters:	Waverly Jong Mrs. Jong (Waverly's mother)
Setting:	San Francisco's Chinatown
Conflict:	Waverly is embarrassed by her mother. Mrs. Jong thinks Waverly is ashamed of her.

Event 1: Waverly pesters her mother for some plums and her mother gets angry. Waverly learns that if she wants something it is better to remain silent. → **Event 2:** Waverly's brother Vincent gets a used chess set for Christmas. → **Event 3:** Waverly learns chess and begins to win several tournaments. She becomes well known for her chess-playing ability.

Climax: Mrs. Jong's habit of introducing Waverly as a chess champion embarrasses her. Waverly tells her to stop, and she runs away when her mother gets angry.

Resolution: Waverly returns home—only to find her mother is giving her the "silent treatment." She goes to her room to ponder her next move in this mother-daughter conflict.

Rules of the Game
from The Joy Luck Club
Amy Tan

There are many differences between the cultures of China and the United States. In China, family and community are most important. An honor given to any family member brings honor to the whole family. In America, people tend to think more in terms of individual goals. These differences are one source of conflict between Waverly and her Chinese mother.

I was six when my mother taught me the art of invisible strength. It was a strategy for winning arguments, respect from others, and eventually, though neither of us knew it at the time, chess games.

"Bite back your tongue," scolded my mother when I cried loudly, yanking her hand toward the store that sold bags of salted plums. At home, she said, "Wise guy, he not go against wind. In Chinese we say, Come from South, blow with wind—poom!—North will follow. Strongest wind cannot be seen."

The next week I bit back my tongue as we entered the store with the forbidden candies. When my mother finished her shopping, she quietly plucked a small bag of plums from the rack and put it on the counter with the rest of the items.

My mother imparted her daily truths so she could help my older brothers and me rise above our circumstances. We lived in San Francisco's Chinatown. Like most of the other Chinese children who played in the back alleys of restaurants and curio shops,[1] I didn't think we were poor. My bowl was always full, three five-course meals every day, beginning with a soup full of mysterious things I didn't want to know the names of.

We lived on Waverly Place, in a warm, clean, two-bedroom flat that sat above a small Chinese bakery specializing in steamed pastries and dim sum.[2] In the early morning, when the alley was still quiet, I could smell fragrant red beans as they were cooked down to a pasty sweetness. By daybreak, our flat was heavy with the odor of fried sesame balls and sweet curried chicken crescents. From my bed, I would listen as my father got ready for work, then locked the door behind him, one-two-three clicks.

At the end of our two-block alley was a small sandlot playground with swings and slides well-shined down the middle with use. The play area was bordered by wood-slat benches where old-country people sat cracking roasted watermelon

---

1. **curio** (kyo͞or′ ē ō) **shops** shops that sell unusual or rare items.
2. **dim sum** (dim′ tso͞om) shells of dough filled with meat and vegetables and served as a light meal.

seeds with their golden teeth and scattering the husks to an impatient gathering of gurgling pigeons. The best playground, however, was the dark alley itself. It was crammed with daily mysteries and adventures. My brothers and I would peer into the medicinal herb shop, watching old Li dole out onto a stiff sheet of white paper the right amount of insect shells, saffron-colored[3] seeds and pungent leaves for his ailing customers. It was said that he once cured a woman dying of an ancestral curse that had eluded the best of American doctors. Next to the pharmacy was a printer who specialized in gold-embossed wedding invitations and festive red banners.

Farther down the street was Ping Yuen Fish Market. The front window displayed a tank crowded with doomed fish and turtles struggling to gain footing on the slimy green-tiled sides. A hand-written sign informed tourists, "Within this store, is all for food, not for pet." Inside, the butchers with their bloodstained white smocks deftly gutted the fish while customers cried out their orders and shouted, "Give me your freshest," to which the butchers always protested, "All are freshest." On less crowded market days, we would inspect the crates of live frogs and crabs which we were warned not to poke, boxes of dried cuttlefish, and row upon row of iced prawns, squid, and slippery fish. The sanddabs made me shiver each time; their eyes lay on one flattened side and reminded me of my mother's story of a careless girl who ran into a crowded street and was crushed by a cab. "Was smash flat," reported my mother.

At the corner of the alley was Hong Sing's, a four-table cafe with a recessed stairwell in front that led to a door marked "Tradesmen." My brothers and I believed the bad people emerged from this door at night. Tourists never went to Hong Sing's, since the menu was printed only in Chinese. A Caucasian[4] man with a big camera once posed me and my playmates in front of the restaurant. He had us move to the side of the picture window so the photo would capture the roasted duck with its head dangling from a juice-covered rope. After he took the picture, I told him he should go into Hong Sing's and eat dinner. When he smiled and asked me what they served, I shouted, "Guts and duck's feet and octopus gizzards!" Then I ran off with my friends, shrieking with laughter as we scampered across the alley and hid in the entryway grotto[5] of the China Gem Company, my heart pounding with hope that he would chase us.

Vocabulary Development **pungent** (pun´ jənt) *adj.* producing a sharp sensation of smell

---

3. **saffron-colored** orange-yellow.
4. **Caucasian** (kô kā´ zhən) *adj.* person of European ancestry.
5. **entryway grotto** (grät´ ō) *n.* the entryway resembled a cave.

My mother named me after the street that we lived on: Waverly Place Jong, my official name for important American documents. But my family called me Meimei,[6] "Little Sister." I was the youngest, the only daughter. Each morning before school, my mother would twist and yank on my thick black hair until she had formed two tightly wound pigtails. One day, as she struggled to weave a hard-toothed comb through my disobedient hair, I had a sly thought.

I asked her, "Ma, what is Chinese torture?" My mother shook her head. A bobby pin was wedged between her lips. She wetted her palm and smoothed the hair above my ear, then pushed the pin in so that it nicked sharply against my scalp.

"Who say this word?" she asked without a trace of knowing how wicked I was being. I shrugged my shoulders and said, "Some boy in my class said Chinese people do Chinese torture."

"Chinese people do many things," she said simply. "Chinese people do business, do medicine, do painting. Not lazy like American people. We do torture. Best torture."

My older brother Vincent was the one who actually got the chess set. We had gone to the annual Christmas party held at the First Chinese Baptist Church at the end of the alley. The missionary ladies had put together a Santa bag of gifts donated by members of another church. None of the gifts had names on them. There were separate sacks for boys and girls of different ages.

One of the Chinese parishioners had donned a Santa Claus costume and a stiff paper beard with cotton balls glued to it. I think the only children who thought he was the real thing were too young to know that Santa Claus was not Chinese. When my turn came up, the Santa man asked me how old I was. I thought it was a trick question; I was seven according to the American formula and eight by the Chinese calendar. I said I was born on March 17, 1951. That seemed to satisfy him. He then solemnly asked if I had been a very, very good girl this year and did I believe in Jesus Christ and obey my parents. I knew the only answer to that. I nodded back with equal solemnity.

Having watched the other children opening their gifts, I already knew that the big gifts were not necessarily the nicest ones. One girl my age got a large coloring book of biblical characters, while a less greedy girl who selected a small box received a glass vial of lavender toilet water. The sound of the box was also important. A ten-year-old boy had chosen a box that jangled when he shook it. It was a tin globe of the world with a slit for inserting money. He must have

---

6. **Meimei** (mā´ mā´)

© Pearson Education, Inc.

_____

_____

_____

Underline the different reactions of the mother and children to the chess set gift. Write the name of each person next to his or her reaction. What do the reactions tell you about the different values of the two generations?

_____

_____

_____

_____

Who initially teaches Waverly how to play chess?

_____

_____

_____

thought it was full of dimes and nickels, because when he saw that it had just ten pennies, his face fell with such undisguised disappointment that his mother slapped the side of his head and led him out of the church hall, apologizing to the crowd for her son who had such bad manners he couldn't appreciate such a fine gift.

As I peered into the sack, I quickly fingered the remaining presents, testing their weight, imagining what they contained. I chose a heavy, compact one that was wrapped in shiny silver foil and a red satin ribbon. It was a twelve-pack of Life Savers and I spent the rest of the party arranging and rearranging the candy tubes in the order of my favorites. My brother Winston chose wisely as well. His present turned out to be a box of intricate plastic parts; the instructions on the box proclaimed that when they were properly assembled he would have an authentic miniature replica of a World War II submarine.

Vincent got the chess set, which would have been a very decent present to get at a church Christmas party except it was obviously used and, as we discovered later, it was missing a black pawn and a white knight. My mother graciously thanked the unknown benefactor, saying, "Too good. Cost too much." At which point, an old lady with fine white, wispy hair nodded toward our family and said with a whistling whisper, "Merry, merry Christmas."

When we got home, my mother told Vincent to throw the chess set away. "She not want it. We not want it," she said, tossing her head stiffly to the side with a tight, proud smile. My brothers had deaf ears. They were already lining up the chess pieces and reading from the dog-eared instruction book.

I watched Vincent and Winston play during Christmas week. The chess board seemed to hold elaborate secrets waiting to be untangled. The chessmen were more powerful than Old Li's magic herbs that cured ancestral curses. And my brothers wore such serious faces that I was sure something was at stake that was greater than avoiding the tradesmen's door to Hong Sing's.

"Let me! Let me!" I begged between games when one brother or the other would sit back with a deep sigh of relief and victory, the other annoyed, unable to let go of the outcome. Vincent at first refused to let me play, but when I offered my Life Savers as replacements for the buttons that filled in for the missing pieces, he relented. He chose the flavors: wild cherry for the black pawn and peppermint for the white knight. Winner could eat both. As our mother sprinkled flour and rolled out small doughy circles for the steamed dumplings that would be our dinner that night, Vincent explained the rules, pointing to each piece. "You have sixteen pieces and so do I. One king and queen, two bishops, two knights, two castles, and eight pawns. The pawns can only move forward one step, except on the first move. Then they can move two. But they can only take men by moving crossways like this, except in the beginning, when you can move ahead and take another pawn."

"Why?" I asked as I moved my pawn. "Why can't they move more steps?"

"Because they're pawns," he said.

"But why do they go crossways to take other men. Why aren't there any women and children?"

"Why is the sky blue? Why must you always ask stupid questions?" asked Vincent. "This is a game. These are the rules. I didn't make them up. See. Here. In the book." He jabbed a page with a pawn in his hand. "Pawn. P-A-W-N. Pawn. Read it yourself."

My mother patted the flour off her hands. "Let me see book," she said quietly. She scanned the pages quickly, not reading the foreign English symbols, seeming to search deliberately for nothing in particular.

"This American rules," she concluded at last. "Every time people come out from foreign country, must know rules. You not know, judge say, Too bad, go back. They not telling you why so you can use their way go forward. They say, Don't know why, you find out yourself. But they knowing all the time. Better you take it, find out why yourself." She tossed her head back with a satisfied smile.

I found out about all the whys later. I read the rules and looked up all the big words in a dictionary. I borrowed books from the Chinatown library. I studied each chess piece, trying to absorb the power each contained.

I learned about opening moves and why it's important to control the center early on; the shortest distance between two points is straight down the middle. I learned about the middle game and why tactics between two adversaries are like clashing ideas; the one who plays better has the clearest plans for both attacking and getting out of traps. I learned why it is essential in the endgame[7] to have foresight, a mathematical understanding of all possible moves, and patience; all weaknesses and advantages become evident to a strong adversary and are obscured to a tiring opponent. I discovered that for the whole game one must gather invisible strengths and see the endgame before the game begins.

I also found out why I should never reveal "why" to others. A little knowledge withheld is a great advantage one should store for future use. That is the power of chess. It is a game of secrets in which one must show and never tell.

---

7. **endgame** (end´ gām´) final stage of a chess game in which each player has only a few pieces left on the board.

◆ Stop to Reflect

Why do rules to complicated games seem strange at first?

_____

_____

_____

◆ Reading Strategy

What differences in perspective between Waverly and her mother are revealed in the bracketed section?

_____

_____

_____

_____

◆ Reading Check

Why is it important to "never reveal 'why' to others" when playing chess?

_____

_____

_____

Waverly Jong is so interested in chess that she studies it intensively. Have you ever had a hobby or interest that you found absorbing?

Why did it interest you so much?

_____

_____

_____

The man does not seem to take Waverly's offer seriously. Why do adults sometimes underestimate the abilities of children?

_____

_____

_____

Underline the different names of chess moves in the bracketed paragraph. What do they suggest about the game?

_____

_____

_____

How does Mrs. Jong react to Waverly's victories in chess?

_____

_____

I loved the secrets I found within the sixty-four black and white squares. I carefully drew a handmade chessboard and pinned it to the wall next to my bed, where at night I would stare for hours at imaginary battles. Soon I no longer lost any games or Life Savers, but I lost my adversaries. Winston and Vincent decided they were more interested in roaming the streets after school in their Hopalong Cassidy[8] cowboy hats.

On a cold spring afternoon, while walking home from school, I detoured through the playground at the end of our alley. I saw a group of old men, two seated across a folding table playing a game of chess, others smoking pipes, eating peanuts, and watching. I ran home and grabbed Vincent's chess set, which was bound in a cardboard box with rubber bands. I also carefully selected two prized rolls of Life Savers. I came back to the park and approached a man who was observing the game.

"Want to play?" I asked him. His face widened with surprise and he grinned as he looked at the box under my arm.

"Little sister, been a long time since I play with dolls," he said, smiling benevolently. I quickly put the box down next to him on the bench and displayed my retort.

Lau Po, as he allowed me to call him, turned out to be a much better player than my brothers. I lost many games and many Life Savers. But over the weeks, with each diminishing roll of candies, I added new secrets. Lau Po gave me the names. The Double Attack from the East and West Shores. Throwing Stones on the Drowning Man. The Sudden Meeting of the Clan. The Surprise from the Sleeping Guard. The Humble Servant Who Kills the King. Sand in the Eyes of Advancing Forces. A Double Killing Without Blood.

There were also the fine points of chess etiquette. Keep captured men in neat rows, as well-tended prisoners. Never announce "Check" with vanity, lest someone with an unseen sword slit your throat. Never hurl pieces into the sandbox after you have lost a game, because then you must find them again, by yourself, after apologizing to all around you. By the end of the summer, Lau Po had taught me all he knew, and I had become a better chess player.

A small weekend crowd of Chinese people and tourists would gather as I played and defeated my opponents one by one. My mother would join the crowds during these outdoor exhibition games. She sat proudly on the bench, telling my admirers with proper Chinese humility, "Is luck."

Vocabulary Development: benevolently (bə nev´ ə lent lē) *adv.* in a kind and well-meaning way
retort (ri tôrt´) *n.* sharp or clever reply

---

8. **Hopalong Cassidy** character in cowboy movies during the 1950s.

A man who watched me play in the park suggested that my mother allow me to play in local chess tournaments. My mother smiled graciously, an answer that meant nothing. I desperately wanted to go, but I bit back my tongue. I knew she would not let me play among strangers. So as we walked home I said in a small voice that I didn't want to play in the local tournament. They would have American rules. If I lost, I would bring shame on my family.

"Is shame you fall down nobody push you," said my mother.

During my first tournament, my mother sat with me in the front row as I waited for my turn. I frequently bounced my legs to unstick them from the cold metal seat of the folding chair. When my name was called, I leapt up. My mother unwrapped something in her lap. It was her chang, a small tablet of red jade which held the sun's fire. "Is luck," she whispered, and tucked it into my dress pocket. I turned to my opponent, a fifteen-year-old boy from Oakland. He looked at me, wrinkling his nose.

As I began to play, the boy disappeared, the color ran out of the room, and I saw only my white pieces and his black ones waiting on the other side. A light wind began blowing past my ears. It whispered secrets only I could hear.

"Blow from the South," it murmured. "The wind leaves no trail." I saw a clear path, the traps to avoid. The crowd rustled. "Shhh! Shhh!" said the corners of the room. The wind blew stronger. "Throw sand from the East to distract him." The knight came forward ready for the sacrifice. The wind hissed, louder and louder. "Blow, blow, blow. He cannot see. He is blind now. Make him lean away from the wind so he is easier to knock down."

"Check," I said, as the wind roared with laughter. The wind died down to little puffs, my own breath.

My mother placed my first trophy next to a new plastic chess set that the neighborhood Tao society[9] had given to me. As she wiped each piece with a soft cloth, she said, "Next time win more, lose less."

"Ma, it's not how many pieces you lose," I said. "Sometimes you need to lose pieces to get ahead."

"Better to lose less, see if you really need."

At the next tournament, I won again, but it was my mother who wore the triumphant grin.

"Lost eight piece this time. Last time was eleven. What I tell you? Better off lose less!" I was annoyed, but I couldn't say anything.

I attended more tournaments, each one farther away from home. I won all games, in all divisions. The Chinese bakery downstairs from our flat displayed my growing collection of

---

9. **Tao** (dou) **society** group of people who believe in Taoism, a Chinese religion that stresses simplicity and unselfishness.

◆ **Reading Strategy**

Waverly knows that her mother is stubborn and does not quit easily. How does Waverly use this knowledge to get Mrs. Jong to agree to let her play in the tournament?

_____

_____

_____

◆ **Reading Check**

Why does the author say that the boy "disappeared" while Waverly was playing against him?

_____

_____

_____

◆ **Literary Analysis**

What is the attitude of Waverly toward her mother in the bracketed passage?

_____

_____

_____

◆ **Reading Check**

What are two indications of Waverly's success as a chess player?

1. _____

2. _____

trophies in its window, amidst the dust-covered cakes that were never picked up. The day after I won an important regional tournament, the window encased a fresh sheet cake with whipped-cream frosting and red script saying, "Congratulations, Waverly Jong, Chinatown Chess Champion." Soon after that, a flower shop, headstone engraver, and funeral parlor offered to sponsor me in national tournaments. That's when my mother decided I no longer had to do the dishes. Winston and Vincent had to do my chores.

"Why does she get to play and we do all the work," complained Vincent.

<u>"Is new American rules," said my mother. "Meimei play, squeeze all her brains out for win chess. You play, worth squeeze towel."</u>

By my ninth birthday, I was a national chess champion. I was still some 429 points away from grand-master status, but I was touted as the Great American Hope, a child prodigy and a girl to boot. They ran a photo of me in *Life* magazine next to a quote in which Bobby Fischer[10] said, "There will never be a woman grand master." "Your move, Bobby," said the caption.

The day they took the magazine picture I wore neatly plaited braids clipped with plastic barrettes trimmed with rhinestones. I was playing in a large high school auditorium that echoed with phlegmy coughs and the squeaky rubber knobs of chair legs sliding across freshly waxed wooden floors. Seated across from me was an American man, about the same age as Lau Po, maybe fifty. I remember that his sweaty brow seemed to weep at my every move. He wore a dark, malodorous suit. One of his pockets was stuffed with a great white kerchief on which he wiped his palm before sweeping his hand over the chosen chess piece with great flourish.

In my crisp pink-and-white dress with scratchy lace at the neck, one of two my mother had sewn for these special occasions, I would clasp my hands under my chin, the delicate points of my elbows poised lightly on the table in the manner my mother had shown me for posing for the press. I would swing my patent leather shoes back and forth like an impatient child riding on a school bus. Then I would pause, suck in my lips, twirl my chosen piece in midair as if undecided, and then firmly plant it in its new threatening place, with a triumphant smile thrown back at my opponent for good measure.

◆ Stop to Reflect

Do you think the deal that Mrs. Jong lays out in the underlined passage is a fair one? Explain.

_____

_____

_____

◆ Reading Check

Explain the caption from the *Life* magazine article after reading the footnote below.

_____

_____

_____

◆ Reading Check

How do Waverly's clothes, posture, and attitude contrast with those of her opponent in the tournament? Underline the relevant description in the text.

Vocabulary Development: prodigy (präd′ ə jē) *n.* person who is amazingly talented or intelligent
malodorous (mal ō′ dər əs) *adj.* having a bad smell

---

10. **Bobby Fischer** born in 1943, this American chess prodigy attained the high rank of grand master in 1958.

I no longer played in the alley of Waverly Place. I never visited the playground where the pigeons and old men gathered. I went to school, then directly home to learn new chess secrets, cleverly concealed advantages, more escape routes.

But I found it difficult to concentrate at home. My mother had a habit of standing over me while I plotted out my games. I think she thought of herself as my protective ally. Her lips would be sealed tight, and after each move I made, a soft "Hmmmmph" would escape from her nose.

"Ma, I can't practice when you stand there like that," I said one day. She retreated to the kitchen and made loud noises with the pots and pans. When the crashing stopped, I could see out of the corner of my eye that she was standing in the doorway. "Hmmmmph!" Only this one came out of her tight throat.

My parents made many <u>concessions</u> to allow me to practice. One time I complained that the bedroom I shared was so noisy that I couldn't think. Thereafter, my brothers slept in a bed in the living room facing the street. I said I couldn't finish my rice; my head didn't work right when my stomach was too full. I left the table with half-finished bowls and nobody complained. But there was one duty I couldn't avoid. I had to accompany my mother on Saturday market days when I had no tournament to play. My mother would proudly walk with me, visiting many shops, buying very little. "This my daughter Wave-ly Jong," she said to whoever looked her way.

One day, after we left a shop I said under my breath, "I wish you wouldn't do that, telling everybody I'm your daughter." My mother stopped walking. Crowds of people with heavy bags pushed past us on the sidewalk, bumping into first one shoulder, then another.

"Aiii-ya. So shame be with mother?" She grasped my hand even tighter as she glared at me.

I looked down. "It's not that, it's just so obvious. It's just so embarrassing."

"Embarrass you be my daughter?" Her voice was cracking with anger.

"That's not what I meant. That's not what I said."

"What you say?"

I knew it was a mistake to say anything more, but I heard my voice speaking. "Why do you have to use me to show off? If you want to show off, then why don't you learn to play chess." My mother's eyes turned into dangerous black slits. She had no words for me, just sharp silence.

Vocabulary Development: **concessions** (kən sesh´ ənz) *n.* things given or granted as privileges

---

◆ Literary Analysis

How does Mrs. Jong react when Waverly tells her that she cannot concentrate with her standing in the doorway?

_____

_____

_____

◆ Reading Check

What sacrifices does Waverly's family make so she can practice her chess?

1. _____

_____

2. _____

_____

◆ Reading Check

Look at the bracketed conversation. On the lines below, give a quick summary of

1. Waverly's point of view:

_____

_____

_____

2. Mrs. Jong's point of view:

_____

_____

_____

Why does Waverly run away from her mother?

_____

_____

_____

◆ Reading Check

Mrs. Jong gives her daughter the "silent treatment" when she returns. How might the way Mrs. Jong expresses her anger push her farther apart from Waverly?

_____

_____

_____

◆ Literary Analysis

Do you think the conflicts are over between Waverly and her mother with this argument?

Why or why not?

_____

_____

_____

I felt the wind rushing around my hot ears. I jerked my hand out of my mother's tight grasp and spun around, knocking into an old woman. Her bag of groceries spilled to the ground.

"Aii-ya! Stupid girl!" my mother and the woman cried. Oranges and tin cans careened down the sidewalk. As my mother stooped to help the old woman pick up the escaping food, I took off.

I raced down the street, dashing between people, not looking back as my mother screamed shrilly, "Meimei! Meimei!" I fled down an alley, past dark curtained shops and merchants washing the grime off their windows. I sped into the sunlight, into a large street crowded with tourists examining trinkets and souvenirs. I ducked into another dark alley, down another street, up another alley. I ran until it hurt and I realized I had nowhere to go, that I was not running from anything. The alleys contained no escape routes.

My breath came out like angry smoke. It was cold. I sat down on an upturned plastic pail next to a stack of empty boxes, cupping my chin with my hands, thinking hard. I imagined my mother, first walking briskly down one street or another looking for me, then giving up and returning home to await my arrival. After two hours, I stood up on creaking legs and slowly walked home.

The alley was quiet and I could see the yellow lights shining from our flat like two tiger's eyes in the night. I climbed the sixteen steps to the door, advancing quietly up each so as not to make any warning sounds. I turned the knob; the door was locked. I heard a chair moving, quick steps, the locks turning—click! click! click!—and then the door opened.

"About time you got home," said Vincent. "Boy, are you in trouble."

He slid back to the dinner table. On a platter were the remains of a large fish, its fleshy head still connected to bones swimming upstream in vain escape. Standing there waiting for my punishment, I heard my mother speak in a dry voice.

"We not concerning this girl. This girl not have concerning for us."

Nobody looked at me. Bone chopsticks[11] clinked against the insides of bowls being emptied into hungry mouths.

I walked into my room, closed the door, and lay down on my bed. The room was dark, the ceiling filled with shadows from the dinnertime lights of neighboring flats.

In my head, I saw a chessboard with sixty-four black and white squares. Opposite me was my opponent, two angry black slits. She wore a triumphant smile. "Strongest wind cannot be seen," she said.

---

11. **chopsticks** (chäp´ stiks´) two small sticks of wood, bone, or ivory, held together in one hand and used as utensils for eating, cooking, and serving food.

Her black men advanced across the plane, slowly marching to each successive level as a single unit. My white pieces screamed as they scurried and fell off the board one by one. As her men drew closer to my edge, I felt myself growing light. I rose up into the air and flew out the window. Higher and higher, above the alley, over the tops of tiled roofs, where I was gathered up by the wind and pushed up toward the night sky until everything below me disappeared and I was alone.

I closed my eyes and pondered my next move.

Reader's Response: Did Waverly's mother react appropriately when Waverly told her to stop introducing her as a chess champion? Why or why not?

_____

_____

_____

Thinking About the Skill: How did thinking about the differences between Waverly and her mother help you to understand the story?

_____

_____

_____

Who is playing chess against Waverly in her dream?

_____

_____

_____

Checkouts

Cynthia Rylant

Summary

In this story, a teenage girl has just moved with her parents to Cincinnati. She is not happy with the move, and she spends a lot of time looking through photographs of her former home. The one activity she does enjoy in her new surroundings is grocery shopping. During one trip to the supermarket, she sees a bag boy whom she finds attractive. It is his first day on the job and he is nervous, but he notices her, too. Soon, the girl and boy are watching for each other at the supermarket. However, though they do occasionally see each other there, they never speak to each other or indicate their feelings. In the end, the boy and girl do find romance—but with other people.

Visual Summary

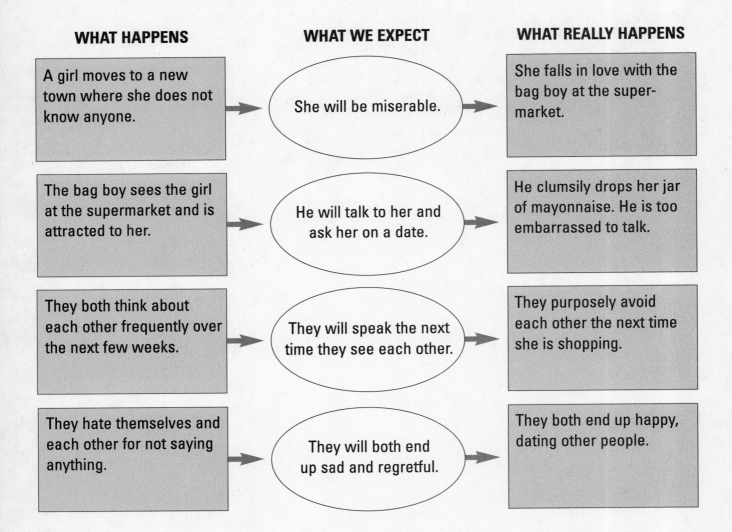

WHAT HAPPENS	WHAT WE EXPECT	WHAT REALLY HAPPENS
A girl moves to a new town where she does not know anyone.	She will be miserable.	She falls in love with the bag boy at the supermarket.
The bag boy sees the girl at the supermarket and is attracted to her.	He will talk to her and ask her on a date.	He clumsily drops her jar of mayonnaise. He is too embarrassed to talk.
They both think about each other frequently over the next few weeks.	They will speak the next time they see each other.	They purposely avoid each other the next time she is shopping.
They hate themselves and each other for not saying anything.	They will both end up sad and regretful.	They both end up happy, dating other people.

Checkouts
Cynthia Rylant

Moving to a new home can be exciting, but it can also be scary. The girl in "Checkouts" is anxious and lonely after her family's move to Cincinnati.

Her parents had moved her to Cincinnati, to a large house with beveled glass[1] windows and several porches and the *history* her mother liked to emphasize. You'll love the house, they said. You'll be lonely at first, they admitted, but you're so nice you'll make friends fast. And as an impulse tore at her to lie on the floor, to hold to their ankles and tell them she felt she was dying, to offer anything, anything at all, so they might allow her to finish growing up in the town of her childhood, they firmed their mouths and spoke from their chests and they said, It's decided.

They moved her to Cincinnati, where for a month she spent the greater part of every day in a room full of beveled glass windows, sifting through photographs of the life she'd lived and left behind. But it is difficult work, suffering, and in its own way a kind of art, and finally she didn't have the energy for it anymore, so she emerged from the beautiful house and fell in love with a bag boy at the supermarket. Of course, this didn't happen all at once, just like that, but in the sequence of things that's exactly the way it happened.

She liked to grocery shop. She loved it in the way some people love to drive long country roads, because doing it she could think and relax and wander. Her parents wrote up the list and handed it to her and off she went without complaint to perform what they regarded as a great sacrifice of her time and a sign that she was indeed a very nice girl. She had never told them how much she loved grocery shopping, only that she was "willing" to do it. She had an <u>intuition</u> which told her that her parents were not safe for sharing such strong, important facts about herself. Let them think they knew her.

Once inside the supermarket, her hands firmly around the handle of the cart, she would lapse into a kind of <u>reverie</u> and wheel toward the produce. Like a Tibetan monk in solitary meditation, she calmed to a point of deep, deep happiness; this feeling came to her, reliably, if strangely, only in the supermarket.

Vocabulary Development: intuition (in´ tōō wish´ ən) *n.* knowledge of something without reasoning
reverie (rev´ ər ē) *n.* dreamy thought of pleasant things

---

1. **beveled** (bev´ əld) **glass** glass having angled or slanted edges.

◆ **Activate Prior Knowledge**

Perhaps you have been in a situation where you felt too shy to talk to someone. Why do you think people sometimes have trouble speaking with people they like or admire?

_____

_____

_____

◆ **Reading Strategy**

There are many elements in this story that you may be able to **relate to personal experience.** Think of an occasion when you were faced with a completely new situation, like summer camp or a new school. What emotions did you experience at the time?

_____

_____

_____

◆ **Reading Check**

Why does the girl not want her parents to know that she likes shopping?

_____

_____

◆ **Reading Check**

What is the girl's frame of mind once she enters the supermarket?

_____

_____

Irony is a literary technique in which the outcome is different from what we expect. Why is the description of how the girl fell in love ironic?

_____

_____

_____

Think of a situation in the past where you experienced embarrassment due to your own clumsiness. Did you react in a similar way as the boy in the story?

_____

_____

Using the definition of **irony** as an unexpected result, how is the underlined sentence ironic?

_____

_____

Circle the characteristics that make the boy attractive to the girl. Why is she attracted to the bag boy?

_____

_____

_____

Then one day the bag boy dropped her jar of mayonnaise and that is how she fell in love.

He was nervous—first day on the job—and along had come this fascinating girl, standing in the checkout line with the unfocused stare one often sees in young children, her face turned enough away that he might take several full looks at her as he packed sturdy bags full of food and the goods of modern life. She interested him because her hair was red and thick, and in it she had placed a huge orange bow, nearly the size of a small hat. That was enough to distract him, and when finally it was her groceries he was packing, she looked at him and smiled and he could respond only by busting her jar of mayonnaise on the floor, <u>shards</u> of glass and oozing cream decorating the area around his feet.

She loved him at exactly that moment, and if he'd known this perhaps he wouldn't have fallen into the brown depression he fell into, which lasted the rest of his shift. He believed he must have looked the fool in her eyes, and he envied the sureness of everyone around him: the cocky cashier at the register, the grim and <u>harried</u> store manager, the bland butcher, and the <u>brazen</u> bag boys who smoked in the warehouse on their breaks. He wanted a second chance. Another chance to be confident and say witty things to her as he threw tin cans into her bags, persuading her to allow him to help her to her car so he might learn just a little about her, check out the floor of the car for signs of hobbies or fetishes and the bumpers for clues as to beliefs and loyalties.

But he busted her jar of mayonnaise and nothing else worked out for the rest of the day.

<u>Strange, how attractive clumsiness can be.</u> She left the supermarket with stars in her eyes, for she had loved the way his long nervous fingers moved from the conveyor belt to the bags, how deftly (until the mayonnaise) they had picked up her items and placed them in her bags. She had loved the way the hair kept falling into his eyes as he leaned over to grab a box or a tin. And the tattered brown shoes he wore with no socks. And the left side of his collar turned in rather than out.

The bag boy seemed a wonderful contrast to the perfectly beautiful house she had been forced to accept as her home, to the _history_ she hated, to the loneliness she had become used to, and she couldn't wait to come back for more of his awkwardness and <u>dishevelment</u>.

Vocabulary Development: shards (shärdz) _n._ broken pieces
harried (har´ ēd) _adj._ worried
brazen (brā´ zən) _adj._ shamelessly bold
dishevelment (di shev´ əl ment) _n._
untidiness

Incredibly, it was another four weeks before they saw each other again. As fate would have it, her visits to the supermarket never coincided with his schedule to bag. Each time she went to the store, her eyes scanned the checkouts at once, her heart in her mouth. And each hour he worked, the bag boy kept one eye on the door, watching for the red-haired girl with the big orange bow.

Yet in their disappointment these weeks there was a kind of ecstasy. It is reason enough to be alive, the hope you may see again some face which has meant something to you. The anticipation of meeting the bag boy eased the girl's painful transition into her new and jarring life in Cincinnati. It provided for her an anchor amid all that was impersonal and unfamiliar, and she spent less time on thoughts of what she had left behind as she concentrated on what might lie ahead. And for the boy, the long and often tedious hours at the supermarket which provided no challenge other than that of showing up the following workday . . . these hours became possibilities of mystery and romance for him as he watched the electric doors for the girl in the orange bow.

And when finally they did meet up again, neither offered a clue to the other that he, or she, had been the object of obsessive thought for weeks. She spotted him as soon as she came into the store, but she kept her eyes strictly in front of her as she pulled out a cart and wheeled it toward the produce. And he, too, knew the instant she came through the door—though the orange bow was gone, replaced by a small but bright yellow flower instead—and he never once turned his head in her direction but watched her from the corner of his vision as he tried to swallow back the fear in his throat.

It is odd how we sometimes deny ourselves the very pleasure we have longed for and which is finally within our reach. For some <u>perverse</u> reason she would not have been able to <u>articulate</u>, the girl did not bring her cart up to the bag boy's checkout when her shopping was done. And the bag boy let her leave the store, pretending no notice of her.

This is often the way of children, when they truly want a thing, to pretend that they don't. And then they grow angry when no one tried harder to give them this thing they so casually rejected, and they soon find themselves in a rage simply because they cannot say yes when they mean yes. Humans are very complicated. (And perhaps cats, who have been known to react in the same way, though the resulting rage can only be guessed at.)

Vocabulary Development: perverse (pər vʉrs´) *adj.* contrary and willful
articulate (är tik´ yə lāt) *v.* express in words

◆ Reading Strategy

Has there been anyone in your own experience that you looked forward to seeing with such eager anticipation?

_____

_____

_____

◆ Stop to Reflect

How does thinking of other things help people deal with boring or difficult situations?

_____

_____

_____

◆ Literary Analysis

What is the **irony** in the way the boy and girl react to one another in the store?

_____

_____

_____

◆ Reading Check

How have the feelings that the boy and girl had for each other changed?

_____

_____

_____

◆ Stop to Reflect

Do you think the outcome would have been different if the boy and girl had found the courage to talk with each other at the store? Why or why not?

_____

_____

_____

The girl hated herself for not checking out at the boy's line, and the boy hated himself for not catching her eye and saying hello, and they most sincerely hated each other without having ever exchanged even two minutes of conversation.

Eventually—in fact, within the week—a kind and intelligent boy who lived very near her beautiful house asked the girl to a movie and she gave up her fancy for the bag boy at the supermarket. And the bag boy himself grew so bored with his job that he made a desperate search for something better and ended up in a bookstore where scores of fascinating girls lingered like honeybees about a hive. Some months later the bag boy and the girl with the orange bow again crossed paths, standing in line with their dates at a movie theater, and, glancing toward the other, each smiled slightly, then looked away, as strangers on public buses often do, when one is moving off the bus and the other is moving on.

Vocabulary Development: lingered (liŋ´ gərd) *v.* stayed on, as if unwilling to leave

---

Reader's Response: Do you think the girl and bag boy were better off not getting together? Why or why not?

_____

_____

_____

Thinking About the Skill: How did **relating the story to your own experiences** contribute to your understanding and enjoyment of the story?

_____

_____

_____

The Interlopers
Saki

Summary

Ulrich and Georg have always been enemies. Their families have been enemies for generations because of a dispute over land ownership. Each man thinks the other man is trespassing on his land. The two men meet in the forest, prepared to kill each other. Before they can act, however, a storm knocks down a tree, pinning both men to the ground. Badly hurt and unable to move, they continue to quarrel, vowing to fight until death. After threatening one another, they lie silently waiting to be rescued. Ulrich manages to open his flask, and he offers Georg a sip of wine. Georg refuses, but Ulrich makes an offer to end the feud. Georg agrees. They discuss what great friends they will be, and how surprised everyone will be to see them not fighting. Together they shout for help and soon hear the sound of movement in the woods. Ulrich can make out nine or ten figures approaching. They are excited and relieved at the thought of being rescued. Unfortunately, the figures are not men but wolves.

Visual Summary

	Conflict	
Ulrich: Ulrich wants to kill Georg because of a land dispute.	vs.	**Georg:** Georg wants to kill Ulrich because of a land dispute.
Ulrich: Ulrich is trapped. He wants to be rescued so he can kill Georg.	vs.	**Georg:** Georg is trapped. He wants to be rescued so he can kill Ulrich.
Ulrich and Georg: Ulrich and Georg try to put off death together by shouting out loudly for help.	vs.	**Nature:** The tree is crushing them. They could die from their injuries, the cold, or a new threat . . . wolves.

The Interlopers
Saki

The title "The Interlopers" refers to intruders. As the story begins, Ulrich von Gradwitz is hunting down his bitter enemy, Georg Znaeym, who he knows is trespassing on his land.

In a forest of mixed growth somewhere on the eastern spurs of the Carpathians,[1] a man stood one winter night watching and listening, as though he waited for some beast of the woods to come within the range of his vision, and, later, of his rifle. But the game for whose presence he kept so keen an outlook was none that figured in the sportsman's calendar as lawful and proper for the chase: Ulrich von Gradwitz[2] patrolled the dark forest in quest of a human enemy.

The forest lands of Gradwitz were of wide extent and well stocked with game; the narrow strip of <u>precipitous</u> woodland that lay on its outskirt was not remarkable for the game it harbored or the shooting it afforded, but it was the most jealously guarded of all its owner's territorial possessions. A famous lawsuit, in the days of his grandfather, had wrested it from the illegal possession of a neighboring family of petty landowners; the dispossessed party had never acquiesced in the judgment of the Courts, and a long series of poaching affrays[3] and similar scandals had embittered the relationships between the families for three generations. The neighbor feud had grown into a personal one since Ulrich had come to be head of his family; if there was a man in the world whom he detested and wished ill to it was Georg Znaeym,[4] the inheritor of the quarrel and the tireless game-snatcher and raider of the disputed border-forest. The feud might, perhaps, have died down or been compromised if the personal ill will of the two men had not stood in the way; as boys they had thirsted for one another's blood, as men each prayed that misfortune might fall on the other, and this wind-scourged winter night Ulrich had banded together his foresters to watch the dark forest, not in quest of four-footed quarry, but to keep a lookout for the prowling thieves whom he suspected of being afoot from across the land boundary. The roebuck,[5] which usually kept in the sheltered hollows during a storm wind, were running like driven things tonight, and there was movement and unrest among the

---

Vocabulary Development: precipitous (pri sip´ ə təs) *adj.* steep

---

1. **Carpathians** (kär pā´ thē ənz) mountains in central Europe.
2. **Ulrich von Gradwitz** (o͞ol´ rik fôn gräd´ vitz)
3. **poaching affrays** (pōch´ iŋ ə frāz´) disputes about hunting on someone else's property.
4. **Georg Znaeym** (gā´ ôrg znä´ im)
5. **roebuck** (rō´ buk´) *n.* male deer.

◆ Activate Prior Knowledge

This story revolves around two feuding men. Why do people hold grudges against one another?

_____

_____

_____

◆ Reading Strategy

To follow a story's action, notice **causes and effects**. A **cause** is a reason that something happens, and the **effect** is the result. In the first paragraph, we learn that Ulrich is searching for his enemy. Now, we know the cause of his actions. What is it?

_____

_____

_____

◆ Reading Check

Who is hunting alongside Ulrich?

_____

_____

_____

creatures that were wont to sleep through the dark hours. Assuredly there was a disturbing element in the forest, and Ulrich could guess the quarter from whence it came.

He strayed away by himself from the watchers whom he had placed in ambush on the crest of the hill, and wandered far down the steep slopes amid the wild tangle of undergrowth, peering through the tree trunks and listening through the whistling and skirling of the wind and the restless beating of the branches for sight or sound of the <u>marauders</u>. If only on this wild night, in this dark, lone spot, he might come across Georg Znaeym, man to man, with none to witness—that was the wish that was uppermost in his thoughts. And as he stepped round the trunk of a huge beech he came face to face with the man he sought.

<u>The two enemies stood glaring at one another for a long silent moment. Each had a rifle in his hand, each had hate in his heart and murder uppermost in his mind. The chance had come to give full play to the passions of a lifetime.</u> But a man who has been brought up under the code of a restraining civilization cannot easily nerve himself to shoot down his neighbor in cold blood and without word spoken, except for an offense against his hearth and honor. And before the moment of hesitation had given way to action a deed of Nature's own violence overwhelmed them both. A fierce shriek of the storm had been answered by a splitting crash over their heads, and ere they could leap aside a mass of falling beech tree had thundered down on them. Ulrich von Gradwitz found himself stretched on the ground, one arm numb beneath him and the other held almost as helplessly in a tight tangle of forked branches, while both legs were pinned beneath the fallen mass. His heavy shooting-boots had saved his feet from being crushed to pieces, but if his fractures were not as serious as they might have been, at least it was evident that he could not move from his present position till someone came to release him. The descending twigs had slashed the skin of his face, and he had to wink away some drops of blood from his eyelashes before he could take in a general view of the disaster. At his side, so near that under ordinary circumstances he could almost have touched him, lay Georg Znaeym, alive and struggling, but obviously as helplessly pinioned down as himself. All round them lay a thick-strewn wreckage of splintered branches and broken twigs.

Relief at being alive and exasperation at his captive plight brought a strange <u>medley</u> of pious thank-offerings and sharp curses to Ulrich's lips. Georg, who was nearly blinded with the blood which trickled across his eyes, stopped his struggling for a moment to listen, and then gave a short, snarling laugh.

Vocabulary Development: marauders (mə rôd´ ərz) *n.* raiders
medley (med´ lē) *n.* mixture

The Interlopers **73**

◆ **Literary Analysis**

Many stories have a **conflict**, or struggle, as part of the plot. Who is involved in the conflict in this story?

_____

_____

_____

◆ **Stop to Reflect**

Circle the words in the underlined sentences that reveal the way the two men feel about each other.

◆ **Literary Analysis**

What change in circumstances occurs in the paragraph with the underlined sentences? How might the new circumstances affect the conflict between the two men?

_____

_____

_____

_____

◆ **Reading Check**

What is Ulrich's initial reaction to the new situation?

_____

_____

_____

When events turn out opposite from what we expect, they are called *ironic*. What is ironic about the two men's situation?

_____

_____

_____

Explain whether the remarks in the bracketed section show that their **conflict** has intensified or weakened after the tree falls.

_____

_____

_____

_____

_____

_____

Briefly summarize the events that have occurred so far in the story.

_____

_____

_____

_____

_____

_____

"So you're not killed, as you ought to be, but you're caught, anyway," he cried; "caught fast. Ho, what a jest, Ulrich von Gradwitz snared in his stolen forest. There's real justice for you!"

And he laughed again, mockingly and savagely.

"I'm caught in my own forest land," retorted Ulrich. "When my men come to release us you will wish, perhaps, that you were in a better plight than caught poaching on a neighbor's land, shame on you."

Georg was silent for a moment; then he answered quietly:

"Are you sure that your men will find much to release? I have men, too, in the forest tonight, close behind me, and *they* will be here first and do the releasing. When they drag me out from under these branches it won't need much clumsiness on their part to roll this mass of trunk right over on the top of you. Your men will find you dead under a fallen beech tree. For form's sake I shall send my <u>condolences</u> to your family."

"It is a useful hint," said Ulrich fiercely. "My men had orders to follow in ten minutes' time, seven of which must have gone by already, and when they get me out—I will remember the hint. Only as you will have met your death poaching on my lands I don't think I can decently send any message of condolence to your family."

"Good," snarled Georg, "good. We fight this quarrel out to the death, you and I and our foresters, with no cursed interlopers to come between us. Death and damnation to you, Ulrich von Gradwitz."

"The same to you, Georg Znaeym, forest-thief, game-snatcher."

Both men spoke with the bitterness of possible defeat before them, for each knew that it might be long before his men would seek him out or find him; it was a bare matter of chance which party would arrive first on the scene.

Both had now given up the useless struggle to free themselves from the mass of wood that held them down; Ulrich limited his endeavors to an effort to bring his one partially free arm near enough to his outer coat pocket to draw out his wine flask. Even when he had accomplished that operation it was long before he could manage the unscrewing of the stopper or get any of the liquid down his throat. But what a heaven-sent draft it seemed! It was an open winter, and little snow had fallen as yet, hence the captives suffered less from the cold than might have been the case at that season of the year; nevertheless, the wine was warming and reviving to the wounded man, and he looked across with something like a throb of pity to where his enemy lay, just keeping the groans

Vocabulary Development: condolence (kən dō´ ləns) *n.* expression of sympathy with a grieving person

of pain and weariness from crossing his lips.

"Could you reach this flask if I threw it over to you?" asked Ulrich suddenly; "there is good wine in it, and one may as well be as comfortable as one can. Let us drink, even if tonight one of us dies."

"No, I can scarcely see anything; there is so much blood caked round my eyes," said Georg, "and in any case I don't drink wine with an enemy."

Ulrich was silent for a few minutes, and lay listening to the weary screeching of the wind. An idea was slowly forming and growing in his brain, an idea that gained strength every time that he looked across at the man who was fighting so grimly against pain and exhaustion. In the pain and languor that Ulrich himself was feeling the old fierce hatred seemed to be dying down.

"Neighbor," he said presently, "do as you please if your men come first. It was a fair compact. But as for me, I've changed my mind. If my men are the first to come you shall be the first to be helped, as though you were my guest. We have quarreled like devils all our lives over this stupid strip of forest, where the trees can't even stand upright in a breath of wind. Lying here tonight, thinking, I've come to think we've been rather fools; there are better things in life than getting the better of a boundary dispute. Neighbor, if you will help me to bury the old quarrel I—I will ask you to be my friend."

Georg Znaeym was silent for so long that Ulrich thought, perhaps, he had fainted with the pain of his injuries. Then he spoke slowly and in jerks.

"How the whole region would stare and gabble if we rode into the market square together. No one living can remember seeing a Znaeym and a von Gradwitz talking to one another in friendship. And what peace there would be among the forester folk if we ended our feud tonight. And if we choose to make peace among our people there is none other to interfere, no interlopers from outside . . . You would come and keep the Sylvester night beneath my roof, and I would come and feast on some high day at your castle . . . I would never fire a shot on your land, save when you invited me as a guest; and you should come and shoot with me down in the marshes where the wildfowl are. In all the countryside there are none that could hinder if we willed to make peace. I never thought to have wanted to do other than hate you all my life, but I think I have changed my mind about things too, this last half-hour. And you offered me your wine flask . . . Ulrich von Gradwitz, I will be your friend."

For a space both men were silent, turning over in their minds the wonderful changes that this dramatic reconciliation

Vocabulary Development: languor (laŋ´ gər) *n.* weakness

◆ Stop to Reflect

What does Ulrich's offer suggest might be changing or about to change?

_____

_____

◆ Literary Analysis

Conflict can be internal as well as external. What ideas or feelings indicate that Ulrich is struggling with an internal conflict in the bracketed paragraph?

_____

_____

_____

◆ Reading Strategy

A long silence is an **effect** in the underlined sentence. What is the cause of the long silence?

_____

_____

_____

◆ Reading Check

Does Georg accept Ulrich's offer of peace?

_____

_____

_____

The **conflict** in the story has changed. It is no longer between Ulrich and Georg. What are the opposing sides in the conflict now?

_____

_____

_____

What do you think will be the effect of their shouts for help?

_____

_____

_____

What is the new source of conflict that appears at the very end of the story?

_____

_____

_____

would bring about. In the cold, gloomy forest, with the wind tearing in fitful gusts through the naked branches and whistling round the tree trunks, they lay and waited for the help that would now bring release and <u>succor</u> to both parties. And each prayed a private prayer that his men might be the first to arrive, so that he might be the first to show honorable attention to the enemy that had become a friend.

Presently, as the wind dropped for a moment, Ulrich broke silence.

"Let's shout for help," he said; "in this lull our voices may carry a little way."

"They won't carry far through the trees and undergrowth," said Georg, "but we can try. Together, then."

The two raised their voices in a prolonged hunting call.

"Together again," said Ulrich a few minutes later, after listening in vain for an answering halloo.

"I heard something that time, I think," said Ulrich.

"I heard nothing but the pestilential wind," said Georg hoarsely.

There was silence again for some minutes, and then Ulrich gave a joyful cry.

"I can see figures coming through the wood. They are following in the way I came down the hillside."

Both men raised their voices in as loud a shout as they could muster.

"They hear us! They've stopped. Now they see us. They're running down the hill toward us," cried Ulrich.

"How many of them are there?" asked Georg.

"I can't see distinctly," said Ulrich; "nine or ten."

"Then they are yours," said Georg; "I had only seven out with me."

"They are making all the speed they can, brave lads," said Ulrich gladly.

"Are they your men?" asked Georg. "Are they your men?" he repeated impatiently as Ulrich did not answer.

"No," said Ulrich with a laugh, the idiotic chattering laugh of a man unstrung with hideous fear.

"Who are they?" asked Georg quickly, straining his eyes to see what the other would gladly not have seen.

"Wolves."

Vocabulary Development: succor (suk´ ər) *n.* aid; help; relief

---

Reader's Response: With whom do you sympathize—Ulrich, Georg, neither, or both? Why?

_____

_____

The Secret Life of Walter Mitty
James Thurber

Summary

Walter Mitty is an ordinary man who escapes from his boring life and nagging wife by daydreaming. The story begins in the middle of one of his dreams. He is a naval officer leading his airplane through a powerful storm. Mitty is jolted from his dreams of heroism by his wife. She is scolding him for driving too fast. All of the dreams that follow are triggered by ordinary events on a shopping trip with his wife. He dreams of being a world-famous surgeon, a sharpshooting criminal, a fearless soldier, and a proud man facing a firing squad. Each time Mitty drifts off, reality intrudes somehow—he almost gets in a car accident, he remembers some errand, or his wife pesters him about something he is doing wrong.

Visual Summary

Daydream	Jolt Back to Reality	Reality	Dream Trigger
Mitty is a commander guiding a seaplane through a storm.	His wife scolds him for driving too fast.	Mitty and his wife are driving into town to go shopping.	Mitty passes a hospital and takes off his gloves.
Mitty is a surgeon operating on a dying patient.	A parking attendant yells at Mitty.	Mitty parks the car to buy rain shoes.	A newsboy is shouting news about a trial.
Mitty is a criminal standing trial in a courtroom.	Mitty remembers he is supposed to buy puppy biscuits.	He buys the biscuits and waits for his wife in a chair.	Mitty sees a newspaper with war photographs.
Mitty is a soldier on a dangerous mission.	His wife returns and scolds him.	His wife goes on another errand.	Mitty smokes a cigarette while he waits.
Mitty is a man facing a firing squad.			

The Secret Life of Walter Mitty
James Thurber

It does not take much to send Walter Mitty off on a daydream. Join him in the middle of a daydream already in progress. Mitty is the commander of an airplane fighting his way through a fierce storm.

"We're going through!" The Commander's voice was like thin ice breaking. He wore his full-dress uniform, with the heavily braided white cap pulled down rakishly over one cold gray eye. "We can't make it, sir. It's spoiling for a hurricane, if you ask me." "I'm not asking you, Lieutenant Berg," said the Commander. "Throw on the power lights! Rev her up to 8,500! We're going through!" The pounding of the cylinders increased: ta-pocketa-pocketa-pocketa-*pocketa-pocketa*. The Commander stared at the ice forming on the pilot window. He walked over and twisted a row of complicated dials. "Switch on No. 8 auxiliary!" he shouted. "Switch on No. 8 auxiliary!" repeated Lieutenant Berg. "Full strength in No. 3 turret!" shouted the Commander. "Full strength in No. 3 turret!" The crew, bending to their various tasks in the huge, hurtling eight-engined Navy hydroplane,[1] looked at each other and grinned. "The Old Man'll get us through," they said to one another. "The Old Man ain't afraid of Hell!". . .

"Not so fast! You're driving too fast!" said Mrs. Mitty. "What are you driving so fast for?"

"Hmm?" said Walter Mitty. He looked at his wife, in the seat beside him, with shocked astonishment. She seemed grossly unfamiliar, like a strange woman who had yelled at him in a crowd. "You were up to fifty-five," she said. "You know I don't like to go more than forty. You were up to fifty-five." Walter Mitty drove on toward Waterbury in silence, the roaring of the SN202 through the worst storm in twenty years of Navy flying fading in the remote, intimate airways of his mind. "You're tensed up again," said Mrs. Mitty. "It's one of your days. I wish you'd let Dr. Renshaw look you over."

Walter Mitty stopped the car in front of the building where his wife went to have her hair done. "Remember to get those overshoes while I'm having my hair done," she said. "I don't need overshoes," said Mitty. She put her mirror back into her bag. "We've been all through that," she said, getting out

---

Vocabulary Development: rakishly (rāk´ ish lē) *adv.* with a careless, casual look; dashing
hurtling (hurt´ liŋ) *adj.* moving swiftly and with great force

---

1. **hydroplane** (hī´ drə plān) *n.* seaplane.

Sidebar

◆ **Activate Prior Knowledge**

When you find yourself daydreaming, what role do you like to imagine for yourself?

_____

_____

_____

_____

◆ **Reading Strategy**

Read ahead, and you find that Walter Mitty is not in a plane. Where is he?

_____

_____

_____

◆ **Literary Analysis**

Point of view is the perspective from which a story is told. In *first person point of view*, the narrator ("I") is one of the characters. In *third person point of view,* the person telling the story does not participate in the action. Read the underlined sentences. Are they written from a first or third person point of view?

_____

_____

_____

◆ **Reading Check**

What is the purpose of the Mittys' trip?

_____

_____

_____

of the car. "You're not a young man any longer." He raced the engine a little. "Why don't you wear your gloves? Have you lost your gloves?" Walter Mitty reached in a pocket and brought out the gloves. He put them on, but after she had turned and gone into the building and he had driven on to a red light, he took them off again. "Pick it up, brother!" snapped a cop as the light changed, and Mitty hastily pulled on his gloves and lurched ahead. He drove around the streets aimlessly for a time, and then he drove past the hospital on his way to the parking lot.

. . . "It's the millionaire banker, Wellington McMillan," said the pretty nurse. "Yes?" said Walter Mitty, removing his gloves slowly. "Who has the case?" "Dr. Renshaw and Dr. Benbow, but there are two specialists here, Dr. Remington from New York and Mr. Pritchard-Mitford from London. He flew over." A door opened down a long, cool corridor and Dr. Renshaw came out. He looked distraught and haggard. "Hello, Mitty," he said. "We're having the devil's own time with McMillan, the millionaire banker and close personal friend of Roosevelt. Obstreosis of the ductal tract.[2] Tertiary. Wish you'd take a look at him." "Glad to," said Mitty.

In the operating room there were whispered introductions: "Dr. Remington, Dr. Mitty. Mr. Pritchard-Mitford, Dr. Mitty." "I've read your book on streptothricosis," said Pritchard-Mitford, shaking hands. "A brilliant performance, sir." "Thank you," said Walter Mitty. "Didn't know you were in the States, Mitty," grumbled Remington. "Coals to Newcastle,[3] bringing Mitford and me up here for tertiary." "You are very kind," said Mitty. A huge, complicated machine, connected to the operating table, with many tubes and wires, began at this moment to go pocketa-pocketa-pocketa. "The new anesthetizer is giving way!" shouted an intern. "There is no one in the East who knows how to fix it!" "Quiet, man!" said Mitty, in a low, cool voice. He sprang to the machine, which was now going pocketa-pocketa-queep-pocketa-queep. He began fingering delicately a row of glistening dials. "Give me a fountain pen!" he snapped. Someone handed him a fountain pen. He pulled a faulty piston out of the machine and inserted the pen in its place.

Vocabulary Development: distraught (di strôt´) *adj.* extremely troubled; confused; distracted
haggard (hag´ ərd) *adj.* having a worn look, as from sleeplessness

---

2. **obstreosis of the ductal tract** Thurber has invented this and other medical terms.
3. **coals to Newcastle** The proverb "bringing coals to Newcastle" means bringing things to a place unnecessarily—Newcastle, England, was a coal center and so did not need coal brought to it.

◆ **Stop to Reflect**

From your brief glimpse of Mrs. Mitty, how would you describe her?

_____

_____

_____

◆ **Reading Strategy**

Read back and **read ahead** to determine the event that occurs between the two underlined sentences. What occurs?

_____

_____

_____

◆ **Literary Analysis**

Names and pronouns, such as "he" or "she," serve as clues that a story is written from the third person **point of view.** Circle names and pronouns that indicate point of view in Mitty's surgeon dream.

◆ **Reading Check**

Why does Mitty need the fountain pen in his surgeon dream?

_____

_____

_____

_____

_____

_____

_____

What nearly happened to Walter Mitty in reality?

_____

_____

Look at the underlined sentence. What causes Mitty to remember the incident with the young garageman? **Read back** to find out.

_____

_____

_____

The third person **point of view** can either be _limited_ or _omniscient._ In omniscient third person, the narrator sees into the thoughts of all the characters. In limited third person, the narrator sees everything through the perspective of a single character. Look at the bracketed paragraph. Is this story written in the limited or omniscient third person? Explain.

_____

_____

"That will hold for ten minutes," he said. "Get on with the operation." A nurse hurried over and whispered to Renshaw, and Mitty saw the man turn pale. "Coreopsis has set in," said Renshaw nervously. "If you would take over, Mitty?" Mitty looked at him and at the craven figure of Benbow, who drank, and at the grave, uncertain faces of the two great specialists. "If you wish," he said. They slipped a white gown on him; he adjusted a mask and drew on thin gloves; nurses handed him shining . . .

"Back it up, Mac! Look out for that Buick!" Walter Mitty jammed on the brakes. "Wrong lane, Mac," said the parking-lot attendant, looking at Mitty closely. "Gee. Yeh," muttered Mitty. He began cautiously to back out of the lane marked "Exit Only." "Leave her sit there," said the attendant. "I'll put her away." Mitty got out of the car. "Hey, better leave the key." "Oh," said Mitty, handing the man the ignition key. The attendant vaulted into the car, backed it up with insolent skill, and put it where it belonged.

They're so cocky, thought Walter Mitty, walking along Main Street; they think they know everything. Once he had tried to take his chains off, outside New Milford, and he had got them wound around the axles. A man had had to come out in a wrecking car and unwind them, a young, grinning garageman. Since then Mrs. Mitty always made him drive to a garage to have the chains taken off. The next time, he thought, I'll wear my right arm in a sling; they won't grin at me then. I'll have my right arm in a sling and they'll see I couldn't possibly take the chains off myself. He kicked at the slush on the sidewalk. "Overshoes," he said to himself, and he began looking for a shoe store.

When he came out into the street again, with the over-shoes in a box under his arm, Walter Mitty began to wonder what the other thing was his wife had told him to get. She had told him, twice, before they set out from their house for Waterbury. In a way he hated these weekly trips to town—he was always getting something wrong. Kleenex, he thought, Squibb's, razor blades? No. Toothpaste, toothbrush, bicarbonate, carborundum, initiative and referendum?[4] He gave it up. But she would remember it. "Where's the what's-its-name?" she would ask. "Don't tell me you forgot the what's-its-name." A newsboy went by shouting something about the Waterbury trial.

> **Vocabulary Development: insolent** (in´ sə lənt) _adj._ boldly disrespectful in speech or behavior

4. **carborundum** (kär´ bə run´ dəm), **initiative** (i nish´ ē ə tiv) **and referendum** (ref ə ren´ dəm) Thurber is purposely making a nonsense list; _carborundum_ is a hard substance used for scraping, _initiative_ is the right of citizens to introduce ideas for laws, and _referendum_ is the right of citizens to vote on laws.

. . . "Perhaps this will refresh your memory." The District Attorney suddenly thrust a heavy automatic at the quiet figure on the witness stand. "Have you ever seen this before?" Walter Mitty took the gun and examined it expertly. "This is my Webley-Vickers 50.80," he said calmly. An excited buzz ran around the courtroom. The Judge rapped for order. "You are a crack shot with any sort of firearms, I believe?" said the District Attorney, insinuatingly. "Objection!" shouted Mitty's attorney. "We have shown that the defendant could not have fired the shot. We have shown that he wore his right arm in a sling on the night of the fourteenth of July." Walter Mitty raised his hand briefly and the bickering attorneys were stilled. "With any known make of gun," he said evenly, "I could have killed Gregory Fitzhurst at three hundred feet *with my left hand.*" Pandemonium broke loose in the courtroom. A woman's scream rose above the bedlam and suddenly a lovely, dark-haired girl was in Walter Mitty's arms. The District Attorney struck at her savagely. Without rising from his chair, Mitty let the man have it on the point of the chin. "You miserable cur!" . . .

"Puppy biscuit," said Walter Mitty. He stopped walking and the buildings of Waterbury rose up out of the misty courtroom and surrounded him again. A woman who was passing laughed. "He said 'Puppy biscuit,'" she said to her companion. "That man said 'Puppy biscuit' to himself." Walter Mitty hurried on. He went into an A. & P., not the first one he came to but a smaller one farther up the street. "I want some biscuit for small, young dogs," he said to the clerk. "Any special brand, sir?" The greatest pistol shot in the world thought a moment. "It says 'Puppies Bark for It' on the box," said Walter Mitty.

His wife would be through at the hairdresser's in fifteen minutes, Mitty saw in looking at his watch, unless they had trouble drying it; sometimes they had trouble drying it. She didn't like to get to the hotel first; she would want him to be there waiting for her as usual. He found a big leather chair in the lobby, facing a window, and he put the overshoes and the puppy biscuit on the floor beside it. He picked up an old copy of *Liberty* and sank down into the chair. "Can Germany Conquer the World Through the Air?" Walter Mitty looked at the pictures of bombing planes and of ruined streets.

◆ **Reading Check**

When does Mitty lapse into his next daydream? Draw a heavy vertical line in the text to indicate the shift from reality.

◆ **Stop to Reflect**

Why would mild-mannered Walter Mitty imagine himself as a dangerous criminal?

_____

_____

_____

◆ **Reading Check**

Why does Walter Mitty suddenly say "Puppy biscuit"?

_____

_____

_____

_____

◆ **Reading Check**

Why is Mitty concerned about how his wife will react if he does not arrive first to the hotel?

_____

_____

_____

_____

Vocabulary Development: insinuatingly (in sin′ yōō āt′ iŋ lē) *adv.* hinting or suggesting indirectly
cur (kʉr) *n.* mean, contemptible person; mean, ugly dog

© Pearson Education, Inc.

The Secret Life of Walter Mitty **81**

_____

_____

_____

_____

Describe the situation that Mitty is facing in this dream.

_____

_____

_____

_____

The limited third person **point of view** lets us in on the thoughts and feelings of only one character—Walter Mitty. How would Mrs. Mitty describe the situation of finding her husband daydreaming in the hotel chair to a friend?

_____

_____

_____

_____

. . . "The cannonading has got the wind up in young Raleigh,[5] sir," said the sergeant. Captain Mitty looked up at him through tousled hair. "Get him to bed," he said wearily. "With the others. I'll fly alone." "But you can't, sir," said the sergeant anxiously. "It takes two men to handle that bomber and the Archies[6] are pounding hell out of the air. Von Richtman's circus[7] is between here and Saulier." "Somebody's got to get that ammunition dump," said Mitty. "I'm going over. Spot of brandy?" He poured a drink for the sergeant and one for himself. War thundered and whined around the dugout and battered at the door. There was a rending of wood and splinters flew through the room. "A bit of a near thing," said Captain Mitty carelessly. "The box barrage is closing in," said the sergeant. "We only live once, Sergeant," said Mitty, with his faint, fleeting smile. "Or do we?" He poured another brandy and tossed it off. "I never see a man could hold his brandy like you, sir," said the sergeant. "Begging your pardon, sir." Captain Mitty stood up and strapped on his huge Webley-Vickers automatic. "It's forty kilometers through hell, sir," said the sergeant. Mitty finished one last brandy. "After all," he said softly, "what isn't?" The pounding of the cannon increased; there was the rat-tat-tatting of machine guns, and from somewhere came the menacing pocketa-pocketa-pocketa of the new flame-throwers. Walter Mitty walked to the door of the dugout humming "Auprès de Ma Blonde."[8] He turned and waved to the sergeant. "Cheerio!" he said . . . .

Something struck his shoulder. "I've been looking all over this hotel for you," said Mrs. Mitty. "Why do you have to hide in this old chair? How did you expect me to find you?" "Things close in," said Walter Mitty vaguely. "What?" Mrs. Mitty said. "Did you get the what's-its-name? The puppy biscuit? What's in that box?" "Overshoes," said Mitty. "Couldn't you have put them on in the store?" "I was thinking," said Walter Mitty. "Does it ever occur to you that I am sometimes thinking?" She looked at him. "I'm going to take your temperature when I get you home," she said.

They went out through the revolving doors that made a faintly derisive whistling sound when you pushed them. It was two blocks to the parking lot. At the drugstore on the

---

Vocabulary Development: cannonading (kan´ ən ād´ iŋ) *n.* continuous firing of artillery
derisive (di rī´ siv) *adj.* showing contempt

---

5. **he has got the wind up in young Raleigh** has made young Raleigh nervous.
6. **Archies:** slang term for antiaircraft guns.
7. **Von Richtman's circus** German airplane squadron.
8. **"Auprès de Ma Blonde"** (ō prā´ də mä blōn´ də) "Next to My Blonde," a popular French song.

corner she said, "Wait here for me. I forgot something. I won't be a minute." She was more than a minute. Walter Mitty lighted a cigarette. It began to rain, rain with sleet in it. He stood up against the wall of the drugstore, smoking. . . . He put his shoulders back and his heels together. "To hell with the handkerchief," said Walter Mitty scornfully. He took one last drag on his cigarette and snapped it away. Then, with that faint, fleeting smile playing about his lips, he faced the firing squad; erect and motionless, proud and disdainful, Walter Mitty the Undefeated, <u>inscrutable</u> to the last.

Vocabulary Development: inscrutable (in skrōōt′ ə bəl) *adj.* baffling; mysterious

---

Reader's Response: Did you laugh at Walter Mitty's dreams or did they make you feel sorry for him? Why do you think you felt this way?

_____

_____

_____

Thinking About the Skill: How did reading back and reading ahead help clear up confusion when Mitty went in and out of his dreams?

_____

_____

_____

◆ Stop to Reflect

In this dream, Mitty is refusing the blindfold that is often given to men before they are executed by firing squad. Why do people imagine doing things in daydreams that they would never do in real life?

_____

_____

_____

_____

_____

_____

Go Deep to the Sewer

Bill Cosby

Summary

In this essay, Bill Cosby remembers what it was like to play as a child on the city streets of Philadelphia. Instead of a grassy playing field with goals and bases, Cosby and his friends used city streets, garbage cans, and parked cars. They had to improvise, or "make do," with the materials they had at hand. Sometimes, Cosby's friends had to invent new rules to deal with unexpected situations—like the time the car serving as third base drove away while the ball was in play. Through it all, Cosby finds the humor in the situation as he describes their creative games of football and stickball.

Visual Summary

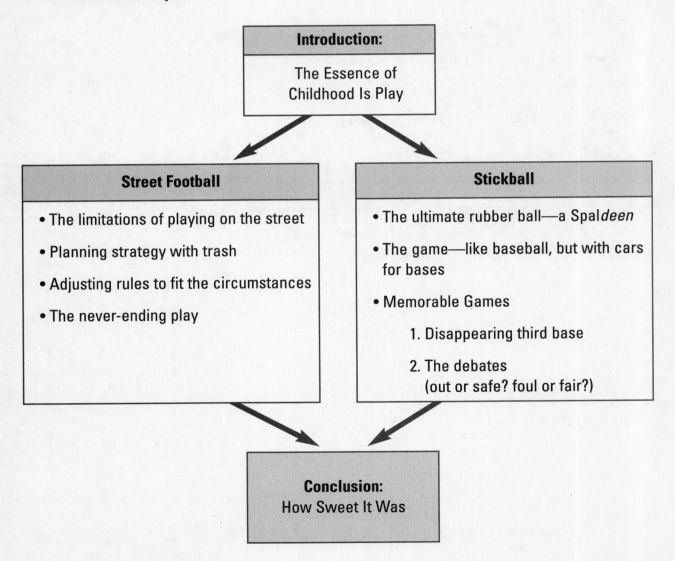

Introduction:
The Essence of Childhood Is Play

Street Football

• The limitations of playing on the street

• Planning strategy with trash

• Adjusting rules to fit the circumstances

• The never-ending play

Stickball

• The ultimate rubber ball—a Spal*deen*

• The game—like baseball, but with cars for bases

• Memorable Games

   1. Disappearing third base

   2. The debates
   (out or safe? foul or fair?)

Conclusion:
How Sweet It Was

Go Deep to the Sewer
Bill Cosby

Bill Cosby grew up playing on the streets of Philadelphia. Many of his humorous stories, like "Go Deep to the Sewer," revolve around memories of his childhood experiences playing with his friends from the neighborhood.

The essence of childhood, of course, is play, which my friends and I did endlessly on streets that we reluctantly shared with traffic. As a daring receiver in touch football, I spent many happy years running up and down those asphalt fields, hoping that a football would hit me before a Chevrolet did.

My mother was often a nervous fan who watched me from her window.

"Bill, don't get run over!" she would cry in a moving concern for me.

"Do you see me getting run over?" I would cleverly reply.

And if I ever *had* been run over, my mother had a seat for it that a scalper[1] would have prized.

Because the narrow fields of those football games allowed almost no lateral movement, an end run was possible only if a car pulled out and blocked for you. And so I worked on my pass-catching, for I knew I had little chance of ever living my dream: taking a handoff and sweeping to glory along the curb, dancing over the dog dung like Red Grange.

The quarterback held this position not because he was the best passer but because he knew how to drop to one knee in the huddle and diagram plays with trash.

"Okay, Shorty," Junior Barnes would say, "this is you: the orange peel."

"I don' wanna be the orange peel," Shorty replied. "The orange peel is Albert. I'm the gum."

"But let's make 'em *think* he's the orange peel," I said, "an' let 'em think Albert's the manhole."

"Okay, Shorty," said Junior, "you go out ten steps an' then cut left behind the black Oldsmobile."

"I'll sorta *go in* it first to shake my man," said Shorty, "an' then, when he don' know where I am, you can hit me at the fender."

"Cool. An' Arnie, you go down to the corner of Locust an' fake takin' the bus. An' Cos, you do a zig out to the bakery. See if you can shake your man before you hit the rolls."

Build Vocabulary: lateral (lat´ ər əl) *adj.* sideways

---

1. **scalper** (skalp´ ər) *n.* person who buys tickets and sells them later at higher-than-regular prices.

♦ **Activate Prior Knowledge**

Think about games you have played with friends or classmates. Did you ever have to "make do" with the equipment or space you had? How did it affect the way the game was played?

_____

_____

_____

_____

♦ **Reading Strategy**

In much of his comedy, Bill Cosby uses **situational humor.** In other words, his colorful descriptions of situations are the source of the humor. In the bracketed paragraph, what is the situation which Cosby describes humorously?

_____

_____

♦ **Literary Analysis**

This whole selection is a **humorous remembrance** of Cosby's childhood. Find and circle phrases and sentences on this page that make you smile or laugh.

♦ **Reading Check**

What are the challenges Cosby and his friends face in playing football on a crowded street?

_____

_____

_____

_____

Cosby chooses to remember his childhood humorously. If Cosby was taking a serious approach, what might he write in the bracketed paragraph about being short and thin?

_____

_____

_____

_____

_____

In Cosby's memory, Junior is the "permanent quarterback." Why do you think some people become leaders?

_____

_____

_____

_____

_____

What is funny about the situation that Cosby describes?

_____

_____

_____

_____

_____

"Suppose I start a fly pattern to the bakery an' then do a zig out to the trash can," I said.

"No, they'll be expecting that."

I spent most of my boyhood trying to catch passes with the easy grace of my heroes at Temple;[2] but easy grace was too hard for me. Because I was short and thin, my hands were too small to catch a football with arms extended on the run. Instead, I had to stagger backwards and smother the ball in my chest. How I yearned to grab the ball in my hands while striding smoothly ahead, rather than receiving it like someone who was catching a load of wet wash. Often, after a pass had bounced off my hands, I returned to the quarterback and glumly said, "Jeeze, Junior, I don' know what happened." He, of course, knew what had happened: he had thrown the ball to someone who should have been catching it with a butterfly net.

Each of these street games began with a quick review of the rules: two-hand touch, either three or four downs, always goal-to-go, forward passing from anywhere, and no touchdowns called back because of traffic in motion. If a receiver caught a ball near an oncoming car while the defender was running for his life, the receiver had guts, and possibly a long excuse from school.

I will never forget one particular play from those days when I was trying so hard to prove my manhood between the manholes. In the huddle, as Junior, our permanent quarterback, dropped to one knee to arrange the garbage offensively, I said, "Hey, Junior, make me a decoy on this one."

Pretending to catch the ball was what I did best.

"What's a decoy?" he said.

"Well, it's—"

"I ain't got time to learn. Okay, Eddie, you're the Dr Pepper cap an' you go deep toward New Jersey."

"An' I'll fool around short," I said.

"No, Cos, you fake goin' deep an' then buttonhook at the DeSoto. An' Harold, you do a zig out between 'em. *Somebody* get free."

Moments later, the ball was snapped to him and I started sprinting down the field with my defender, Jody, who was matching me stride for stride. Wondering if I would be able to get free for a pass sometime within the next hour, I stopped at the corner and began sprinting back to Junior, whose arm had been cocked for about fifteen seconds,

---

Vocabulary Development: yearned (yūrnd) *v.* longed for; desired

decoy (dē´ koi) *n.* person used to lure others into a trap

---

2. **Temple** Temple University in Philadelphia, Pennsylvania.

as if he'd been posing for a trophy. Since Eddie and Harold also were covered, and since running from scrimmage was impossible on that narrow field, I felt that this might be touch football's first eternal play: Junior still standing there long after Eddie, Harold, and I had dropped to the ground, his arm still cocked as he tried to find some way to pass to himself.

But unlimited time was what we had and it was almost enough for us. Often we played in the street until the light began to fade and the ball became a blur in the dusk. If there is one memory of my childhood that will never disappear, it is a bunch of boys straining to find a flying football in the growing darkness of a summer night.

There were, of course, a couple of streetlamps on our field, but they were useful only if your pattern took you right up to one of them to make your catch. The rest of the field was lost in the night; and what an adventure it was to refuse to surrender to that night, to hear the quarterback cry "Ball!" and then stagger around in a kind of gridiron blindman's buff.

"Hey, you guys, dontcha think we should call the game?" said Harold one summer evening.

"Why do a stupid thing like that?" Junior replied.

"'Cause I can't see the ball."

"Harold, that don't make you special. Nobody can see the ball. But y' *know* it's up there."

And we continued to stagger around as night fell on Philadelphia and we kept looking for a football that could have been seen only on radar screens.

One day last year in a gym, I heard a boy say to his father, "Dad, what's a Spal*deen*?"

This shocking question left me depressed, for it is one thing not to know the location of the White House or the country that gave its name to Swiss cheese, but when a boy doesn't know what a Spal*deen* is, our educational system has failed. For those of you ignorant of basic American history, a Spal*deen* was a pink rubber ball with more bounce than can be imagined today. Baseball fans talk about the lively ball, but a lively baseball is a sinking stone compared to a Spal*deen*, which could be dropped from your eye level and bounce back there again, if you wanted to do something boring with it. And when you connected with a Spal*deen* in stickball, you put a pink rocket in orbit, perhaps even over the house at the corner and into another neighborhood, where it might gently bop somebody's mother sitting on a stoop.

I love to remember all the street games that we could play with a Spal*deen*. First, of course, was stickball, an organized version of which is also popular and known as baseball. The playing field was the same rectangle that we used for football: it was the first rectangular diamond. And for this

Cosby talks about having "unlimited time." Why do you think time can seem unlimited when we are young children?

_____

_____

_____

_____

_____

_____

◆ Literary Analysis

Why does Cosby exaggerate when describing the memory in the bracketed paragraph?

_____

_____

_____

_____

_____

_____

◆ Reading Check

What is a Spal*deen*?

_____

_____

_____

_____

_____

◆ Reading Strategy

List the circumstances that make the situation in the first bracketed passage humorous.

_____

_____

_____

_____

◆ Literary Analysis

What humorous comment does Cosby write about each of his friends in the second bracketed passage?

Junior _____

_____

Albert _____

_____

game, we had outfield walls in which people happened to live and we had bases that lacked a certain uniformity: home and second were manhole covers, and first and third were the fenders of parked cars.

One summer morning, this offbeat infield caused a memorable interpretation of the official stickball rules. Junior hit a two-sewer shot and was running toward what should have been third when third suddenly drove away in first. While the bewildered Junior tried to arrive safely in what had become a twilight zone, Eddie took my throw from center field and tagged him out.

"I'm not out!" cried Junior in outrage. "I'm right here on third!"

And he did have a point, but so did Eddie, who replied, not without a certain logic of his own, "But third ain't there anymore."

In those games, our first base was as mobile as our third; and it was a floating first that set off another lively division of opinion on the day that Fat Albert hit a drive over the spot from which first base had just driven away, leaving us without a good part of the right field foul line. The hit would have been at least a double for anyone with movable legs, but Albert's destination was first, where the play might have been close had the right fielder hit the cutoff man instead of a postman.

"Foul ball!" cried Junior, taking a guess that happened to be in his favor.

"You're out of your mind, Junior!" cried Albert, an observation that often was true, no matter what Junior was doing. "It went right over the fender!"

"What fender?"

"If that car comes back, you'll see it's got a fender," said Albert, our automotive authority.

However, no matter how many pieces of our field drove away, nothing could ever take away the sweetness of having your stick connect with a Spal*deen* in a magnificent *whoppp* and drive it so high and far that it bounced off a window with a view of New Jersey and then caromed back to the street, where Eddie would have fielded it like Carl Furillo[3] had he not backed into a coal shute.

---

3. **Carl Furillo** (kärl fər il′ ō) baseball player for the Brooklyn Dodgers in the 1950s.

Reader's Response: Do you think you would have enjoyed spending time with Cosby and his friends? Why or why not?

_____

_____

Talk

African (Ashanti) Folk Tale

retold by Harold Courlander and George Herzog

Summary

"Talk" is a strange and humorous folk tale set in West Africa. In this story, various objects talk to a farmer, startling and frightening him. The tale begins with the farmer digging yams. One yam tells the farmer to go away and leave him alone. Next, the dog speaks up, the palm tree responds, and a stone talks. Frightened, the farmer runs toward the village. As he meets others along the way, they too hear objects talking: a fish trap, a bundle of cloth, the river, and finally the chief's stool. The chief's stool speaks the final line of the story when it says, "Imagine, a talking yam."

Visual Summary

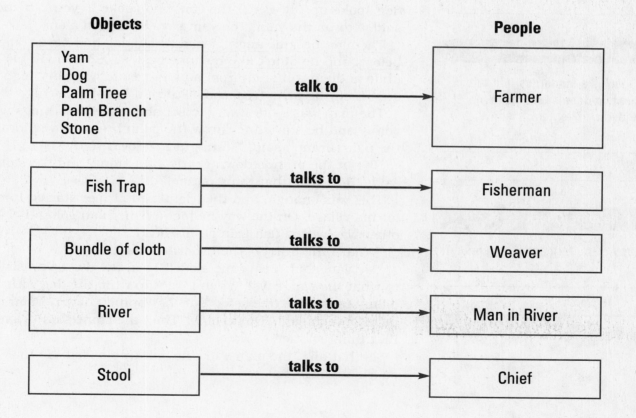

Objects		People
Yam Dog Palm Tree Palm Branch Stone	talk to	Farmer
Fish Trap	talks to	Fisherman
Bundle of cloth	talks to	Weaver
River	talks to	Man in River
Stool	talks to	Chief

African (Ashanti) Folk Tale
Retold by Harold Courlander and
George Herzog

We would probably be surprised if our food suddenly started to talk to us. As this African folk tale begins, a farmer is startled when a vegetable he is digging up scolds him.

Once, not far from the city of Accra on the Gulf of Guinea, a country man went out to his garden to dig up some yams to take to market. While he was digging, one of the yams said to him, "Well, at last you're here. You never weeded me, but now you come around with your digging stick. Go away and leave me alone!"

The farmer turned around and looked at his cow in amazement. The cow was chewing her cud and looking at him.

"Did you say something?" he asked.

The cow kept on chewing and said nothing, but the man's dog spoke up. "It wasn't the cow who spoke to you," the dog said. "It was the yam. The yam says leave him alone."

The man became angry, because his dog had never talked before, and he didn't like his tone besides. So he took his knife and cut a branch from a palm tree to whip his dog. Just then the palm tree said, "Put that branch down!"

The man was getting very upset about the way things were going, and he started to throw the palm branch away, but the palm branch said, "Man, put me down softly!"

He put the branch down gently on a stone, and the stone said, "Hey, take that thing off me!"

This was enough, and the frightened farmer started to run for his village. On the way he met a fisherman going the other way with a fish trap on his head.

"What's the hurry?" the fisherman asked.

"My yam said, 'Leave me alone!' Then the dog said, 'Listen to what the yam says!' When I went to whip the dog with a palm branch the tree said, 'Put that branch down!' Then the palm branch said, 'Do it softly!' Then the stone said, 'Take that thing off me!'"

"Is that all?" the man with the fish trap asked. "Is that so frightening?"

◆ **Activate Prior Knowledge**

Have you ever talked to something that cannot talk back? For example, have you ever told a phone to ring or a computer to hurry? How would you feel if these objects answered you?

_____

_____

◆ **Reading Strategy**

An illogical situation is one that does not make sense. In the bracketed paragraph, what is the illogical situation?

_____

_____

◆ **Literary Analysis**

"Talk" is a **humorous folk tale.** List two details that make the underlined sentence funny.

1. _____

2. _____

◆ **Reading Check**

Why is the farmer running away?

_____

_____

"Well," the man's fish trap said, "did he take it off the stone?"

"Wah!" the fisherman shouted. He threw the fish trap on the ground and began to run with the farmer, and on the trail they met a weaver with a bundle of cloth on his head.

"Where are you going in such a rush?" he asked them.

"My yam said, 'Leave me alone!'" the farmer said. "The dog said, 'Listen to what the yam says!' The tree said, 'Put that branch down!' The branch said, 'Do it softly!' And the stone said, 'Take that thing off me!'"

"And then," the fisherman continued, "the fish trap said, 'Did he take it off?'"

"That's nothing to get excited about," the weaver said. "No reason at all."

"Oh, yes it is," his bundle of cloth said. "If it happened to you you'd run too!"

"Wah!" the weaver shouted. He threw his bundle on the trail and started running with the other men.

They came panting to the <u>ford</u> in the river and found a man bathing. "Are you chasing a gazelle?" he asked them.

The first man said breathlessly, "My yam talked at me, and it said, 'Leave me alone!' And my dog said, 'Listen to your yam!' And when I cut myself a branch the tree said, 'Put that branch down!' And the branch said, 'Do it softly!' And the stone said, "Take that thing off me!'"

The fisherman panted. "And my trap said, 'Did he?'"

The weaver wheezed. "And my bundle of cloth said, 'You'd run too!'"

"Is that why you're running?" the man in the river asked.

"Well, wouldn't you run if you were in their position?" the river said.

The man jumped out of the water and began to run with the others. They ran down the main street of the village to the house of the chief. The chief's servant brought his stool out, and he came and sat on it to listen to their complaints. The men began to recite their troubles.

"I went out to my garden to dig yams," the farmer said, waving his arms. "Then everything began to talk! My yam said, 'Leave me alone!' My dog said, 'Pay attention to your yam!' The tree said, 'Put that branch down!' The branch said, 'Do it softly!' And the stone said, 'Take it off me!'"

"And my fish trap said, 'Well, did he take it off?'" the fisherman said.

"And my cloth said, 'You'd run too!'" the weaver said.

Vocabulary Development: ford (förd) *n.* shallow place in a river that can be crossed

---

◆ **Literary Analysis**

Why is the fisherman's reaction especially funny when the fish trap starts speaking?

_____

_____

_____

◆ **Reading Strategy**

Name three things that happen in this folk tale that could not happen in real life.

1. _____

2. _____

3. _____

◆ **Literary Analysis**

Circle the lines spoken by all of the animals and objects so far in the folk tale. What attitude do they have in common?

_____

_____

_____

◆ **Reading Check**

Where did the men ultimately take their complaints?

_____

_____

_____

What is most illogical in the underlined sentence:

(a) the stool talking?

(b) the stool thinking a talking yam was odd, when the stool itself could talk?

(c) the stool agreeing with the chief?

Circle the letter of your answer. Then explain your choice.

_____

_____

_____

_____

"And the river said the same," the bather said hoarsely, his eyes bulging.

The chief listened to them patiently, but he couldn't refrain from scowling. "Now this is really a wild story," he said at last. "You'd better all go back to your work before I punish you for disturbing the peace."

So the men went away, and the chief shook his head and mumbled to himself, "Nonsense like that upsets the community."

"Fantastic, isn't it?" his stool said. "Imagine, a talking yam!"

Vocabulary Development: refrain (ri frān´) v. to hold back
scowling (skoul´ iŋ) v. contracting the eyebrows and frowning to show displeasure

---

Reader's Response: What was your favorite part of the story? Why?

_____

_____

_____

Thinking About the Skill: How did recognizing illogical situations help you to understand the story?

_____

_____

_____

from The Road Ahead
Bill Gates

Summary

In this nonfiction excerpt, computer pioneer Bill Gates tells about the direction technology will take in our homes in the future. Gates remembers how frustrating it was when he was a child to miss a television show on the day and time it was broadcast. Today, videocassette recorders (VCRs) allow viewing whenever one wishes, although there is the inconvenience of timers and tapes. In the future, however, movies, television shows, and other kinds of digital information will be stored on servers. Computers will then access video-on-demand for home televisions connected to large home networks. Users will be able to call up selections from a large menu without the use of a VCR. Gates believes that in the near future video-on-demand will become a "killer app"—a use of technology that becomes a vital moneymaking venture.

Visual Summary

Television in the Future

- Digitized data will be stored on servers.
- Data will be retrieved from servers and routed on demand to televisions, computers, and telephones.
- Individuals will be able to control when to view television shows, movies, and other kinds of video.

Television Today

- People can use VCRs to tape shows for later viewing.
- They can rent movies to watch on television via VCRs.
- Bandwidth is currently available in corporate networks for limited video-on-demand.

Television Before the 1980s

- People had to watch shows when they aired.
- If traveling, they would miss a show.
- Missing a show meant missing out on discussions of the show the next day.

What is the newest video device you have in your home? What does it permit you to do that older devices did not make possible?

_____

_____

_____

_____

_____

_____

◆ Reading Strategy

You can sometimes **recognize a writer's bias** by looking for words that convey positive or negative feelings. Put a plus next to each of these words from the bracketed paragraph that conveys a positive feeling and a minus next to each one that conveys a negative feeling:

• flexibility   • luxury

• fuss   • convenient

• freedom

◆ Literary Analysis

In **expository writing,** a writer provides details or examples to help explain information. Underline an example Gates provides to show that people have been converting synchronous communications into asynchronous forms for a long time.

from The Road Ahead
Bill Gates

Imagine a time, not too long from now, when you will be able to request the television shows and movies you want exactly when you want to view them. You'll be the one in charge!

When I was a kid, *The Ed Sullivan Show* came on at eight o'clock on Sunday nights. Most Americans with television sets tried to be at home to watch it because that might be the only time and place to see the Beatles, Elvis Presley, the Temptations, or that guy who could spin ten plates <u>simultaneously</u> on the noses of ten dogs. But if you were driving back from your grandparents' house or on a Cub Scout camping trip, too bad. Not being at home on Sunday at eight meant that you also missed out on the Monday morning talk about Sunday night's show.

Conventional television allows us to decide what we watch but not when we watch it. The technical term for this sort of broadcasting is "synchronous."[1] Viewers have to synchronize their schedules with the time of a broadcast that's sent to everybody at the same time. That's how I watched *The Ed Sullivan Show* thirty years ago, and it's how most of us will watch the news tonight.

In the early 1980's the videocassette recorder gave us more flexibility. If you cared enough about a program to fuss with timers and tapes in advance, you could watch it whenever you liked. You could claim from the broadcasters the freedom and luxury to serve as your own program scheduler—and millions of people do. When you tape a television show, or when you let your answering machine take an incoming message so that you don't have to pick up the phone, you're converting synchronous communications into a more convenient form: "asynchronous" communications.

It's human nature to find ways to convert synchronous communications into asynchronous forms. Before the invention of writing 5,000 years ago, the only form of communication was the spoken word and the listener had to be in the presence of the speaker or miss his message. Once the message could be written, it could be stored and read later by anybody, at his or her convenience. I'm writing these words at home on a summer evening, but I have no idea where or when you'll read them. One of the benefits the communications revolution will bring to all of us is more control over our schedules.

Vocabulary Development: simultaneously (sī΄ məl tā΄ nē əs lē) *adv.* at the same time

---

1. **synchronous** (siŋ΄ krə nəs) *adj.* happening at the same time; simultaneous.

Once a form of communication is asynchronous, you also get an increase in the variety of selection possibilities. Even people who rarely record television programs routinely rent movies from the thousands of choices available at local video rental stores for just a few dollars each. The home viewer can spend any evening with Elvis, the Beatles—or Greta Garbo.

Television has been around for fewer than sixty years, but in that time it has become a major influence in the life of almost everyone in the developed nations. In some ways, though, television was just an enhancement of commercial radio, which had been bringing electronic entertainment into homes for twenty years. But no broadcast medium we have right now is comparable to the communications media we'll have once the Internet evolves to the point at which it has the broadband capacity[2] necessary to carry high-quality video.

Because consumers already understand the value of movies and are used to paying to watch them, video-on-demand is an obvious development. There won't be any intermediary VCR. You'll simply select what you want from countless available programs.

No one knows when residential broadband networks capable of supporting video-on-demand will be available in the United States and other developed countries, let alone in developing countries. Many corporate networks already have enough bandwidth,[3] but . . . even in the U.S. most homes will have to make do for some time—maybe more than a decade—with narrowband and midband access. Fortunately, these lower-capacity bandwidths work fine for many Internet-based services such as games, electronic mail, and banking. For the next few years, interactivity in homes will be limited to these kinds of services, which will be delivered to personal computers and other information appliances.

Even after broadband residential networks have become common, television shows will continue to be broadcast as they are today, for synchronous consumption. But after they air, these shows—as well as thousands of movies and virtually all other kinds of video—will also be available whenever you want to view them. If a new episode of *Seinfeld* is on at 9:00 P.M. on Thursday night, you'll also be able to see it at 9:13 P.M., 9:45 P.M., or 11:00 A.M. on Saturday. And there will be thousands of other choices. Your request for a specific movie or TV show episode will register, and the bits[4] will be routed to you across the network. It will feel as if there's no intermediary machinery between you and the object of your interest. You'll indicate what you want, and presto! you'll get it.

---

2. **broadband capacity** *n.* ability to transmit a huge amount of electronic information quickly.
3. **bandwidth** *n.* amount of electronic information that can be transmitted in a given amount of time; capacity.
4. **bits** *n.* units of electronic information.

◆ **Stop to Reflect**

In the first underlined sentence, Gates says that television has become a major influence in the life of almost everyone. Describe a way that television influences your life.

_____

_____

_____

◆ **Literary Analysis**

What example does Gates provide to explain why consumers will easily adjust to the idea of video-on-demand?

_____

_____

_____

◆ **Reading Check**

Based on the second underlined sentence, why are most homes in the United States unable to have video-on-demand now?

_____

_____

_____

◆ **Reading Strategy**

In what way might Gates's **bias** toward technology affect his feelings about video-on-demand?

_____

_____

_____

Underline a sentence in the bracketed paragraph in which Gates explains how video-on-demand will work.

◆ **Reading Check**

Why do you think Gates refers to television, computers, and telephones as "information appliances"?

_____

_____

_____

_____

◆ **Reading Strategy**

Circle words that Gates includes in the final paragraph (on pages 96 and 97) that show his positive **bias** toward video-on-demand.

Movies, TV shows, and other kinds of digital information will be stored on "servers," which are computers with <u>capacious</u> disks. Servers will provide information for use anywhere on the network, just as they do for today's Internet. If you ask to see a particular movie, check a fact, or retrieve your electronic mail, your request will be routed by switches to the server or servers storing that information. You won't know whether the movie, TV show, query response, or e-mail that arrives at your house is stored on a server down the road or on the other side of the country, and it won't matter to you.

The digitized data will be retrieved from the server and routed by switches back to your television, personal computer, or telephone—your "information appliance." These digital devices will succeed for the same reason their analog <u>precursors</u> did—they'll make some aspect of life easier. Unlike the dedicated word processors[5] that brought the first microprocessors to many offices, most of these information appliances will be general-purpose, programmable computers connected to the network.

Even if a show is being broadcast live, you'll be able to use your <u>infrared</u> remote control to start it, stop it, or go to any earlier part of the program, at any time. If somebody comes to the door, you'll be able to pause the program for as long as you like. You'll be in absolute control—except, of course, you won't be able to forward past part of a live show as it's taking place.

Most viewers can appreciate the benefits of video-on-demand and will welcome the convenience it gives them. Once the costs to build a broadband network are low enough, video-on-demand has the potential to be what in computer <u>parlance</u> is called a "killer application," or just "killer app"—a use of technology so attractive to consumers that it fuels market forces and makes the underlying

---

Vocabulary Development: capacious (kə pā´ shəs) *adj.* able to hold much; roomy
precursors (prē kʉr´ sərz) *n.* things that prepare the way for what will follow
infrared (in´ frə red´) *adj.* of light waves that lie just beyond the red end of the visible spectrum
parlance (pär´ ləns) *n.* style of speaking or writing; language

---

5. **dedicated word processors** *n.* machines that can be used only for word processing. Unlike personal computers, dedicated machines perform only one function.

invention on which it depends all but indispensable. Killer applications change technological advances from curiosities into moneymaking essentials.

Reader's Response: Would you like to have video-on-demand available in your house? Why or why not?

_____

_____

_____

Thinking About the Skill: How does recognizing a writer's bias help you to evaluate the information you read?

_____

_____

_____

◆ Stop to Reflect

What are some other "killer apps" in your home? Why are they indispensable?

_____

_____

_____

_____

The Machine That Won the War

Isaac Asimov

Summary

In this futuristic story, a giant computer named Multivac is credited with winning a war between Earth and a rival planet named Deneb. As the three main characters discuss the victory, they reveal their own activities during the war. Henderson, Chief Programmer for Multivac, admits he was forced to "correct" computer data that had become meaningless. Jablonsky, whose job is to analyze Multivac's data, admits that he knew Multivac was unreliable but did nothing about it. To protect his job, he, too, adjusted data until it looked right. Finally, Swift, the Director, admits that he hadn't taken the data presented to him seriously anyway. In fact, when he had to make war decisions, he used the oldest computing device available: the flip of a coin.

Visual Summary

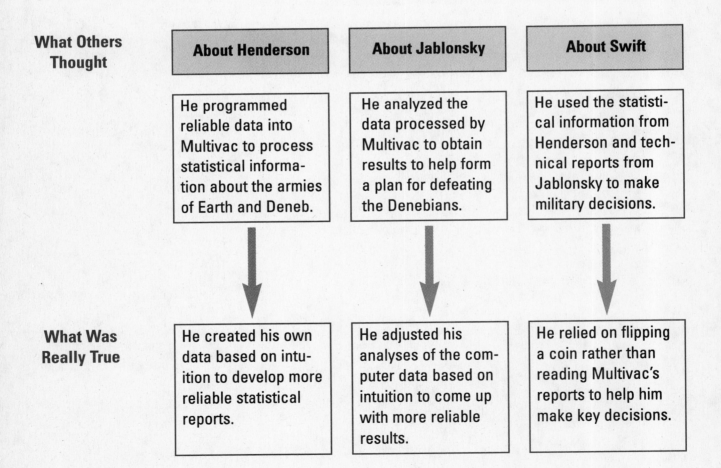

What Others Thought

About Henderson	About Jablonsky	About Swift
He programmed reliable data into Multivac to process statistical information about the armies of Earth and Deneb.	He analyzed the data processed by Multivac to obtain results to help form a plan for defeating the Denebians.	He used the statistical information from Henderson and technical reports from Jablonsky to make military decisions.

What Was Really True

He created his own data based on intuition to develop more reliable statistical reports.	He adjusted his analyses of the computer data based on intuition to come up with more reliable results.	He relied on flipping a coin rather than reading Multivac's reports to help him make key decisions.

The Machine That Won the War
Isaac Asimov

If your country was at war, which would you trust more to plan a winning strategy—people or computers? This science-fiction story may help you answer the question.

The celebration had a long way to go and even in the silent depths of Multivac's underground chambers, it hung in the air.

If nothing else, there was the mere fact of isolation and silence. For the first time in a decade, technicians were not scurrying about the vitals of the giant computer, the soft lights did not wink out their <u>erratic</u> patterns, the flow of information in and out had halted.

It would not be halted long, of course, for the needs of peace would be pressing. Yet now, for a day, perhaps for a week, even Multivac might celebrate the great time, and rest.

Lamar Swift took off the military cap he was wearing and looked down the long and empty main corridor of the enormous computer. He sat down rather wearily in one of the technician's swing-stools, and his uniform, in which he had never been comfortable, took on a heavy and wrinkled appearance.

He said, "I'll miss it all after a <u>grisly</u> fashion. It's hard to remember when we weren't at war with Deneb, and it seems against nature now to be at peace and to look at the stars without anxiety."

The two men with the Executive Director of the Solar Federation were both younger than Swift. Neither was as gray. Neither looked quite as tired.

John Henderson, thin-lipped and finding it hard to control the relief he felt in the midst of triumph, said, "They're destroyed! They're destroyed! It's what I keep saying to myself over and over and I still can't believe it. We all talked so much, over so many years, about the menace hanging over Earth and all its worlds, over every human being, and all the time it was true, every word of it. And now we're alive and it's the Denebians who are shattered and destroyed. They'll be no menace now, ever again."

"Thanks to Multivac," said Swift, with a quiet glance at the <u>imperturbable</u> Jablonsky, who through all the war had been Chief Interpreter of science's <u>oracle</u>. "Right, Max?"

Vocabulary Development: **erratic** (er at´ ik) *adj.* irregular; random
grisly (griz´ lē) *adj.* horrifying; gruesome
imperturbable (im´ pər tʉr´ bə bəl) *adj.* unable to be excited or disturbed
oracle (ō´ rə kəl) *n.* source of knowledge or wise counsel

◆ **Activate Prior Knowledge**

Describe a job in which people use computers to solve problems or help them make decisions.

_____

_____

_____

◆ **Reading Strategy**

Use **relevant details** from the opening paragraphs of the story to answer the following questions:

Why are the people celebrating?

_____

What is Multivac?

_____

How long did the war last?

_____

◆ **Literary Analysis**

Science-fiction writing often deals with events that are set in space. Circle three details in the bracketed passage that involve events in space.

◆ **Reading Check**

What role did Multivac play in the war with Deneb?

_____

_____

_____

Which word in the underlined sentence shows that Jablonsky doesn't like or respect Multivac?

_____

_____

Circle several details in Henderson's bracketed remarks that show that this is a **science-fiction** story.

List two **details** about Henderson's job that are **relevant** to the plot of the story.

1._____

_____

_____

2._____

_____

_____

Jablonsky shrugged. He said, "Well, that's what *they* say." His broad thumb moved in the direction of his right shoulder, aiming upward.

"Jealous, Max?"

"Because they're shouting for Multivac? Because Multivac is the big hero of mankind in this war?" Jablonsky's craggy face took on an air of suitable contempt. "What's that to me? Let Multivac be the machine that won the war, if it pleases them."

Henderson looked at the other two out of the corners of his eyes. In this short interlude that the three had instinctively sought out in the one peaceful corner of a metropolis gone mad; in this entr'acte[1] between the dangers of war and the difficulties of peace; when, for one moment, they might all find surcease; he was conscious only of his weight of guilt.

Suddenly, it was as though that weight were too great to be borne longer. It had to be thrown off, along with the war; now!

Henderson said, "Multivac had nothing to do with victory. It's just a machine."

"A big one," said Swift.

"Then just a big machine. No better than the data fed it." For a moment, he stopped, suddenly unnerved at what he was saying.

Jablonsky looked at him. "You should know. You supplied the data. Or is it just that you're taking the credit?"

"*No,*" said Henderson angrily. "There is no credit. What do you know of the data Multivac had to use: predigested from a hundred subsidiary computers here on Earth, on the Moon, on Mars, even on Titan. With Titan always delayed and always feeling that its figures would introduce an unexpected bias."

"It would drive anyone mad," said Swift, with gentle sympathy.

Henderson shook his head. "It wasn't just that. I admit that eight years ago when I replaced Lepont as Chief Programmer, I was nervous. But there was an exhilaration about things in those days. The war was still long range; an adventure without real danger. We hadn't reached the point where manned vessels had had to take over and where interstellar warps could swallow up a planet clean, if aimed correctly. But then, when the real difficulties began—"

Angrily—he could finally permit anger—he said, "You know nothing about it."

"Well," said Swift. "Tell us. The war is over. We've won."

"Yes." Henderson nodded his head. He had to remember that. Earth had won, so all had been for the best. "Well, the data became meaningless."

Vocabulary Development: surcease (sər sēs´) *n.* an end
subsidiary (səb sid´ ē er´ ē) *adj.* secondary; supporting

1. **entr'acte** (än trakt´) *n.* interval.

"Meaningless? You mean that literally?" said Jablonsky.

"Literally. What would you expect? The trouble with you two was that you weren't out in the thick of it. You never left Multivac, Max, and you, Mr. Director, never left the Mansion except on state visits where you saw exactly what they wanted you to see."

"I was not as unaware of that," said Swift, "as you may have thought."

"Do you know," said Henderson, "to what extent data concerning our production capacity, our resource potential, our trained manpower—everything of importance to the war effort, in fact—had become unreliable and untrustworthy during the last half of the war? Group leaders, both civilian and military, were intent on projecting their own improved image, so to speak, so they obscured the bad and magnified the good. Whatever the machines might do, the men who programmed them and interpreted the results had their own skins to think of and competitors to stab. There was no way of stopping that. I tried, and failed."

"Of course," said Swift, in quiet consolation. "I can see that you would."

"Yet I presume you provided Multivac with data in your programming?" Jablonsky said. "You said nothing to us about unreliability."

"How could I tell you? And if I did, how could you afford to believe me?" demanded Henderson, savagely. "Our entire war effort was geared to Multivac. It was the one great weapon on our side, for the Denebians had nothing like it. What else kept up morale in the face of doom but the assurance that Multivac would always predict and circumvent any Denebian move, and would always direct and prevent the circumvention of our moves? Great Space, after our Spy-warp was blasted out of hyperspace we lacked any reliable Denebian data to feed Multivac and we didn't dare make _that_ public."

"True enough," said Swift.

"Well, then," said Henderson, "if I told you the data was unreliable, what could you have done but replace me and refuse to believe me? I couldn't allow that."

"What did you do?" said Jablonsky.

"Since the war is won, I'll tell you what I did. I corrected the data."

"How?" asked Swift.

"Intuition, I presume. I juggled them till they looked right. At first, I hardly dared. I changed a bit here and there to correct what were obvious impossibilities. When the sky didn't collapse about us, I got braver. Toward the end, I scarcely cared. I just wrote out the necessary data as it was

---

Vocabulary Development: circumvent (sur´ kəm vent´) v. avoid; go around

◆ **Reading Strategy**

What **relevant detail** presented in the first bracketed paragraph explains why the data entered into Multivac had become unreliable and untrustworthy?

_____

_____

_____

_____

_____

_____

_____

◆ **Literary Analysis**

Mark the Text

Circle any words or terms used in the second bracketed paragraph that suggest the story takes place in the future.

◆ **Reading Check**

Why didn't Henderson tell his bosses that the data was unreliable?

_____

_____

_____

_____

_____

Why is the fact that Jablonsky didn't act on the reports about unauthorized use of the Annex **relevant** to the story's plot?

_____

_____

_____

_____

_____

Why was Multivac not in working order during the last years of the war?

_____

_____

_____

_____

In the bracketed passage, what **relevant detail** does Swift reveal to the other two men that surprises them?

_____

_____

_____

_____

_____

needed. I even had the Multivac Annex prepare data for me according to a private programming pattern I had devised for the purpose."

"Random figures?" said Jablonsky.

"Not at all. I introduced a number of necessary biases."

Jablonsky smiled, quite unexpectedly, his dark eyes sparkling behind the crinkling of the lower lids. "Three times a report was brought to me about unauthorized uses of the Annex, and I let it go each time. If it had mattered, I would have followed it up and spotted you, John, and found out what you were doing. But, of course, nothing about Multivac mattered in those days, so you got away with it."

"What do you mean, nothing mattered?" asked Henderson, suspiciously.

"Nothing did. I suppose if I had told you this at the time, it would have spared you your agony, but then if you had told me what you were doing, it would have spared me mine. What made you think Multivac was in working order, whatever the data you supplied it?"

"Not in working order?" said Swift.

"Not really. Not reliably. After all, where were my technicians in the last years of the war? I'll tell you, they were feeding computers on a thousand different space devices. They were gone! I had to make do with kids I couldn't trust and veterans who were out-of-date. Besides, do you think I could trust the solid-state components coming out of Cryogenics[2] in the last years? Cryogenics wasn't any better placed as far as personnel was concerned than I was. To me, it didn't matter whether the data being supplied Multivac were reliable or not. The results weren't reliable. That much I knew."

"What did you do?" asked Henderson.

"I did what you did, John. I introduced the bugger factor. I adjusted matters in accordance with intuition—and that's how the machine won the war."

Swift leaned back in the chair and stretched his legs out before him. "Such revelations. It turns out then that the material handed me to guide me in my decision-making capacity was a man-made interpretation of man-made data. Isn't that right?"

"It looks so," said Jablonsky.

"Then I perceive I was correct in not placing too much reliance upon it," said Swift.

"You didn't?" Jablonsky, despite what he had just said, managed to look professionally insulted.

"I'm afraid I didn't. Multivac might seem to say, Strike here, not there; do this, not that; wait, don't act. But I could never be certain that what Multivac seemed to say, it really

---

2. **Cryogenics** (krī ō jen´ iks) here, a department concerned with the science of low-temperature phenomena.

did say; or what it really said, it really meant. I could never be certain."

"But the final report was always plain enough, sir," said Jablonsky.

"To those who did not have to make the decision, perhaps. Not to me. The horror of the responsibility of such decisions was unbearable and not even Multivac was sufficient to remove the weight. But the point is I was justified in doubting and there is tremendous relief in that."

Caught up in the conspiracy of mutual confession, Jablonsky put titles aside. "What was it you did then, Lamar? After all, you did make decisions. How?"

"Well, it's time to be getting back perhaps, but—I'll tell you first. Why not? I did make use of a computer, Max, but an older one than Multivac, much older."

He groped in his own pocket and brought out a scattering of small change; old-fashioned coins dating to the first years before the metal shortage had brought into being a credit system tied to a computer-complex.

Swift smiled rather sheepishly. "I still need these to make money seem substantial to me. An old man finds it hard to abandon the habits of youth." He dropped the coins, one by one, back into his pocket.

He held the last coin between his fingers, staring absently at it. "Multivac is not the first computer, friends, nor the best-known, nor the one that can most efficiently lift the load of decision from the shoulders of the executive. A machine *did* win the war, John; at least a very simple computing device did; one that I used every time I had a particularly hard decision to make."

With a faint smile of reminiscence, he flipped the coin he held. It glinted in the air as it spun and came down in Swift's outstretched palm. His hand closed over it and brought it down on the back of his left hand. His right hand remained in place, hiding the coin.

"Heads or tails, gentlemen?" said Swift.

Reader's Response: Did your opinion of Multivac change from the beginning to the end of the story? Explain.

_____

_____

Thinking About the Skill: How does focusing on relevant details help you read a story more effectively?

_____

_____

What was Swift's role during the war?

_____

_____

Circle words or phrases Swift uses in the bracketed paragraph that show that his responsibilities troubled him.

◆ Reading Strategy

Why is it **relevant** that Swift still has coins from the old-fashioned money system?

_____

_____

_____

_____

◆ Stop to Reflect

Do you think the ending of the story was meant to be funny or sarcastic?

_____

What message do you think the author tries to convey through the ending about how much we rely on computers today?

_____

_____

_____

_____

_____

from Silent Spring
Rachel Carson

Summary

In this short fable, the author warns that environmental disasters might one day destroy many of the plants, animals, and natural settings that people in America enjoy today. She begins by describing a time when there were prosperous fields of grain, fruitful orchards, continuous migrations of birds, and streams filled with fish. Then, a blight crept over the land, wiping out plant and animal life on farms and in orchards and streams. The blight seems to have been caused by a white powder. At the end, the author notes that the town does not actually exist. However, all of the disasters she describes have happened in different places and might happen everywhere unless Americans change the way they treat the environment.

Visual Summary

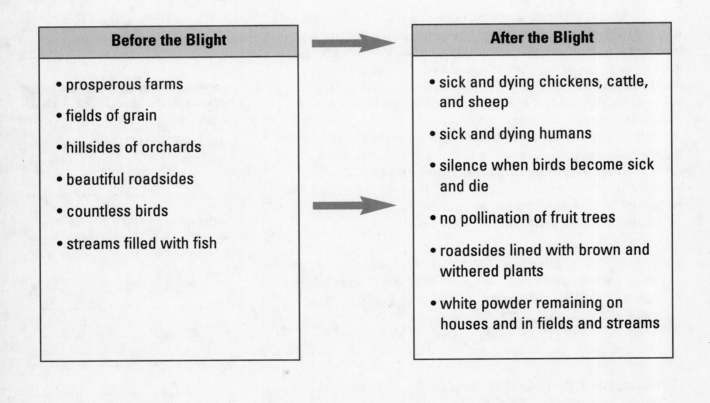

Before the Blight

- prosperous farms
- fields of grain
- hillsides of orchards
- beautiful roadsides
- countless birds
- streams filled with fish

After the Blight

- sick and dying chickens, cattle, and sheep
- sick and dying humans
- silence when birds become sick and die
- no pollination of fruit trees
- roadsides lined with brown and withered plants
- white powder remaining on houses and in fields and streams

from Silent Spring
Rachel Carson

This short fable is part of a longer book in which Rachel Carson, an environmentalist, warns that using pesticides without careful controls might destroy nature as we know it. Carson wants to persuade people to act differently.

There was once a town in the heart of America where all life seemed to live in harmony with its surroundings. The town lay in the midst of a checkerboard of prosperous farms, with fields of grain and hillsides of orchards where, in spring, white clouds of bloom drifted above the green fields. In autumn, oak and maple and birch set up a blaze of color that flamed and flickered across a backdrop of pines. Then foxes barked in the hills and deer silently crossed the fields, half hidden in the mists of the fall mornings.

Along the roads, laurel, viburnum and alder, great ferns and wildflowers delighted the traveler's eye through much of the year. Even in winter the roadsides were places of beauty, where countless birds came to feed on the berries and on the seed heads of the dried weeds rising above the snow. The countryside was, in fact, famous for the abundance and variety of its bird life, and when the flood of migrants was pouring through in spring and fall people traveled from great distances to observe them. Others came to fish the streams, which flowed clear and cold out of the hills and contained shady pools where trout lay. So it had been from the days many years ago when the first settlers raised their houses, sank their wells, and built their barns.

Then a strange <u>blight</u> crept over the area and everything began to change. Some evil spell had settled on the community: mysterious maladies swept the flocks of chickens; the cattle and sheep sickened and died. Everywhere was a shadow of death. The farmers spoke of much illness among their families. In the town the doctors had become more and more puzzled by new kinds of sickness appearing among their patients. There had been several sudden and unexplained deaths, not only among adults but even among children, who would be stricken suddenly while at play and die within a few hours.

There was a strange stillness. The birds, for example— where had they gone? Many people spoke of them, puzzled and disturbed. The feeding stations in the backyards were

---

Vocabulary Development: blight (blīt) *n.* something that destroys or prevents growth

Describe an environmental disaster you have read or heard about.

_____

_____

_____

_____

_____

Underline **facts** in the bracketed passage that support Carson's **opinion** that all life around the town "seemed to live in harmony with its surroundings."

How does Carson's use of the phrase "strange blight" make you feel about the setting in the fable?

_____

_____

_____

_____

What was unusual about the deadly illnesses that struck children in the town?

_____

_____

_____

_____

List two **facts** that Carson provides in the bracketed passage to support her statement that the birds were moribund.

1._____

_____

2._____

_____

◆ Literary Analysis

A **persuasive appeal** is a warning designed to get people to act differently. What warning is Carson presenting in the underlined sentence?

_____

_____

_____

◆ Literary Analysis

Circle words the author uses in the last paragraph to make her warning have a stronger impact on readers.

deserted. The few birds seen anywhere were moribund; they trembled violently and could not fly. It was a spring without voices. On the mornings that had once throbbed with the dawn chorus of robins, catbirds, doves, jays, wrens, and scores of other bird voices there was now no sound; only silence lay over the fields and woods and marsh.

On the farms the hens brooded, but no chicks hatched. The farmers complained that they were unable to raise any pigs—the litters were small and the young survived only a few days. The apple trees were coming into bloom but no bees droned among the blossoms, so there was no pollination and there would be no fruit.

The roadsides, once so attractive, were now lined with browned and withered vegetation as though swept by fire. These, too, were silent, deserted by all living things. Even the streams were now lifeless. Anglers no longer visited them, for all the fish had died.

In the gutters under the eaves and between the shingles of the roofs, a white granular powder still showed a few patches; some weeks before it had fallen like snow upon the roofs and the lawns, the fields and streams.

No witchcraft, no enemy action had silenced the rebirth of new life in this stricken world. The people had done it themselves.

This town does not actually exist, but it might easily have a thousand counterparts in America or elsewhere in the world. I know of no community that has experienced all the misfortunes I describe. Yet every one of these disasters has actually happened somewhere, and many real communities have already suffered a substantial number of them. A grim specter has crept upon us almost unnoticed, and this imagined tragedy may easily become a stark reality we all shall know.

Vocabulary Development: moribund (môr´ ə bund´) *adj.* dying

Reader's Response: Do you think Carson's technique of creating a fictional town was an effective way to get across her message? Why or why not?

_____

_____

Thinking About the Skill: Why is it useful to be able to separate facts from opinions when you are reading a persuasive essay?

_____

_____

The Gift of the Magi
O. Henry

Summary

This story is about Jim and Della, a couple in love. Della is introduced to us first. She is thinking of a present for her husband Jim on Christmas Eve. Della is heartbroken that she does not have enough money to buy Jim the perfect present—a watch chain for his favorite watch. Suddenly, she has the idea to sell her most treasured possession—her hair—so that she can afford the watch chain. When Jim arrives home, he is shocked by Della's appearance. Jim had sold his watch so that he could afford a set of combs for Della's hair—hair that now no longer exists. Both presents are useless for the moment, but it does not matter. Such sacrifices are wise, the narrator concludes, since they are made in the true spirit of giving.

Visual Summary

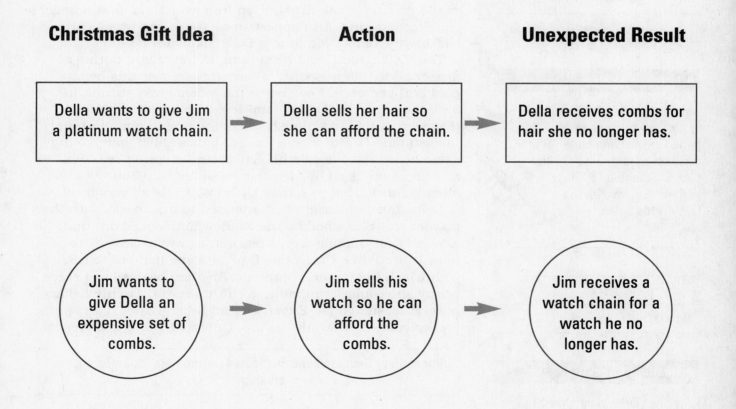

Christmas Gift Idea	Action	Unexpected Result
Della wants to give Jim a platinum watch chain.	Della sells her hair so she can afford the chain.	Della receives combs for hair she no longer has.
Jim wants to give Della an expensive set of combs.	Jim sells his watch so he can afford the combs.	Jim receives a watch chain for a watch he no longer has.

As the story opens, Della is in tears because she does not have enough money to buy her husband a Christmas present.

One dollar and eighty-seven cents. That was all. And sixty cents of it was in pennies. Pennies saved one and two at a time by bulldozing the grocer and the vegetable man and the butcher until one's cheeks burned with the silent imputation of parsimony[1] that such close dealing implied. Three times Della counted it. One dollar and eighty-seven cents. And the next day would be Christmas.

There was clearly nothing to do but flop down on the shabby little couch and howl. So Della did it. Which instigates the moral reflection that life is made up of sobs, sniffles, and smiles, with sniffles predominating.

While the mistress of the home is gradually subsiding from the first stage to the second, take a look at the home. A furnished flat[2] at $8 per week. It did not exactly beggar description,[3] but it certainly had that word on the lookout for the mendicancy squad.[4]

In the vestibule below was a letter-box into which no letter would go, and an electric button from which no mortal finger could coax a ring. Also appertaining thereunto was a card bearing the name "Mr. James Dillingham Young."

The "Dillingham" had been flung to the breeze during a former period of prosperity when its possessor was being paid $30 per week. Now, when the income was shrunk to $20, the letters of "Dillingham" looked blurred, as though they were thinking seriously of contracting to a modest and unassuming D. But whenever Mr. James Dillingham Young came home and reached his flat above he was called "Jim" and greatly hugged by Mrs. James Dillingham Young, already introduced to you as Della. Which is all very good.

Della finished her cry and attended to her cheeks with the powder rag. She stood by the window and looked out dully at a gray cat walking a gray fence in a gray backyard. To-morrow would be Christmas Day, and she had only $1.87 with which to buy Jim a present. She had been saving every penny she could for months, with this result. Twenty dollars a week doesn't go far. Expenses had been greater than she had calculated. They always are. Only $1.87 to buy a present

---

Vocabulary Development: instigates (in´ stə gāts´) *v.* urges on; stirs up

---

1. **silent imputation** (im pyoo tā´ shən) **of parsimony** (pär´ sə mō´ nē) silent accusation of stinginess.
2. **flat** (flat) *n.* apartment.
3. **beggar description** resist description.
4. **mendicancy** (men´ di kən´ sē) **squad** police who arrest beggars.

◆ **Activate Prior Knowledge**

Think of a time when you wanted to buy something that you could not afford. What sacrifices did you make in order to save enough money to afford it?

_____

_____

_____

◆ **Reading Strategy**

While you read, **ask questions** about characters and events to understand the details of a story. As you read further, you can find the answers to your questions. What question could you ask about Della's behavior in the bracketed paragraph?

_____

_____

_____

◆ **Literary Analysis**

A **plot** consists of the events of a story. Only two events have happened in the story so far. Find the passages that deal with plot and place a "P" next to them. Summarize the two events below.

1. _____

_____

2. _____

_____

◆ **Reading Check**

Why does Della only have $1.87 to spend on Jim's Christmas present?

_____

_____

for Jim. Her Jim. Many a happy hour she had spent planning for something nice for him. Something fine and rare and sterling—something just a little bit near to being worthy of the honor of being owned by Jim.

There was a pier glass[5] between the windows of the room. Perhaps you have seen a pier glass in an $8 flat. A very thin and very agile person may, by observing his reflection in a rapid sequence of longitudinal strips, obtain a fairly accurate conception of his looks. Della, being slender, had mastered the art.

Suddenly she whirled from the window and stood before the glass. Her eyes were shining brilliantly, but her face had lost its color within twenty seconds. Rapidly she pulled down her hair and let it fall to its full length.

Now, there were two possessions of the James Dillingham Youngs in which they both took a mighty pride. One was Jim's gold watch that had been his father's and his grand-father's. The other was Della's hair. Had the Queen of Sheba[6] lived in the flat across the airshaft, Della would have let her hair hang out the window some day to dry just to depreciate Her Majesty's jewels and gifts. Had King Solomon been the janitor, with all his treasures piled up in the basement, Jim would have pulled out his watch every time he passed, just to see him pluck at his beard from envy.

So now Della's beautiful hair fell about her rippling and shining like a cascade of brown waters. It reached below her knee and made itself almost a garment for her. And then she did it up again nervously and quickly. Once she faltered for a minute and stood still while a tear or two splashed on the worn red carpet.

On went her old brown jacket; on went her old brown hat. With a whirl of skirts and with the brilliant sparkle still in her eyes, she fluttered out the door and down the stairs to the street.

Where she stopped the sign read: "Mme. Sofronie. Hair Goods of All Kinds." One flight up Della ran, and collected herself, panting. Madame, large, too white, chilly, hardly looked the "Sofronie."

"Will you buy my hair?" asked Della.

"I buy hair," said Madame. "Take yer hat off and let's have a sight at the looks of it."

Down rippled the brown cascade.

"Twenty dollars," said Madame, lifting the mass with a practiced hand.

Vocabulary Development: depreciate (di prē´ shē āt) *v.* reduce in value
cascade (kas kād´) *n.* waterfall

---

5. **pier** (pir) **glass** tall mirror.
6. **Queen of Sheba** the biblical queen who visited King Solomon to test his wisdom.

◆ Stop to Reflect

Why do you think people feel the impulse to give other people expensive gifts?

_____

_____

_____

◆ Reading Strategy

Sudden, unexplained changes in the action are a good place to **ask questions.** What question does the first bracketed paragraph raise?

_____

_____

◆ Literary Analysis

Even a minor event can be considered part of the **plot.** Can the underlined sentence be considered part of the plot? Why or why not?

_____

_____

_____

◆ Reading Check

The conversation in the second bracketed passage might provide the answer to a question you might have had earlier. What decision has Della made?

_____

_____

_____

_____

_____

_____

_____

◆ Literary Analysis

Della's decision to use the curling irons was the result of which **plot** event?

_____

_____

_____

_____

_____

◆ Reading Check

Why is Della anxious about Jim's lateness?

_____

_____

_____

_____

"Give it to me quick," said Della.

Oh, and the next two hours tripped by on rosy wings. Forget the hashed metaphor. She was ransacking the stores for Jim's present.

She found it at last. It surely had been made for Jim and no one else. There was no other like it in any of the stores, and she had turned all of them inside out. It was a platinum fob chain[7] simple and <u>chaste</u> in design, properly proclaiming its value by substance alone and not by <u>meretricious</u> ornamentation—as all good things should do. It was even worthy of The Watch. As soon as she saw it she knew that it must be Jim's. It was like him. Quietness and value—the description applied to both. Twenty-one dollars they took from her for it, and she hurried home with the 87 cents. With that chain on his watch Jim might be properly anxious about the time in any company. Grand as the watch was he sometimes looked at it on the sly on account of the old leather strap that he used in place of a chain.

When Della reached home her intoxication gave way a little to prudence and reason. She got out her curling irons and lighted the gas and went to work repairing the <u>ravages</u> made by generosity added to love. Which is always a tremendous task, dear friends—a mammoth task.

Within forty minutes her head was covered with tiny, close-lying curls that made her look wonderfully like a truant schoolboy. She looked at her reflection in the mirror long, carefully, and critically.

"If Jim doesn't kill me," she said to herself, "before he takes a second look at me, he'll say I look like a Coney Island[8] chorus girl. But what could I do—oh! what could I do with a dollar and eighty-seven cents?"

At 7 o'clock the coffee was made and the frying-pan was on the back of the stove hot and ready to cook the chops.

Jim was never late. Della doubled the fob chain in her hand and sat on the corner of the table near the door that he always entered. Then she heard his step on the stair away down on the first flight, and she turned white for just a moment. She had a habit of saying little silent prayers about the simplest everyday things, and now she whispered: "Please God, make him think I am still pretty."

Vocabulary Development: chaste (chāst) *adj.* pure or clean in style; not ornate
meretricious (mer´ ə trish´ əs) *adj.* attractive in a cheap, flashy way
ravages (rav´ ij iz) *n.* ruins; devastating damages

---

7. **fob** (fäb) **chain** small chain connecting a watch to its pocket.
8. **Coney Island** beach and amusement park in Brooklyn, New York.

The door opened and Jim stepped in and closed it. He looked thin and very serious. Poor fellow, he was only twenty-two—and to be burdened with a family! He needed a new overcoat and he was without gloves.

Jim stopped inside the door, as immovable as a setter at the scent of quail. His eyes were fixed upon Della, and there was an expression in them that she could not read, and it terrified her. It was not anger, nor surprise, nor disapproval, nor horror, nor any of the sentiments that she had been prepared for. He simply stared at her fixedly with that peculiar expression on his face.

Della wriggled off the table and went for him.

"Jim, darling," she cried, "don't look at me that way. I had my hair cut off and sold it because I couldn't have lived through Christmas without giving you a present. It'll grow out again—you won't mind, will you? I just had to do it. My hair grows awfully fast. Say 'Merry Christmas!' Jim, and let's be happy. You don't know what a nice—what a beautiful, nice gift I've got for you."

"You've cut off your hair?" asked Jim, laboriously, as if he had not arrived at that patent fact yet even after the hardest mental labor.

"Cut it off and sold it," said Della. "Don't you like me just as well, anyhow? I'm me without my hair, ain't I?"

Jim looked about the room curiously.

"You say your hair is gone?" he said, with an air almost of idiocy.

"You needn't look for it," said Della. "It's sold, I tell you— sold and gone, too. It's Christmas Eve, boy. Be good to me, for it went for you. Maybe the hairs of my head were numbered," she went on with a sudden serious sweetness, "but nobody could ever count my love for you. Shall I put the chops on, Jim?"

Out of his trance Jim seemed quickly to wake. He enfolded his Della. For ten seconds let us regard with discreet scrutiny some inconsequential object in the other direction. Eight dollars a week or a million a year—what is the difference? A mathematician or a wit would give you the wrong answer. The Magi brought valuable gifts, but that was not among them. This dark assertion will be illuminated later on.

Jim drew a package from his overcoat pocket and threw it upon the table.

"Don't make any mistake, Dell," he said, "about me. I don't think there's anything in the way of a haircut or a shave or a shampoo that could make me like my girl any less. But if you'll unwrap that package you may see why you had me going a while at first."

Vocabulary Development: discreet (dis krēt´) *adj.* tactful; respectful

© Pearson Education, Inc.

◆ **Reading Strategy**

A question that arises from the bracketed paragraph is: "Why does Jim have such a strange expression on his face?" Write down your answer. Then, read ahead to see if you guessed correctly.

_____

_____

_____

_____

_____

_____

◆ **Literary Analysis**

Which **plot** event does Jim find it hard to understand?

_____

_____

_____

_____

_____

_____

◆ **Reading Check**

Does Jim really mind the fact that Della cut her hair, as Della fears?

_____

_____

_____

_____

_____

_____

_____

_____

_____

_____

◆ Literary Analysis

Which event on this page is the final event in the story's **plot**?

_____

_____

_____

_____

_____

_____

◆ Stop to Reflect

Why do you think the author describes the couple as "foolish" in one sentence and then "wise" in the next?

_____

_____

_____

_____

_____

White fingers and nimble tore at the string and paper. And then an ecstatic scream of joy; and then, alas! a quick feminine change to hysterical tears and wails, necessitating the immediate employment of all the comforting powers of the lord of the flat.

For there lay The Combs—the set of combs, side and back, that Della had worshipped for long in a Broadway window. Beautiful combs, pure tortoise shell, with jeweled rims—just the shade to wear in the beautiful vanished hair. They were expensive combs, she knew, and her heart had simply craved and yearned over them without the least hope of possession. And now, they were hers, but the tresses that should have adorned the coveted adornments were gone.

But she hugged them to her bosom, and at length she was able to look up with dim eyes and a smile and say: "My hair grows so fast, Jim!"

And then Della leaped up like a little singed cat and cried, "Oh, oh!"

Jim had not yet seen his beautiful present. She held it out to him eagerly upon her open palm. The dull precious metal seemed to flash with a reflection of her bright and ardent spirit.

"Isn't it a dandy, Jim? I hunted all over town to find it. You'll have to look at the time a hundred times a day now. Give me your watch. I want to see how it looks on it."

Instead of obeying, Jim tumbled down on the couch and put his hands under the back of his head and smiled.

"Dell," said he, "let's put our Christmas presents away and keep 'em a while. They're too nice to use just at present. I sold the watch to get the money to buy your combs. And now suppose you put the chops on."

The Magi, as you know, were wise men—wonderfully wise men—who brought gifts to the Babe in the manger. They invented the art of giving Christmas presents. Being wise, their gifts were no doubt wise ones, possibly bearing the privilege of exchange in case of duplication. And here I have lamely related to you the uneventful chronicle of two foolish children in a flat who most unwisely sacrificed for each other the greatest treasures of their house. But in a last word to the wise of these days let it be said that of all who give gifts these two were the wisest. Of all who give and receive gifts, such as they are wisest. Everywhere they are wisest. They are the magi.

Reader's Response: Do you think that Jim and Della were foolish to spend money they did not have on gifts for each other? Why or why not?

_____

_____

The Scarlet Ibis

James Hurst

Summary

The narrator of this story remembers his boyhood with his brother, Doodle. Doodle was a disappointment to his brother because he was weak and frail. When Doodle was born, the narrator had looked forward to having a new playmate. Instead, he often had to take care of Doodle and he resented this responsibility. Still, a bond developed between them, despite Doodle's physical disabilities. Pride drove the narrator to teach Doodle to walk. Encouraged by his success, the narrator decided he would teach Doodle how to run, swim, climb trees, and fight before Doodle started school. The deadline approached and the narrator knew that Doodle would not succeed. He was angry because of this failure and left Doodle behind in a lightning storm. When he returned to look for Doodle, the narrator was devastated to find Doodle lying dead under a bush.

Visual Summary

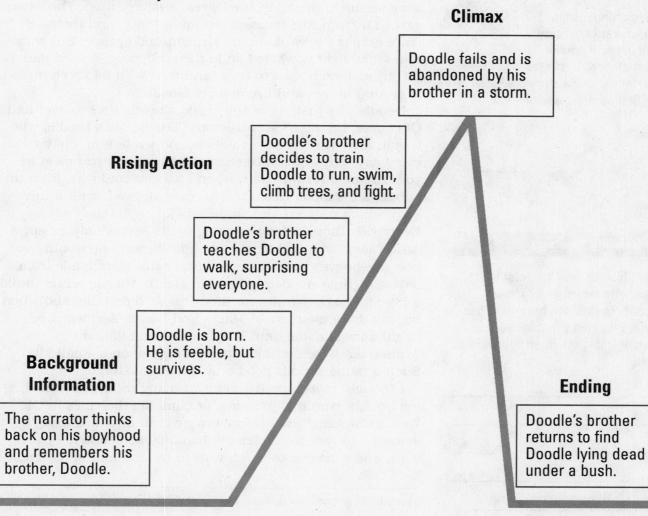

Climax
Doodle fails and is abandoned by his brother in a storm.

Rising Action
Doodle's brother decides to train Doodle to run, swim, climb trees, and fight.

Doodle's brother teaches Doodle to walk, surprising everyone.

Doodle is born. He is feeble, but survives.

Background Information
The narrator thinks back on his boyhood and remembers his brother, Doodle.

Ending
Doodle's brother returns to find Doodle lying dead under a bush.

The Scarlet Ibis
James Hurst

As the story begins, the narrator remembers the sights, sounds, and smells of his boyhood. In particular, he remembers his brother, Doodle.

It was in the clove of seasons, summer was dead but autumn had not yet been born, that the ibis lit in the bleeding tree. The flower garden was stained with rotting brown magnolia petals and ironweeds grew rank amid the purple phlox. The five o'clocks by the chimney still marked time, but the oriole nest in the elm was untenanted and rocked back and forth like an empty cradle. The last graveyard flowers were blooming, and their smell drifted across the cotton field and through every room of our house, speaking softly the names of our dead.

It's strange that all this is still so clear to me, now that the summer has long since fled and time has had its way. A grindstone stands where the bleeding tree stood, just outside the kitchen door, and now if an oriole sings in the elm, its song seems to die up in the leaves, a silvery dust. The flower garden is prim, the house a gleaming white, and the pale fence across the yard stands straight and spruce. But sometimes (like right now), as I sit in the cool, green-draped parlor, the grindstone begins to turn, and time with all its changes is ground away—and I remember Doodle.

Doodle was just about the craziest brother a boy ever had. Of course, he wasn't a crazy crazy like old Miss Leedie, who was in love with President Wilson and wrote him a letter every day, but was a nice crazy, like someone you meet in your dreams. He was born when I was six and was, from the outset, a disappointment. He seemed all head, with a tiny body which was red and shriveled like an old man's. Everybody thought he was going to die—everybody except Aunt Nicey, who had delivered him. She said he would live because he was born in a caul[1] and cauls were made from Jesus' nightgown. Daddy had Mr. Heath, the carpenter, build a little mahogany coffin for him. But he didn't die, and when he was three months old Mama and Daddy decided they might as well name him. They named him William Armstrong, which was like tying a big tail on a small kite. Such a name sounds good only on a tombstone.

I thought myself pretty smart at many things, like holding my breath, running, jumping, or climbing the vines in Old Woman Swamp, and I wanted more than anything else someone to race to Horsehead Landing, someone to box with, and someone to perch with in the top fork of the great

---

1. **caul** (kôl) *n.* membrane enclosing a baby at birth.

pine behind the barn, where across the fields and swamps you could see the sea. I wanted a brother. But Mama, crying, told me that even if William Armstrong lived, he would never do these things with me. He might not, she sobbed, even be "all there." He might, as long as he lived, lie on the rubber sheet in the center of the bed in the front bedroom where the white marquisette curtains billowed out in the afternoon sea breeze, rustling like palmetto fronds.[2]

It was bad enough having an invalid brother, but having one who possibly was not all there was unbearable, so I began to make plans to kill him by smothering him with a pillow. However, one afternoon as I watched him, my head poked between the iron posts of the foot of the bed, he looked straight at me and grinned. I skipped through the rooms, down the echoing halls, shouting, "Mama, he smiled. He's all there! He's all there!" and he was.

When he was two, if you laid him on his stomach, he began to try to move himself, straining terribly. The doctor said that with his weak heart this strain would probably kill him, but it didn't. Trembling, he'd push himself up, turning first red, then a soft purple, and finally collapse back onto the bed like an old worn-out doll. I can still see Mama watching him, her hand pressed tight across her mouth, her eyes wide and unblinking. But he learned to crawl (it was his third winter), and we brought him out of the front bedroom, putting him on the rug before the fireplace. For the first time he became one of us.

As long as he lay all the time in bed, we called him William Armstrong, even though it was formal and sounded as if we were referring to one of our ancestors, but with his creeping around on the deerskin rug and beginning to talk, something had to be done about his name. It was I who renamed him. When he crawled, he crawled backwards, as if he were in reverse and couldn't change gears. If you called him, he'd turn around as if he were going in the other direction, then he'd back right up to you to be picked up. Crawling backward made him look like a doodle-bug, so I began to call him Doodle, and in time even Mama and Daddy thought it was a better name than William Armstrong. Only Aunt Nicey disagreed. She said caul babies should be treated with special respect since they might turn out to be saints. Renaming my brother was perhaps the kindest thing I ever did for him, because nobody expects much from someone called Doodle.

Although Doodle learned to crawl, he showed no signs of walking, but he wasn't idle. He talked so much that we all quit listening to what he said. It was about this time that

---

2. **palmetto fronds** palm leaves.

◆ **Stop to Reflect**

Why do you think this one event in the underlined passage changes the narrator's mind about his brother?

_____

_____

_____

_____

◆ **Literary Analysis**

A first person narrator describes events as he or she sees or remembers them. What does the narrator specifically remember about Doodle and about Mama in the bracketed paragraph?

Doodle: _____

_____

_____

Mama: _____

_____

_____

◆ **Reading Check**

What difficulties has Doodle so far overcome?

_____

_____

_____

_____

_____

_____

_____

_____

_____

_____

First person **point of view** reveals a single character's thoughts and feelings. What are the narrator's thoughts and feelings about his brother Doodle in the bracketed passage?

_____

_____

_____

_____

_____

Do you agree with the narrator that many of us have a cruel streak that is connected with love? Explain, by offering an example.

_____

_____

_____

_____

Daddy built him a go-cart and I had to pull him around. At first I just paraded him up and down the piazza, but then he started crying to be taken out into the yard and it ended up by my having to lug him wherever I went. If I so much as picked up my cap, he'd start crying to go with me and Mama would call from wherever she was, "Take Doodle with you."

He was a burden in many ways. The doctor had said that he mustn't get too excited, too hot, too cold, or too tired and that he must always be treated gently. A long list of don'ts went with him, all of which I ignored once we got out of the house. To discourage his coming with me, I'd run with him across the ends of the cotton rows and career him around corners on two wheels. Sometimes I accidentally turned him over, but he never told Mama. His skin was very sensitive, and he had to wear a big straw hat whenever he went out. When the going got rough and he had to cling to the sides of the go-cart, the hat slipped all the way down over his ears. He was a sight. Finally, I could see I was licked. Doodle was my brother and he was going to cling to me forever, no matter what I did, so I dragged him across the burning cotton field to share with him the only beauty I knew, Old Woman Swamp. I pulled the go-cart through the saw-tooth fern, down into the green dimness where the palmetto fronds whispered by the stream. I lifted him out and set him down in the soft rubber grass beside a tall pine. His eyes were round with wonder as he gazed about him, and his little hands began to stroke the rubber grass. Then he began to cry.

"For heaven's sake, what's the matter?" I asked, annoyed.

"It's so pretty," he said. "So pretty, pretty, pretty."

After that day Doodle and I often went down into Old Woman Swamp. I would gather wildflowers, wild violets, honeysuckle, yellow jasmine, snakeflowers, and water lilies, and with wire grass we'd weave them into necklaces and crowns. We'd bedeck ourselves with our handiwork and loll about thus beautified, beyond the touch of the everyday world. Then when the slanted rays of the sun burned orange in the tops of the pines, we'd drop our jewels into the stream and watch them float away toward the sea.

There is within me (and with sadness I have watched it in others) a knot of cruelty borne by the stream of love, much as our blood sometimes bears the seed of our destruction, and at times I was mean to Doodle. One day I took him up to the barn loft and showed him his casket, telling him how we all had believed he would die. It was covered with a film of Paris green[3] sprinkled to kill the rats, and screech owls had built a nest inside it.

Doodle studied the mahogany box for a long time, then said, "It's not mine."

---

3. **Paris green** poisonous green powder.

"It is," I said. "And before I'll help you down from the loft, you're going to have to touch it."

"I won't touch it," he said sullenly.

"Then I'll leave you here by yourself," I threatened, and made as if I were going down.

Doodle was frightened of being left. "Don't go leave me, Brother," he cried, and he leaned toward the coffin. His hand, trembling, reached out, and when he touched the casket he screamed. A screech owl flapped out of the box into our faces, scaring us and covering us with Paris green. Doodle was paralyzed, so I put him on my shoulder and carried him down the ladder, and even when we were outside in the bright sunshine, he clung to me, crying, "Don't leave me. Don't leave me."

When Doodle was five years old, I was embarrassed at having a brother of that age who couldn't walk, so I set out to teach him. We were down in Old Woman Swamp and it was spring and the sick-sweet smell of bay flowers hung everywhere like a mournful song. "I'm going to teach you to walk, Doodle," I said.

He was sitting comfortably on the soft grass, leaning back against the pine. "Why?" he asked.

I hadn't expected such an answer. "So I won't have to haul you around all the time."

"I can't walk, Brother," he said.

"Who says so?" I demanded.

"Mama, the doctor—everybody."

"Oh, you can walk," I said, and I took him by the arms and stood him up. He collapsed onto the grass like a half-empty flour sack. It was as if he had no bones in his little legs.

"Don't hurt me, Brother," he warned.

"Shut up. I'm not going to hurt you. I'm going to teach you to walk." I heaved him up again, and again he collapsed.

This time he did not lift his face up out of the rubber grass. "I just can't do it. Let's make honeysuckle wreaths."

"Oh yes you can, Doodle," I said. "All you got to do is try. Now come on," and I hauled him up once more.

It seemed so hopeless from the beginning that it's a miracle I didn't give up. But all of us must have something or someone to be proud of, and Doodle had become mine. I did not know then that pride is a wonderful, terrible thing, a seed that bears two vines, life and death. Every day that summer we went to the pine beside the stream of Old Woman Swamp, and I put him on his feet at least a hundred times each afternoon. Occasionally I too became discouraged because it didn't seem as if he was trying, and I would say, "Doodle, don't you *want* to learn to walk?"

He'd nod his head, and I'd say, "Well, if you don't keep trying, you'll never learn." Then I'd paint for him a picture of

---

◆ **Reading Strategy**

Imagine how it must have felt for Doodle to touch his own coffin. Write down a list of words to describe the feelings you imagine.

_____

_____

_____

_____

_____

◆ **Literary Analysis**

Circle the words in the bracketed passage that reveal the narrator's feelings.

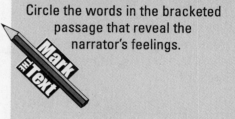

◆ **Stop to Reflect**

What is the best way to motivate people to do something they think they cannot do?

_____

_____

_____

_____

◆ **Reading Check**

What activity is Doodle's brother trying to get Doodle to accomplish?

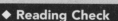

_____

_____

Put yourself in Doodle's brother's place. How would it feel to accomplish something that you never thought you would?

_____

_____

_____

_____

_____

Why does the narrator go to such great lengths to make sure the others do not peek before Doodle is ready?

_____

_____

_____

_____

_____

_____

What emotions is Doodle's brother feeling in the bracketed paragraph? Explain.

_____

_____

_____

_____

_____

_____

us as old men, white-haired, him with a long white beard and me still pulling him around in the go-cart. This never failed to make him try again.

Finally one day, after many weeks of practicing, he stood alone for a few seconds. When he fell, I grabbed him in my arms and hugged him, our laughter pealing through the swamp like a ringing bell. Now we knew it could be done. Hope no longer hid in the dark palmetto thicket but perched like a cardinal in the lacy toothbrush tree, brilliantly visible. "Yes, yes," I cried, and he cried it too, and the grass beneath us was soft and the smell of the swamp was sweet.

With success so <u>imminent</u>, we decided not to tell anyone until he could actually walk. Each day, barring rain, we sneaked into Old Woman Swamp, and by cotton-picking time Doodle was ready to show what he could do. He still wasn't able to walk far, but we could wait no longer. Keeping a nice secret is very hard to do, like holding your breath. We chose to reveal all on October eighth, Doodle's sixth birthday, and for weeks ahead we mooned around the house, promising everybody a most spectacular surprise. Aunt Nicey said that, after so much talk, if we produced anything less tremendous than the Resurrection,[4] she was going to be disappointed.

At breakfast on our chosen day, when Mama, Daddy, and Aunt Nicey were in the dining room, I brought Doodle to the door in the go-cart just as usual and had them turn their backs, making them cross their hearts and hope to die if they peeked. I helped Doodle up, and when he was standing alone I let them look. There wasn't a sound as Doodle walked slowly across the room and sat down at his place at the table. Then Mama began to cry and ran over to him, hugging him and kissing him. Daddy hugged him too, so I went to Aunt Nicey, who was thanks praying in the doorway, and began to waltz her around. We danced together quite well until she came down on my big toe with her brogans, hurting me so badly I thought I was crippled for life.

Doodle told them it was I who had taught him to walk, so everyone wanted to hug me, and I began to cry.

"What are you crying for?" asked Daddy, but I couldn't answer. They did not know that I did it for myself; that pride, whose slave I was, spoke to me louder than all their voices, and that Doodle walked only because I was ashamed of having a crippled brother.

Within a few months Doodle had learned to walk well and his go-cart was put up in the barn loft (it's still there) beside

---

Vocabulary Development: imminent (im′ ə nent) *adj.* likely to happen soon

---

4. **the Resurrection** (res′ e rek′ shen) the rising of Jesus Christ from the dead after his death and burial.

his little mahogany coffin. Now, when we roamed off together, resting often, we never turned back until our destination had been reached, and to help pass the time, we took up lying. From the beginning Doodle was a terrible liar and he got me in the habit. Had anyone stopped to listen to us, we would have been sent off to Dix Hill.

My lies were scary, involved, and usually pointless, but Doodle's were twice as crazy. People in his stories all had wings and flew wherever they wanted to go. His favorite lie was about a boy named Peter who had a pet peacock with a ten-foot tail. Peter wore a golden robe that glittered so brightly that when he walked through the sunflowers they turned away from the sun to face him. When Peter was ready to go to sleep, the peacock spread his magnificent tail, enfolding the boy gently like a closing go-to-sleep flower, burying him in the gloriously iridescent, rustling vortex. Yes, I must admit it. Doodle could beat me lying.

Doodle and I spent lots of time thinking about our future. We decided that when we were grown we'd live in Old Woman Swamp and pick dog-tongue for a living. Beside the stream, he planned, we'd build us a house of whispering leaves and the swamp birds would be our chickens. All day long (when we weren't gathering dog-tongue) we'd swing through the cypresses on the rope vines, and if it rained we'd huddle beneath an umbrella tree and play stickfrog. Mama and Daddy could come and live with us if they wanted to. He even came up with the idea that he could marry Mama and I could marry Daddy. Of course, I was old enough to know this wouldn't work out, but the picture he painted was so beautiful and serene that all I could do was whisper Yes, yes.

Once I had succeeded in teaching Doodle to walk, I began to believe in my own infallibility and I prepared a terrific development program for him, unknown to Mama and Daddy, of course. I would teach him to run, to swim, to climb trees, and to fight. He, too, now believed in my infallibility, so we set the deadline for these accomplishments less than a year away, when, it had been decided, Doodle could start to school.

That winter we didn't make much progress, for I was in school and Doodle suffered from one bad cold after another. But when spring came, rich and warm, we raised our sights again. Success lay at the end of summer like a pot of gold,

---

Vocabulary Development: **iridescent** (ir´ ə des´ ənt) *adj.* having shifting, rainbowlike colors
vortex (vôr´ teks) *n.* center of a situation, which draws in all that surrounds it
infallibility (in fal´ ə bil´ ə tē) *n.* inability to fail

What can you tell about Doodle's personality from the lies that he tells?

_____

_____

_____

_____

Identify with Doodle and his brother as they dream of their future. Why does the future they dream of seem so beautiful?

_____

_____

_____

_____

_____

What is the deadline that is set for Doodle?

_____

_____

_____

_____

_____

_____

_____

_____

_____

_____

◆ Reading Check

Why does Daddy curse the bad weather?

_____

_____

_____

_____

_____

◆ Reading Strategy

Put yourself in the place of the narrator. How does he feel as the deadline approaches?

_____

_____

_____

_____

_____

and our campaign got off to a good start. On hot days, Doodle and I went down to Horsehead Landing and I gave him swimming lessons or showed him how to row a boat. Sometimes we descended into the cool greenness of Old Woman Swamp and climbed the rope vines or boxed scientifically beneath the pine where he had learned to walk. Promise hung about us like the leaves, and wherever we looked, ferns unfurled and birds broke into song.

That summer, the summer of 1918, was blighted. In May and June there was no rain and the crops withered, curled up, then died under the thirsty sun. One morning in July a hurricane came out of the east, tipping over the oaks in the yard and splitting the limbs of the elm trees. That afternoon it roared back out of the west, blew the fallen oaks around, snapping their roots and tearing them out of the earth like a hawk at the <u>entrails</u> of a chicken. Cotton bolls were wrenched from the stalks and lay like green walnuts in the valleys between the rows, while the cornfield leaned over uniformly so that the tassels touched the ground. Doodle and I followed Daddy out into the cotton field, where he stood, shoulders sagging, surveying the ruin. When his chin sank down onto his chest, we were frightened, and Doodle slipped his hand into mine. Suddenly Daddy straightened his shoulders, raised a giant knuckly fist, and with a voice that seemed to rumble out of the earth itself began cursing heaven, hell, the weather, and the Republican Party. Doodle and I, prodding each other and giggling, went back to the house, knowing that everything would be all right.

And during that summer, strange names were heard through the house: Château Thierry, Amiens, Soissons, and in her blessing at the supper table, Mama once said, "And bless the Pearsons, whose boy Joe was lost at Belleau Wood."[5]

So we came to that clove of seasons. School was only a few weeks away, and Doodle was far behind schedule. He could barely clear the ground when climbing up the rope vines and his swimming was certainly not passable. We decided to double our efforts, to make that last drive and reach our pot of gold. I made him swim until he turned blue and row until he couldn't lift an oar. Wherever we went, I purposely walked fast, and although he kept up, his face turned red and his eyes became glazed. Once, he could go no further, so he collapsed on the ground and began to cry.

Vocabulary Development: entrails (en´ trālz) *n.* internal organs, specifically intestines

---

5. **Château Thierry** (shä tō tē e rē´), **Amiens** (à myan´), **Soissons** (swä sôn´), . . . **Belleau** (belō´) **Wood** places in France where battles were fought during World War I.

"Aw, come on, Doodle," I urged. "You can do it. Do you want to be different from everybody else when you start school?"

"Does it make any difference?"

"It certainly does," I said. "Now, come on," and I helped him up.

As we slipped through dog days, Doodle began to look feverish, and Mama felt his forehead, asking him if he felt ill. At night he didn't sleep well, and sometimes he had nightmares, crying out until I touched him and said, "Wake up, Doodle. Wake up."

It was Saturday noon, just a few days before school was to start. I should have already admitted defeat, but my pride wouldn't let me. The excitement of our program had now been gone for weeks, but still we kept on with a tired doggedness. It was too late to turn back, for we had both wandered too far into a net of expectations and had left no crumbs behind.

Daddy, Mama, Doodle, and I were seated at the dining-room table having lunch. It was a hot day, with all the windows and doors open in case a breeze should come. In the kitchen Aunt Nicey was humming softly. After a long silence, Daddy spoke. "It's so calm, I wouldn't be surprised if we had a storm this afternoon."

"I haven't heard a rain frog," said Mama, who believed in signs, as she served the bread around the table.

"I did," declared Doodle. "Down in the swamp."

"He didn't," I said contrarily.

"You did, eh?" said Daddy, ignoring my denial.

"I certainly did," Doodle reiterated, scowling at me over the top of his iced-tea glass, and we were quiet again.

Suddenly, from out in the yard, came a strange croaking noise. Doodle stopped eating, with a piece of bread poised ready for his mouth, his eyes popped round like two blue buttons. "What's that?" he whispered.

I jumped up, knocking over my chair, and had reached the door when Mama called, "Pick up the chair, sit down again, and say excuse me."

By the time I had done this, Doodle had excused himself and had slipped out into the yard. He was looking up into the bleeding tree. "It's a great big red bird!" he called.

The bird croaked loudly again, and Mama and Daddy came out into the yard. We shaded our eyes with our hands against the hazy glare of the sun and peered up through the still leaves. On the topmost branch a bird the size of a chicken, with scarlet feathers and long legs, was perched precariously. Its wings hung down loosely, and as we watched, a feather dropped away and floated slowly down through the green leaves.

Vocabulary Development: precariously (prē ker´ ē əs lē) *adv.*
insecurely

◆ **Reading Check**

What strategy does the narrator use to try to motivate Doodle?

_____

_____

_____

_____

_____

◆ **Stop to Reflect**

What point is the narrator making in the underlined sentence about why they could not turn back?

_____

_____

_____

_____

_____

◆ **Reading Check**

What does Doodle see in the tree?

_____

_____

_____

_____

_____

Why do you think the narrator remembers the death of the bird in such vivid detail?

_____

_____

_____

_____

_____

How does the description in the bracketed paragraph allow you to **identify** with the scarlet ibis?

_____

_____

_____

_____

_____

Why do you think it is so important to Doodle to bury the scarlet ibis?

_____

_____

_____

_____

_____

"It's not even frightened of us," Mama said.

"It looks tired," Daddy added. "Or maybe sick."

Doodle's hands were clasped at his throat, and I had never seen him stand still so long. "What is it?" he asked.

Daddy shook his head. "I don't know, maybe it's—"

At that moment the bird began to flutter, but the wings were uncoordinated, and amid much flapping and a spray of flying feathers, it tumbled down, bumping through the limbs of the bleeding tree and landing at our feet with a thud. Its long, graceful neck jerked twice into an S, then straightened out, and the bird was still. A white veil came over the eyes and the long white beak unhinged. Its legs were crossed and its clawlike feet were delicately curved at rest. Even death did not mar its grace, for it lay on the earth like a broken vase of red flowers, and we stood around it, awed by its exotic beauty.

"It's dead," Mama said.

"What is it?" Doodle repeated.

"Go bring me the bird book," said Daddy.

I ran into the house and brought back the bird book. As we watched, Daddy thumbed through its pages. "It's a scarlet ibis," he said, pointing to a picture. "It lives in the tropics— South America to Florida. A storm must have brought it here."

Sadly, we all looked back at the bird. A scarlet ibis! How many miles it had traveled to die like this, in our yard, beneath the bleeding tree.

"Let's finish lunch," Mama said, nudging us back toward the dining room.

"I'm not hungry," said Doodle, and he knelt down beside the ibis.

"We've got peach cobbler for dessert," Mama tempted from the doorway.

Doodle remained kneeling. "I'm going to bury him."

"Don't you dare touch him," Mama warned. "There's no telling what disease he might have had."

"All right," said Doodle. "I won't."

Daddy, Mama, and I went back to the dining-room table, but we watched Doodle through the open door. He took out a piece of string from his pocket and, without touching the ibis, looped one end around its neck. Slowly, while singing softly "Shall We Gather at the River," he carried the bird around to the front yard and dug a hole in the flower garden, next to the petunia bed. Now we were watching him through the front window, but he didn't know it. His awkwardness at digging the hole with a shovel whose handle was twice as long as he was made us laugh, and we covered our mouths with our hands so he wouldn't hear.

When Doodle came into the dining room, he found us seriously eating our cobbler. He was pale and lingered just inside the screen door. "Did you get the scarlet ibis buried?" asked Daddy.

Doodle didn't speak but nodded his head.

"Go wash your hands, and then you can have some peach cobbler," said Mama.

"I'm not hungry," he said.

"Dead birds is bad luck," said Aunt Nicey, poking her head from the kitchen door. "Specially red dead birds!"

As soon as I had finished eating, Doodle and I hurried off to Horsehead Landing. Time was short, and Doodle still had a long way to go if he was going to keep up with the other boys when he started school. The sun, gilded with the yellow cast of autumn, still burned fiercely, but the dark green woods through which we passed were shady and cool. When we reached the landing, Doodle said he was too tired to swim, so we got into a skiff and floated down the creek with the tide. Far off in the marsh a rail was scolding, and over on the beach locusts were singing in the myrtle trees. Doodle did not speak and kept his head turned away, letting one hand trail limply in the water.

After we had drifted a long way, I put the oars in place and made Doodle row back against the tide. Black clouds began to gather in the southwest, and he kept watching them, trying to pull the oars a little faster. When we reached Horsehead Landing, lightning was playing across half the sky and thunder roared out, hiding even the sound of the sea. The sun disappeared and darkness descended, almost like night. Flocks of marsh crows flew by, heading inland to their roosting trees, and two egrets, squawking, arose from the oyster-rock shallows and careened away.

Doodle was both tired and frightened, and when he stepped from the skiff he collapsed onto the mud, sending an armada of fiddler crabs rustling off into the marsh grass. I helped him up, and as he wiped the mud off his trousers, he smiled at me ashamedly. He had failed and we both knew it, so we started back home, racing the storm. We never spoke (What are the words that can solder cracked pride?), but I knew he was watching me, watching for a sign of mercy. The lightning was near now, and from fear he walked so close behind me he kept stepping on my heels. The faster I walked, the faster he walked, so I began to run. The rain was coming, roaring through the pines, and then, like a bursting Roman candle, a gum tree ahead of us was shattered by a bolt of lightning. When the deafening peal of thunder had died, and in the moment before the rain arrived, I heard Doodle, who had fallen behind, cry out, "Brother, Brother, don't leave me! Don't leave me!"

◆ **Literary Analysis**

First person **point of view** only allows you to see the story from the narrator's perspective. Rewrite the bracketed sentences from Doodle's point of view. How does this change the way you feel about Doodle?

_____

_____

_____

_____

_____

_____

_____

_____

_____

◆ **Reading Strategy**

Put yourself in Doodle's position. Why do you think he feels "tired and frightened"?

_____

_____

_____

_____

◆ **Reading Check**

Why does Doodle's brother begin to run?

_____

_____

_____

_____

_____

_____

What makes Doodle's brother go back and look for Doodle?

_____

_____

_____

_____

Why does the narrator compare Doodle to the scarlet ibis in the final line?

_____

_____

_____

_____

_____

The knowledge that Doodle's and my plans had come to naught was bitter, and that streak of cruelty within me awakened. I ran as fast as I could, leaving him far behind with a wall of rain dividing us. The drops stung my face like nettles, and the wind flared the wet glistening leaves of the bordering trees. Soon I could hear his voice no more.

I hadn't run too far before I became tired, and the flood of childish spite _evanesced_ as well. I stopped and waited for Doodle. The sound of rain was everywhere, but the wind had died and it fell straight down in parallel paths like ropes hanging from the sky. As I waited, I peered through the downpour, but no one came. Finally I went back and found him huddled beneath a red nightshade bush beside the road. He was sitting on the ground, his face buried in his arms, which were resting on his drawn-up knees. "Let's go, Doodle," I said.

He didn't answer, so I placed my hand on his forehead and lifted his head. Limply, he fell backwards onto the earth. He had been bleeding from the mouth, and his neck and the front of his shirt were stained a brilliant red.

"Doodle! Doodle!" I cried, shaking him, but there was no answer but the ropy rain. He lay very awkwardly, with his head thrown far back, making his vermilion neck appear unusually long and slim. His little legs, bent sharply at the knees, had never before seemed so fragile, so thin.

I began to weep, and the tear-blurred vision in red before me looked very familiar. "Doodle!" I screamed above the pounding storm and threw my body to the earth above his. For a long long time, it seemed forever, I lay there crying, sheltering my fallen scarlet ibis from the heresy[6] of rain.

Vocabulary Development: evanesced (ev ə nest´) _v._ faded away

---

6. **heresy** (her´ i sē) idea opposed to the beliefs of a religion or philosophy.

Reader's Response: What was your response to the end of the story?

_____

_____

Thinking About the Skill: Which character did you feel closest to in the story? Why?

_____

_____

The Necklace
Guy de Maupassant

Summary

This story takes place in nineteenth-century Paris. Madame Loisel is the unhappy wife of a middle class government official. She constantly dreams of being rich. Her husband is content, but he knows his wife is miserable. To please her, he obtains an invitation to an exclusive dinner party. Madame Loisel borrows a diamond necklace from a friend so she can look respectable at the party. After a wonderful evening, they are horrified to discover that the necklace is missing. Quietly, the Loisels buy a replacement for the diamond necklace. They can only afford this expensive purchase by taking out an enormous loan. It takes them ten years of saving to repay the loan. At that time, Madame Loisel finally tells the owner of the necklace what really happened. She is shocked when the owner tells her that the necklace she borrowed was inexpensive jewelry that contained only fake diamonds.

Visual Summary

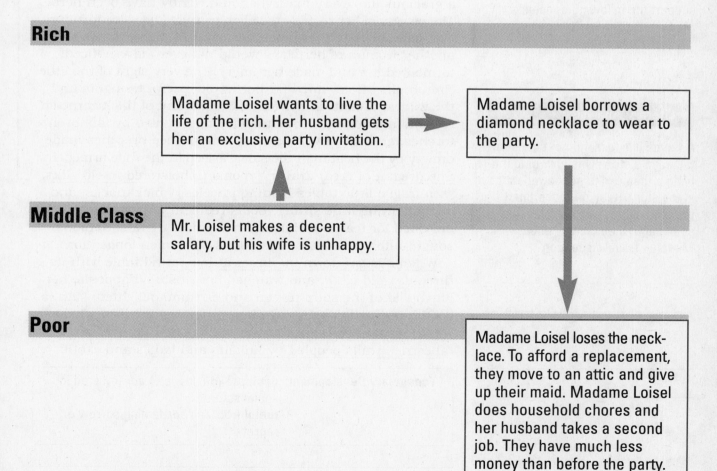

Rich

Madame Loisel wants to live the life of the rich. Her husband gets her an exclusive party invitation.

Madame Loisel borrows a diamond necklace to wear to the party.

Middle Class

Mr. Loisel makes a decent salary, but his wife is unhappy.

Poor

Madame Loisel loses the necklace. To afford a replacement, they move to an attic and give up their maid. Madame Loisel does household chores and her husband takes a second job. They have much less money than before the party.

The Necklace
Guy de Maupassant

In nineteenth-century France, social classes were fairly rigid. A person who came from a middle class family, was expected to remain middle class. As the story begins, we meet Madame Loisel, a middle class woman who would rather be rich.

She was one of those pretty, charming young women who are born, as if by an error of Fate, into a petty official's family. She had no dowry,[1] no hopes, not the slightest chance of being appreciated, understood, loved, and married by a rich and distinguished man; so she slipped into marriage with a minor civil servant at the Ministry of Education.

Unable to afford jewelry, she dressed simply: but she was as wretched as a <u>déclassé</u>, for women have neither caste nor breeding—in them beauty, grace, and charm replace pride of birth. Innate refinement, instinctive elegance, and suppleness of wit give them their place on the only scale that counts, and these qualities make humble girls the peers of the grandest ladies.

She suffered constantly, feeling that all the attributes of a gracious life, every luxury, should rightly have been hers. The poverty of her rooms—the shabby walls, the worn furniture, the ugly upholstery—caused her pain. All these things that another woman of her class would not even have noticed, tormented her and made her angry. The very sight of the little Breton girl who cleaned for her awoke <u>rueful</u> thoughts and the wildest dreams in her mind. She dreamt of thick carpeted reception rooms with Oriental hangings, lighted by tall, bronze torches, and with two huge footmen in knee breeches made drowsy by the heat from the stove, asleep in the wide armchairs. She dreamt of great drawing rooms upholstered in old silks, with fragile little tables holding priceless knickknacks, and of enchanting little sitting rooms redolent of perfume, designed for tea-time chats with intimate friends—famous, sought-after men whose attentions all women longed for.

When she sat down to dinner at her round table with its three-day-old cloth, and watched her husband opposite her lift the lid of the soup tureen and exclaim, delighted: " Ah, a good homemade beef stew! There's nothing better . . ." she would visualize elegant dinners with gleaming silver amid tapestried walls peopled by knights and ladies and exotic

---

Vocabulary Development: déclassé (dā′ klä sā′) *adj.* lowered in social status
rueful (rōō′ fəl) *adj.* feeling sorrow or regret

---

1. **dowry** (dou′ rē) *n.* property that a woman brought to her husband at marriage.

birds in a fairy forest; she would think of exquisite dishes served on gorgeous china, and of gallantries whispered and received with sphinx-like smiles[2] while eating the pink flesh of trout or wings of grouse.

She had no proper wardrobe, no jewels, nothing. And those were the only things that she loved—she felt she was made for them. She would have so loved to charm, to be envied, to be admired and sought after.

She had a rich friend, a schoolmate from the convent she had attended, but she didn't like to visit her because it always made her so miserable when she got home again. She would weep for whole days at a time from sorrow, regret, despair, and distress.

Then one evening her husband arrived home looking triumphant and waving a large envelope.

"There," he said, "there's something for you."

She tore it open eagerly and took out a printed card which said:

"The Minister of Education and Madame Georges Ramponneau[3] request the pleasure of the company of M. and Mme. Loisel[4] at an evening reception at the Ministry on Monday, January 18th."

Instead of being delighted, as her husband had hoped, she tossed the invitation on the table and muttered, annoyed:

"What do you expect me to do with that?"

"Why, I thought you'd be pleased, dear. You never go out and this would be an occasion for you, a great one! I had a lot of trouble getting it. Everyone wants an invitation; they're in great demand and there are only a few reserved for the employees. All the officials will be there."

She looked at him, irritated, and said impatiently:

"I haven't a thing to wear. How could I go?"

It had never even occurred to him. He stammered:

"But what about the dress you wear to the theater? I think it's lovely. . . ."

He fell silent, amazed and bewildered to see that his wife was crying. Two big tears escaped from the corners of her eyes and rolled slowly toward the corners of her mouth. He mumbled:

"What is it? What is it?"

But, with great effort, she had overcome her misery; and now she answered him calmly, wiping her tear-damp cheeks:

"It's nothing. It's just that I have no evening dress and so I can't go to the party. Give the invitation to one of your colleagues whose wife will be better dressed than I would be."

He was overcome. He said:

---

2. **gallantries whispered and received with sphinx** (sfiŋks)-**like smiles** flirtatious compliments whispered and received with mysterious smiles.
3. **Madame Georges Ramponneau** (ma dam´ zhôrzh ram pə nō´)
4. **Loisel** (lwa zel´)

◆ Stop to Reflect

If you could speak to Madame Loisel at this point in the story, what advice would you give her?

_____

_____

_____

_____

◆ Reading Strategy

In the bracketed section, what conclusion can you draw about Madame Loisel, based on her reaction to the invitation?

_____

_____

_____

_____

◆ Reading Check

Why does Madame Loisel feel unable to go to the reception at the Ministry of Education?

_____

_____

_____

_____

_____

_____

_____

_____

_____

One **theme** in this story is the foolishness of trying to appear to be someone you are not. Explain why the underlined statements reflect this theme.

_____

_____

_____

_____

_____

A "tale of woe" is usually about a great tragedy. Why do you think the author uses this phrase to describe Madame Loisel's situation?

_____

_____

_____

"Listen, Mathilde,[5] how much would an evening dress cost—a suitable one that you could wear again on other occasions, something very simple?"

She thought for several seconds, making her calculations and at the same time estimating how much she could ask for without eliciting an immediate refusal and an exclamation of horror from this economical government clerk.

At last, not too sure of herself, she said:

"It's hard to say exactly but I think I could manage with four hundred francs."

He went a little pale, for that was exactly the amount he had put aside to buy a rifle so that he could go hunting the following summer near Nanterre, with a few friends who went shooting larks around there on Sundays.

However, he said:

"Well, all right, then. I'll give you four hundred francs. But try to get something really nice."

As the day of the ball drew closer, Madame Loisel seemed depressed, disturbed, worried—despite the fact that her dress was ready. One evening her husband said:

"What's the matter? You've really been very strange these last few days."

And she answered:

"I hate not having a single jewel, not one stone, to wear. I shall look so dowdy.[6] I'd almost rather not go to the party."

He suggested:

"You can wear some fresh flowers. It's considered very chic[7] at this time of year. For ten francs you can get two or three beautiful roses."

That didn't satisfy her at all.

"No . . . there's nothing more humiliating than to look poverty-stricken among a lot of rich women."

Then her husband exclaimed:

"Wait—you silly thing! Why don't you go and see Madame Forestier[8] and ask her to lend you some jewelry. You certainly know her well enough for that, don't you think?"

She let out a joyful cry.

"You're right. It never occurred to me."

The next day she went to see her friend and related her tale of woe.

Madame Forestier went to her mirrored wardrobe, took out a big jewel case, brought it to Madame Loisel, opened it, and said:

"Take your pick, my dear."

Her eyes wandered from some bracelets to a pearl necklace, then to a gold Venetian cross set with stones, of very fine

5. **Mathilde** (ma tēld´)
6. **dowdy** (dou´dē) *adj.* shabby.
7. **chic** (shēk) *adj.* fashionable.
8. **Forestier** (fô rə styā´)

workmanship. She tried on the jewelry before the mirror, hesitating, unable to bring herself to take them off, to give them back. And she kept asking:

"Do you have anything else, by chance?"

"Why yes. Here, look for yourself. I don't know which ones you'll like."

All at once, in a box lined with black satin, she came upon a superb diamond necklace, and her heart started beating with overwhelming desire. Her hands trembled as she picked it up. She fastened it around her neck over her high-necked dress and stood there gazing at herself ecstatically.

Hesitantly, filled with terrible anguish, she asked:

"Could you lend me this one—just this and nothing else?"

"Yes, of course."

She threw her arms around her friend's neck, kissed her ardently, and fled with her treasure.

The day of the party arrived. Madame Loisel was a great success. She was the prettiest woman there—resplendent graceful, beaming, and deliriously happy. All the men looked at her, asked who she was, tried to get themselves introduced to her. All the minister's aides wanted to waltz with her. The minister himself noticed her.

She danced enraptured—carried away, intoxicated with pleasure, forgetting everything in this triumph of her beauty and the glory of her success, floating in a cloud of happiness formed by all this homage, all this admiration, all the desires she had stirred up—by this victory so complete and so sweet to the heart of a woman.

When she left the party, it was almost four in the morning. Her husband had been sleeping since midnight in a small, deserted sitting room, with three other gentlemen whose wives were having a wonderful time.

He brought her wraps so that they could leave and put them around her shoulders—the plain wraps from her everyday life whose shabbiness jarred with the elegance of her evening dress. She felt this and wanted to escape quickly so that the other women, who were enveloping themselves in their rich furs, wouldn't see her.

Loisel held her back.

"Wait a minute. You'll catch cold out there. I'm going to call a cab."

But she wouldn't listen to him and went hastily downstairs. Outside in the street, there was no cab to be found; they set out to look for one, calling to the drivers they saw passing in the distance.

Vocabulary Development: resplendent (ri splen´ dənt) *adj.* shining brightly

---

◆ **Literary Analysis**

Reread the first bracketed paragraph. Why do you think Madame Loisel is so happy with what she sees when she puts on the necklace?

_____

_____

_____

_____

_____

◆ **Reading Strategy**

Sometimes it is easier to **draw a conclusion** if you start with a question. Ask yourself, "What is important to Madame Loisel?" Circle details in the second bracketed passage that help you answer the question. Then, write your conclusion here.

_____

_____

_____

_____

_____

◆ **Reading Check**

Why does Madame Loisel want to leave quickly when the party is over?

_____

_____

_____

_____

How does the bracketed paragraph contrast in mood with the atmosphere of the party?

_____

_____

_____

_____

_____

◆ Reading Strategy

A description can often help you to **draw a conclusion.** What possible conclusions can you draw from the underlined description of Madame Loisel sitting on the chair?

_____

_____

_____

_____

◆ Stop to Reflect

Why do you think the Loisels choose to lie about what happened to the necklace?

_____

_____

_____

_____

They walked toward the Seine,[9] shivering and miserable. Finally, on the embankment, they found one of those ancient nocturnal broughams[10] which are only to be seen in Paris at night, as if they were ashamed to show their shabbiness in daylight.

It took them to their door in the Rue des Martyrs, and they went sadly upstairs to their apartment. For her, it was all over. And he was thinking that he had to be at the Ministry by ten.

She took off her wraps before the mirror so that she could see herself in all her glory once more. Then she cried out. The necklace was gone; there was nothing around her neck.

Her husband, already half undressed, asked:

"What's the matter?"

She turned toward him in a frenzy:

"The . . . the . . . necklace—it's gone."

He got up, thunderstruck.

"What did you say? . . . What! . . . Impossible!"

And they searched the folds of her dress, the folds of her wrap, the pockets, everywhere. They didn't find it.

He asked:

"Are you sure you still had it when we left the ball?"

"Yes. I remember touching it in the hallway of the Ministry."

"But if you had lost it in the street, we would have heard it fall. It must be in the cab."

"Yes, most likely. Do you remember the number?"

"No. What about you—did you notice it?"

"No."

They looked at each other in utter dejection. Finally Loisel got dressed again.

"I'm going to retrace the whole distance we covered on foot," he said, "and see if I can't find it."

And he left the house. She remained in her evening dress, too weak to go to bed, sitting crushed on a chair, lifeless and blank.

Her husband returned at about seven o'clock. He had found nothing.

He went to the police station, to the newspapers to offer a reward, to the offices of the cab companies—in a word, wherever there seemed to be the slightest hope of tracing it.

She spent the whole day waiting, in a state of utter hopelessness before such an appalling catastrophe.

Loisel returned in the evening, his face lined and pale; he had learned nothing.

"You must write to your friend," he said, "and tell her that you've broken the clasp of the necklace and that you're getting it mended. That'll give us time to decide what to do."

9. **Seine** (sān) river flowing through Paris.
10. **broughams** (brōōms) *n.* horse-drawn carriages.

She wrote the letter at his dictation.

By the end of the week, they had lost all hope.

Loisel, who had aged five years, declared: "We'll have to replace the necklace."

The next day they took the case in which it had been kept and went to the jeweler whose name appeared inside it. He looked through his ledgers:

"I didn't sell this necklace, madame. I only supplied the case."

Then they went from one jeweler to the next, trying to find a necklace like the other, racking their memories, both of them sick with worry and distress.

In a fashionable shop near the Palais Royal, they found a diamond necklace which they decided was exactly like the other. It was worth 40,000 francs. They could have it for 36,000 francs.

They asked the jeweler to hold it for them for three days, and they stipulated that he should take it back for 34,000 francs if the other necklace was found before the end of February.

Loisel possessed 18,000 francs left him by his father. He would borrow the rest.

He borrowed, asking a thousand francs from one man, five hundred from another, a hundred here, fifty there. He signed promissory notes,[11] borrowed at exorbitant rates, dealt with usurers and the entire race of moneylenders. He compromised his whole career, gave his signature even when he wasn't sure he would be able to honor it, and horrified by the anxieties with which his future would be filled, by the black misery about to descend upon him, by the prospect of physical privation and moral suffering, went to get the new necklace, placing on the jeweler's counter 36,000 francs.

When Madame Loisel went to return the necklace, Madame Forestier said in a faintly waspish tone:

"You could have brought it back a little sooner! I might have needed it."

She didn't open the case as her friend had feared she might. If she had noticed the substitution, what would she have thought? What would she have said? Mightn't she have taken Madame Loisel for a thief?

Madame Loisel came to know the awful life of the poverty-stricken. However, she resigned herself to it with unexpected fortitude. The crushing debt had to be paid. She would pay it. They dismissed the maid; they moved into an attic under the roof.

She came to know all the heavy household chores, the loathsome work of the kitchen. She washed the dishes, wearing down her pink nails on greasy casseroles and the

---

11. **promissory** (präm´ i sôr´ē) **notes** written promises to pay back borrowed money.

© Pearson Education, Inc.

◆ **Reading Strategy**

In the underlined sentence, the author states that Loisel "had aged five years." Since this is not literally true, what conclusion do you think the author wants you to draw about the aging and its cause?

_____

_____

_____

_____

_____

◆ **Literary Analysis**

Madame Loisel has to pay the consequences of losing a valuable item. Explain the connection between this idea and the theme of trying to appear as someone you are not.

_____

_____

_____

_____

◆ **Reading Check**

Why is Madame Loisel now responsible for doing all the heavy household chores?

_____

_____

_____

_____

_____

_____

_____

_____

_____

_____

_____

_____

_____

_____

_____

bottoms of saucepans. She did the laundry, washing shirts and dishcloths which she hung on a line to dry; she took the garbage down to the street every morning, and carried water upstairs, stopping at every floor to get her breath. Dressed like a working-class woman, she went to the fruit store, the grocer, and the butcher with her basket on her arm, bargaining, outraged, contesting each sou[12] of her pitiful funds.

Every month some notes had to be honored and more time requested on others.

Her husband worked in the evenings, putting a shopkeeper's ledgers in order, and often at night as well, doing copying at twenty-five centimes a page.

And it went on like that for ten years.

After ten years, they had made good on everything, including the usurious rates and the compound interest.

Madame Loisel looked old now. She had become the sort of strong woman, hard and coarse, that one finds in poor families. Disheveled, her skirts askew, with reddened hands, she spoke in a loud voice, slopping water over the floors as she washed them. But sometimes, when her husband was at the office, she would sit down by the window and muse over that party long ago when she had been so beautiful, the belle of the ball.

How would things have turned out if she hadn't lost that necklace? Who could tell? How strange and fickle life is! How little it takes to make or break you!

Then one Sunday when she was strolling along the Champs Elysées[13] to forget the week's chores for a while, she suddenly caught sight of a woman taking a child for a walk. It was Madame Forestier, still young, still beautiful, still charming.

Madame Loisel started to tremble. Should she speak to her? Yes, certainly she should. And now that she had paid everything back, why shouldn't she tell her the whole story?

She went up to her.

"Hello, Jeanne."

The other didn't recognize her and was surprised that this plainly dressed woman should speak to her so familiarly. She murmured:

"But . . . madame! . . . I'm sure . . . You must be mistaken."

"No, I'm not. I am Mathilde Loisel."

Her friend gave a little cry.

Vocabulary Development: disheveled (di shevʹ əld) *adj.*
disarranged and untidy

---

12. **sou** (soo) *n.* former French coin, worth very little; the centime (sän tēmʹ), mentioned later, was also of little value.
13. **Champs Elysées** (shän zā lē zāʹ) fashionable street in Paris.

"Oh! Oh, my poor Mathilde, how you've changed!"

"Yes, I've been through some pretty hard times since I last saw you and I've had plenty of trouble—and all because of you!"

"Because of me? What do you mean?"

"You remember the diamond necklace you lent me to wear to the party at the Ministry?"

"Yes. What about it?"

"Well, I lost it."

"What are you talking about? You returned it to me."

"What I gave back to you was another one just like it. And it took us ten years to pay for it. You can imagine it wasn't easy for us, since we were quite poor . . . Anyway, I'm glad it's over and done with."

Madame Forestier stopped short.

"You say you bought a diamond necklace to replace that other one?"

"Yes. You didn't even notice then? They really were exactly alike."

And she smiled, full of a proud, simple joy.

Madame Forestier, <u>profoundly</u> moved, took Mathilde's hands in her own.

"Oh, my poor, poor Mathilde! Mine was false. It was worth five hundred francs at the most!"

◆ **Reading Check**

What does Madame Forestier tell Madame Loisel about the value of the necklace?

_____

_____

_____

_____

_____

_____

Vocabulary Development: profoundly (prō foͧnd′ lē) *adj.* deeply and intensely

---

Reader's Response: How did you react to the twist at the end? Why do you think you reacted in the way that you did?

_____

_____

_____

_____

_____

Thinking About the Skill: How can drawing conclusions from the details of a story improve your reading in other areas?

_____

_____

_____

Single Room, Earth View

Sally Ride

Summary

In this nonfiction account, Sally Ride tells about her space shuttle voyage. Ride is amazed by the way the Earth looks from space. Although she is 200 miles away, she is able to see many details on Earth. For example, she can see the different colors of the oceans, environmental problems such as air pollution, natural events like typhoons forming, and man-made structures like skyscrapers in New York City.

Visual Summary

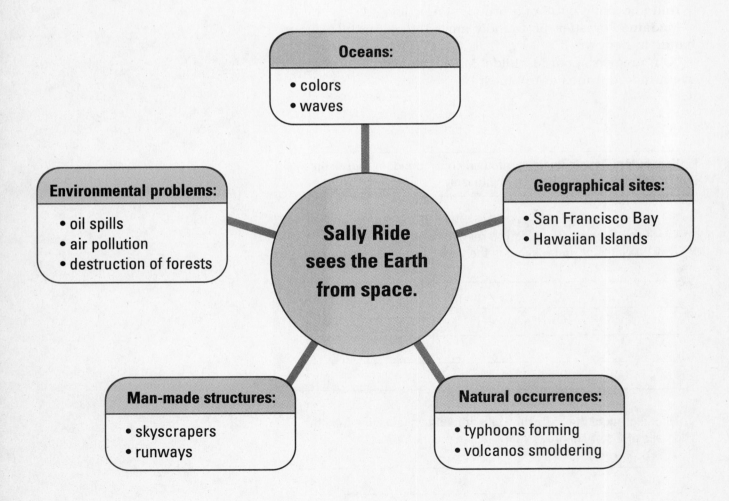

Single Room, Earth View
Sally Ride

*Imagine seeing a sunrise every ninety minutes or looking down on a
lightning storm. These are just some of the things Sally Ride sees on her
first trip to space.*

Everyone I've met has a glittering, if vague, mental image
of space travel. And naturally enough, people want to hear
about it from an astronaut: "How did it feel . . . ?" "What did
it look like . . . ?" "Were you scared?" Sometimes, the
questions come from reporters, their pens poised and their
tape recorders silently reeling in the words; sometimes, it's
wide-eyed, ten-year-old girls who want answers. I find a way
to answer all of them, but it's not easy.

Imagine trying to describe an airplane ride to someone
who has never flown. An <u>articulate</u> traveler could describe
the sights but would find it much harder to explain the
difference in perspective provided by the new view from a
greater distance, along with the feelings, impressions, and
insights that go with the new perspective. And the difference
is enormous: Spaceflight moves the traveler another giant
step farther away. Eight and one-half thunderous minutes
after launch, an astronaut is orbiting high above the Earth,
suddenly able to watch typhoons form, volcanoes smolder,
and meteors streak through the atmosphere below.

While flying over the Hawaiian Islands, several astronauts
have marveled that the islands look just as they do on a
map. When people first hear that, they wonder what should
be so surprising about Hawaii looking the way it does in the
atlas. Yet, to the astronauts it is an absolutely startling
sensation: The islands really *do* look as if that part of the
world has been carpeted with a big page torn out of
Rand-McNally,[1] and all we can do is try to convey the <u>surreal</u>
quality of that scene.

In orbit, racing along at five miles per second, the space
shuttle circles the Earth once every 90 minutes. I found that
at this speed, unless I kept my nose pressed to the window,
it was almost impossible to keep track of where we were at
any given moment—the world below simply changes too fast.
If I turned my concentration away for too long, even just to
change film in a camera, I could miss an entire land mass.

Vocabulary Development: articulate (är tik´ yōō lit) *adj.* expressing
oneself clearly and easily
surreal (sə rē´ əl) *adj.* strange

---

1. **Rand-McNally** publishers of atlases.

_____

_____

_____

_____

_____

_____

◆ Literary Analysis

In the underlined sentence, what **observation** does Ride make about the way the Earth looks from 200 miles away?

_____

_____

_____

_____

_____

◆ Literary Analysis

Underline three geographical features Ride **observes** in the second bracketed passage.

It's embarrassing to float up to a window, glance outside, and then have to ask a crewmate, "What continent is this?"

We could see smoke rising from fires that dotted the entire east coast of Africa, and in the same orbit only moments later, ice floes jostling for position in the Antarctic. We could see the Ganges River dumping its murky, sediment-laden water into the Indian Ocean and watch <u>ominous</u> hurricane clouds expanding and rising like biscuits in the oven of the Caribbean.

Mountain ranges, volcanoes, and river deltas appeared in salt-and-flour relief, all leading me to assume the role of a <u>novice</u> geologist. In such moments, it was easy to imagine the dynamic upheavals that created jutting mountain ranges and the internal wrenchings that created rifts and seas. I also became an instant believer in plate tectonics;[2] India really *is* crashing into Asia, and Saudi Arabia and Egypt really *are* pulling apart, making the Red Sea wider. Even though their respective motion is really no more than mere inches a year, the view from overhead makes theory come alive.

<u>Spectacular as the view is from 200 miles up, the Earth is not the awe-inspiring "blue marble" made famous by the photos from the moon.</u> From space shuttle height, we can't see the entire globe at a glance, but we can look down the entire boot of Italy, or up the East Coast of the United States from Cape Hatteras to Cape Cod. The panoramic view inspires an appreciation for the scale of some of nature's phenomena. One day, as I scanned the sandy expanse of Northern Africa, I couldn't find any of the familiar landmarks—colorful outcroppings of rock in Chad, irrigated patches of the Sahara. Then I realized they were obscured by a huge dust storm, a cloud of sand that enveloped the continent from Morocco to the Sudan.

Since the space shuttle flies fairly low (at least by orbital standards; it's more than 22,000 miles lower than a typical TV satellite), we can make out both natural and man-made features in surprising detail. Familiar geographical features like San Francisco Bay, Long Island, and Lake Michigan are easy to recognize, as are many cities, bridges, and airports. The Great Wall of China is *not* the only man-made object visible from space.

The signatures of civilization are usually seen in straight lines (bridges or runways) or sharp delineations (abrupt transitions from desert to irrigated land, as in California's

---

Vocabulary Development: ominous (äm´ ə nəs) *adj.* threatening
novice (näv´ is) *adj.* beginner

---

2. **plate tectonics** theory that the Earth's surface consists of plates whose constant motion explains continental drift, mountain building, large earthquakes, and so forth.

Imperial Valley). A modern city like New York doesn't leap from the canvas of its surroundings, but its straight piers and concrete runways catch the eye—and around them, the city materializes. I found Salina, Kansas (and pleased my in-laws, who live there) by spotting its long runway amid the wheat fields near the city. Over Florida, I could see the launch pad where we had begun our trip, and the landing strip, where we would eventually land.

Some of civilization's more unfortunate effects on the environment are also evident from orbit. Oil slicks glisten on the surface of the Persian Gulf, patches of pollution-damaged trees dot the forests of central Europe. Some cities look out of focus, and their colors <u>muted</u>, when viewed through a pollutant haze. Not surprisingly, the effects are more noticeable now than they were a decade ago. An astronaut who has flown in both Skylab and the space shuttle reported that the horizon didn't seem quite as sharp, or the colors quite as bright, in 1983 as they had in 1973.

Of course, informal observations by individual astronauts are one thing, but more precise measurements are continually being made from space: The space shuttle has carried infrared film to document damage to citrus trees in Florida and in rain forests along the Amazon. It has carried even more sophisticated sensors in the payload bay. Here is one example: sensors used to measure atmospheric carbon monoxide levels, allowing scientists to study the environmental effects of city emissions and land-clearing fires.

Most of the Earth's surface is covered with water, and at first glance it all looks the same: blue. But with the right lighting conditions and a couple of orbits of practice, it's possible to make out the intricate patterns in the oceans—<u>eddies</u> and spirals become visible because of the <u>subtle</u> differences in water color or reflectivity.

Observations and photographs by astronauts have contributed significantly to the understanding of ocean dynamics, and some of the more intriguing discoveries prompted the National Aeronautics and Space Administration to fly an oceanographic observer for the express purpose of studying the ocean from orbit. Scientists' understanding of the energy balance in the oceans has increased significantly as a result of the discoveries of circular and spiral eddies tens of kilometers in diameter, of standing waves hundreds of kilometers long, and of spiral eddies that sometimes trail into one another for thousands of kilometers. If a scientist

---

Vocabulary Development: muted (myo͞ot′ əd) *adj.* weaker; less
intense
eddies (ed′ ēz) *n.* circular currents
subtle (sut′ əl) *adj.* not obvious

◆ **Reading Strategy**

If you want to find the single comment from the Skylab astronaut, should you skim the bracketed paragraph or read slowly? Explain.

_____

_____

_____

_____

◆ **Reading Check**

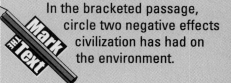

In the bracketed passage, circle two negative effects civilization has had on the environment.

◆ **Literary Analysis**

At first, Ride thinks that all of the Earth's oceans are blue. After looking more closely, what does she **observe** about the oceans?

_____

_____

_____

_____

_____

◆ **Reading Check**

What kind of expert was sent to space to study the oceans?

_____

_____

_____

_____

_____

What **observation** does Ride make about the way the Earth looks at night?

_____

_____

_____

_____

_____

What does Ride say is the most spectacular sight from orbit?

_____

_____

Underline the words in the bracketed passage that describe how often astronauts see a sunrise.

wants to study features on this scale, it's much easier from an orbiting vehicle than from the vantage point of a boat.

Believe it or not, an astronaut can also see the wakes of large ships and the contrails[3] of airplanes. The sun angle has to be just right, but when the lighting conditions are perfect, you can follow otherwise invisible oil tankers on the Persian Gulf and trace major shipping lanes through the Mediterranean Sea. Similarly, when atmospheric conditions allow contrail formation, the thousand-mile-long condensation trails let astronauts trace the major air routes across the northern Pacific Ocean.

Part of every orbit takes us to the dark side of the planet. In space, night is very, very black—but that doesn't mean there's nothing to look at. The lights of cities sparkle; on nights when there was no moon, it was difficult for me to tell the Earth from the sky—the twinkling lights could be stars or they could be small cities. On one nighttime pass from Cuba to Nova Scotia, the entire East Coast of the United States appeared in twinkling outline.

When the moon is full, it casts an eerie light on the Earth. In its light, we see ghostly clouds and bright reflections on the water. One night, the Mississippi River flashed into view, and because of our viewing angle and orbital path, the reflected moonlight seemed to flow downstream—as if Huck Finn[4] had tied a candle to his raft.

Of all the sights from orbit, the most spectacular may be the magnificent displays of lightning that ignite the clouds at night. On Earth, we see lightning from below the clouds; in orbit, we see it from above. Bolts of lightning are underlined_diffused by the clouds into bursting balls of light. Sometimes, when a storm extends hundreds of miles, it looks like a transcontinental brigade is tossing fireworks from cloud to cloud.

As the shuttle races the sun around the Earth, we pass from day to night and back again during a single orbit—hurtling into darkness, then bursting into daylight. The sun's appearance unleashes spectacular blue and orange bands along the horizon, a clockwork miracle that astronauts witness every 90 minutes. But, I really can't describe a sunrise in orbit. The drama set against the black backdrop of space and the magic of the materializing colors can't be captured in an astronomer's equations or an astronaut's photographs.

Vocabulary Development: eerie (ir´ ē) *adj.* mysterious
                          diffused (di fyo͞ozd´) *v.* spread out

---

3. **contrails** (kän´ trāls´) *n.* white trails of condensed water vapor that sometimes form in the wake of aircraft.
4. **Huck Finn** hero of Mark Twain's novel *The Adventures of Huckleberry Finn.*

I once heard someone (not an astronaut) suggest that it's possible to imagine what spaceflight is like by simply <u>extrapolating</u> from the sensations you experience on an airplane. All you have to do, he said, is mentally raise the airplane 200 miles, mentally eliminate the air noise and the turbulence, and you get an accurate mental picture of a trip in the space shuttle.

Not true. And while it's natural to try to liken spaceflight to familiar experiences, it can't be brought "down to Earth"— not in the final sense. The environment is different, the perspective is different. Part of the fascination with space travel is the element of the unknown—the conviction that it's different from earthbound experiences. And it is.

Vocabulary Development: extrapolating (ek strap´ ə lāt´ iŋ) *v.* arriving at a conclusion by making inferences based on known facts

Reader's Response: Did any of Ride's observations about Earth surprise you? Why?

_____

_____

_____

_____

_____

Thinking About the Skill: How can varying your reading rate help you to become a more efficient reader?

_____

_____

_____

_____

_____

◆ **Literary Analysis**

What comment did someone make about imagining space flight, without actually having **observed** it for himself?

_____

_____

_____

◆ **Reading Check**

Mark the Text

Does Ride agree or disagree with this person's comment about space travel? Explain. Underline details in the last paragraph that help you answer this question.

_____

_____

_____

_____

_____

On Summer

Lorraine Hansberry

Summary

The author of "On Summer" explains that as a young person, summer was not her favorite season. She thought the season was too intense; with bright, long days, loud noises, and other unpleasant aspects. She preferred the sadness of autumn, and the bleakness of winter, to summer's heat and glare. Over time, her opinion of summer changed. She came to associate summer with strong-willed people—her grandmother and a woman she met one summer in Maine who was fighting cancer.

Visual Summary

Feelings about the seasons when young

Spring
She is connected to spring because she was born in May.

Winter
She admires its cold distance as an older child.

Autumn
As a teenager, she loves its sadness.

Summer
Summer is too hot and loud, and the days are too long. Summer seems like a mistake.

What happens to her in the summer

- She enjoys sleeping outside.
- She meets her grandmother.
- She visits many places.
- She meets a woman in Maine whom she admires. This woman loves summer. Seeing summer through this woman's eyes helps the author appreciate summer.

Realizations about the seasons when older

Spring
It can provide false promises.

Winter
It shuts dying people up inside.

Autumn
Its sadness can seem artificial.

Summer
It offers life at its fullest.

On Summer
Lorraine Hansberry

"On Summer" is a persuasive essay. The author tells how she went from disliking to appreciating summer. She hopes to persuade the reader to appreciate summer as well.

It has taken me a good number of years to come to any measure of respect for summer. I was, being May-born, literally an "infant of the spring" and, during the later childhood years, tended, for some reason or other, to rather worship the cold <u>aloofness</u> of winter. The adolescence, admittedly lingering still, brought the traditional passionate commitment to melancholy autumn—and all that. For the longest kind of time I simply thought that *summer* was a mistake.

In fact, my earliest memory of anything at all is of waking up in a darkened room where I had been put to bed for a nap on a summer's afternoon, and feeling very, very hot. I acutely disliked the feeling then and retained the bias for years. It had originally been a matter of the heat but, over the years, I came actively to associate displeasure with most of the usually celebrated natural features and social by-products of the season: the too-grainy texture of sand; the too-cold coldness of the various waters we constantly try to escape into, and the icky-perspiry feeling of bathing caps.

It also seemed to me, esthetically[1] speaking, that nature had got inexcusably carried away on the summer question and let the whole thing get to be rather much. By duration alone, for instance, a summer's day seemed maddeningly excessive; an utter overstatement. Except for those few hours at either end of it, objects always appeared in too sharp a relief against backgrounds; shadows too pronounced and light too blinding. It always gave me the feeling of walking around in a motion picture which had been too artsily-craftsily exposed. Sound also had a way of coming to the ear without that muting influence, marvelously common to winter, across patios or beaches or through the woods. I suppose I found it too stark and yet too intimate a season.

My childhood Southside[2] summers were the ordinary city kind, full of the street games which the other rememberers have turned into fine ballets these days and rhymes that anticipated what some people insist on calling modern poetry:

Vocabulary Development: **aloofness** (ə lōōf´ nis) *n.* state of being distant, removed, or uninvolved

---

1. **esthetically** (es thet´ ik lē) *adv.* artistically.
2. **Southside** section of Chicago, Illinois.

◆ **Activate Prior Knowledge**

What is your favorite season? What is your least favorite? Explain your feelings about each season.

_____

_____

_____

_____

◆ **Literary Analysis**

A **persuasive essay** tries to influence the reader to think or act in a certain way. Underline the parts of the first bracketed section where the writer describes what she dislikes about summer. How does she want you to feel about summer at this point?

_____

_____

_____

◆ **Reading Strategy**

You can **identify the author's attitude** by the words he or she uses. Circle the words in the second bracketed paragraph that show the author's attitude toward summer.

◆ **Reading Check**

What does Hansberry dislike about summer?

_____

_____

_____

A **persuasive essay** usually consists of three parts: an *introduction*, where authors state their views, a *body*, where they make their arguments, and a *conclusion*, where they summarize their views. Which part of the essay does the bracketed paragraph represent? Explain.

_____

_____

_____

_____

If the author's purpose is to persuade us that summers are unpleasant, why do you think she includes some pleasant summer memories?

_____

_____

_____

_____

_____

_____

When did the author's trip to visit her grandmother take place?

_____

_____

_____

_____

Oh, Mary Mack, Mack, Mack
With the silver buttons, buttons, buttons
All down her back, back, back
She asked her mother, mother, mother
For fifteen cents, cents, cents
To see the elephant, elephant, elephant
Jump the fence, fence, fence
Well, he jumped so high, high, high
'Til he touched the sky, sky, sky
And he didn't come back, back, back
'Til the Fourth of Ju-ly, ly, ly!

Evenings were spent mainly on the back porches where screen doors slammed in the darkness with those really very special summertime sounds. And, sometimes, when Chicago nights got too steamy, the whole family got into the car and went to the park and slept out in the open on blankets. Those were, of course, the best times of all because the grownups were invariably reminded of having been children in rural parts of the country and told the best stories then. And it was also cool and sweet to be on the grass and there was usually the scent of freshly cut lemons or melons in the air. And Daddy would lie on his back, as fathers must, and explain about how men thought the stars above us came to be and how far away they were. I never did learn to believe that anything could be as far away as *that*. Especially the stars.

My mother first took us south to visit her Tennessee birthplace one summer when I was seven or eight, I think. I woke up on the back seat of the car while we were still driving through some place called Kentucky and my mother was pointing out to the beautiful hills on both sides of the highway and telling my brothers and my sister about how her father had run away and hidden from his master in those very hills when he was a little boy. She said that his mother had wandered among the wooded slopes in the moonlight and left food for him in secret places. They were very beautiful hills and I looked out at them for miles and miles after that wondering who and what a *master* might be.

I remember being startled when I first saw my grandmother rocking away on her porch. All my life I had heard that she was a great beauty and no one had ever remarked that they meant a half century before. The woman that I met was as wrinkled as a prune and could hardly hear and barely see and always seemed to be thinking of other times. But she could still rock and talk and even make wonderful cupcakes which were like cornbread, only sweet. She was captivated by automobiles and, even though it was well into the

Thirties,[3] I don't think she had ever been in one before we came down and took her driving. She was a little afraid of them and could not seem to negotiate the windows, but she loved driving. She died the next summer and that is all that I remember about her, except that she was born in slavery and had memories of it and they didn't sound anything like *Gone With the Wind*.[4]

Like everyone else, I have spent whole or bits of summers in many different kinds of places since then: camps and resorts in the Middle West and New York State; on an island; in a tiny Mexican village; Cape Cod, perched atop the Truro bluffs at Longnook Beach that Millay[5] wrote about; or simply strolling the streets of Provincetown[6] before the hours when the parties begin.

And, lastly, I do not think that I will forget days spent, a few summers ago, at a beautiful lodge built right into the rocky cliffs of a bay on the Maine coast. We met a woman there who had lived a purposeful and courageous life and who was then dying of cancer. She had, characteristically, just written a book and taken up painting. She had also been of radical viewpoint all her life; one of those people who energetically believe that the world *can* be changed for the better and spend their lives trying to do just that. And that was the way she thought of cancer; she absolutely refused to award it the stature of tragedy, a devastating instance of the brooding doom and inexplicability[7] of the absurdity of human destiny, etc., etc. The kind of characterization given, lately, as we all know, to far less formidable foes in life than cancer.

But for this remarkable woman it was a matter of nature in imperfection, implying, as always, work for man to do. It was an *enemy*, but a palpable one with shape and effect and source; and if it existed, it could be destroyed. She saluted it accordingly, without despondency, but with a lively, beautiful and delightfully ribald anger. There was one thing, she felt, which would prove equal to its relentless ravages and that was the genius of man. Not his mysticism, but man with tubes and slides and the stubborn human notion that the stars are very much within our reach.

The last time I saw her she was sitting surrounded by her paintings with her manuscript laid out for me to read, because, she said, she wanted to know what a *young person* would think of her thinking; one must always keep up with what *young people* thought about things because, after all, they were *change*.

---

3. **Thirties** the 1930s.
4. *Gone With the Wind* novel set in the South during the Civil War period.
5. **Millay** Edna St. Vincent Millay (1892–1950), American poet.
6. **Provincetown** resort town at the northern tip of Cape Cod, Massachusetts.
7. **inexplicability** (in eks′ pli kə bil′ ə tē) *n.* condition that cannot be explained.

© Pearson Education, Inc.

On Summer 143

© Pearson Education, Inc.

◆ Reading Check

Why does the author associate travel with summer?

_____

_____

_____

_____

_____

_____

◆ Reading Strategy

Circle three words or phrases in the bracketed passage that show Hansberry's admiration for the woman with cancer.

◆ Reading Check

Why did the woman with cancer care about what the author thought of her manuscript?

_____

_____

_____

_____

_____

_____

_____

_____

Why does meeting the woman in Maine have such a lasting effect on Hansberry?

_____

_____

_____

_____

_____

_____

Every now and then her jaw set in anger as we spoke of things people should be angry about. And then, for relief, she would look out at the lovely bay at a mellow sunset settling on the water. Her face softened with love of all that beauty and, watching her, I wished with all my power what I knew that she was wishing: that she might live to see at least one more _summer_. Through her eyes I finally gained the sense of what it might mean; more than the coming autumn with its pretentious melancholy; more than an austere and silent winter which must shut dying people in for precious months; more even than the frivolous spring, too full of too many false promises, would be the gift of another summer with its stark and intimate assertion of neither birth nor death but life at the apex; with the gentlest nights and, above all, the longest days.

I heard later that she did live to see another summer. And I have retained my respect for the noblest of the seasons.

Reader's Response: How do Hansberry's ideas about summer compare with your own?

_____

_____

_____

_____

Thinking About the Skill: In what way did evaluating the author's attitude help you understand Hansberry's changing feelings about summer?

_____

_____

_____

A Celebration of Grandfathers
Rudolfo A. Anaya

Summary

In "A Celebration of Grandfathers," the author remembers the quiet ways of the "old ones" of his grandfather's generation. They understood the seasons, worked hard, appreciated the land in which they lived, and had a deep inner strength. The author believes today's world puts too much emphasis on youth and ignores the reality of aging. He urges us to understand and respect our grandparents.

Visual Summary

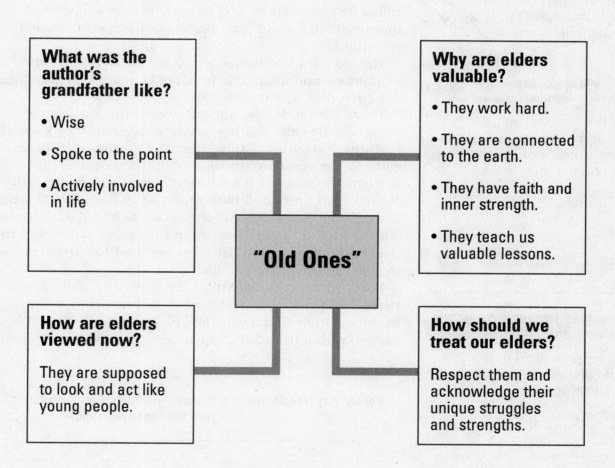

What was the author's grandfather like?

- Wise
- Spoke to the point
- Actively involved in life

Why are elders valuable?

- They work hard.
- They are connected to the earth.
- They have faith and inner strength.
- They teach us valuable lessons.

"Old Ones"

How are elders viewed now?

They are supposed to look and act like young people.

How should we treat our elders?

Respect them and acknowledge their unique struggles and strengths.

Has a grandparent or other older person had an impact on your life? Explain.

_____

_____

_____

In a **reflective essay,** an author records thoughts on a topic of importance to him or her. Read the bracketed passage and decide what the central idea is. Underline the passage that shows the topic of this reflective essay.

What is the **author's attitude** toward the old people in his past? List two words or phrases from the text to support your view.

_____

_____

1. _____

2. _____

What are some of the qualities Anaya remembers about old people from his childhood?

_____

_____

_____

_____

A Celebration of Grandfathers
Rudolfo A. Anaya

Rudolfo Anaya was born in Pastura, New Mexico. His writing reflects his Mexican American heritage. This essay reflects on his past and the values he learned from his grandfather.

"Buenos días le de Dios, abuelo."[1] God give you a good day, grandfather. This is how I was taught as a child to greet my grandfather, or any grown person. It was a greeting of respect, a cultural value to be passed on from generation to generation, this respect for the old ones.

The old people I remember from my childhood were strong in their beliefs, and as we lived daily with them we learned a wise path of life to follow. They had something important to share with the young, and when they spoke the young listened. These old abuelos and abuelitas[2] had worked the earth all their lives, and so they knew the value of nurturing, they knew the sensitivity of the earth. The daily struggle called for cooperation, and so every person contributed to the social fabric, and each person was respected for his contribution.

The old ones had looked deep into the web that connects all animate and inanimate forms of life, and they recognized the great design of the creation.

These *ancianos*[3] from the cultures of the Rio Grande, living side by side, sharing, growing together, they knew the rhythms and cycles of time, from the preparation of the earth in the spring to the digging of the acequias[4] that brought the water to the dance of harvest in the fall. They shared good times and hard times. They helped each other through the epidemics and the personal tragedies, and they shared what little they had when the hot winds burned the land and no rain came. They learned that to survive one had to share in the process of life.

Hard workers all, they tilled the earth and farmed, ran the herds and spun wool, and carved their saints and their kachinas[5] from cottonwood late in the winter nights. All worked with a deep faith which <u>perplexes</u> the modern mind.

> **Vocabulary Development: perplexes** (pər′ pleks′ iz) *v.* confuses or makes hard to understand

1. **Buenos días le de Dios, abuelo** (bwe′ nôs dē′ äs lā dā dē′ ōs ä bwä′ lō)
2. **abuelitas** (a bwä lē′ täs) grandmothers.
3. *ancianos* (än cē ä′ nōs) old people; ancestors.
4. **acequias** (ä sä′ kē əs) irrigation ditches.
5. **kachinas** (kə chē′ nəz) small wooden dolls, representing the spirit of an ancestor or a god.

Their faith shone in their eyes; it was in the strength of their grip, in the creases time wove into their faces. When they spoke, they spoke plainly and with few words, and they meant what they said. When they prayed, they went straight to the source of life. When there were good times, they knew how to dance in celebration and how to prepare the foods of the fiestas.[6] All this they passed on to the young, so that a new generation would know what they had known, so the string of life would not be broken.

Today we would say that the old abuelitos lived authentic lives.

Newcomers to New Mexico often say that time seems to move slowly here. I think they mean they have come in contact with the inner strength of the people, a strength so solid it causes time itself to pause. Think of it. Think of the high, northern New Mexico villages, or the lonely ranches on the open llano.[7] Think of the Indian pueblo[8] which lies as solid as rock in the face of time. Remember the old people whose eyes seem like windows that peer into a distant past that makes absurdity of our contemporary world. That is what one feels when one encounters the old ones and their land, a pausing of time.

We have all felt time stand still. We have all been in the presence of power, the knowledge of the old ones, the majestic peace of a mountain stream or an aspen grove or red buttes rising into blue sky. We have all felt the light of dusk permeate the earth and cause time to pause in its flow.

I felt this when first touched by the spirit of Ultima, the old *curandera*[9] who appears in my first novel, *Bless Me, Ultima.* This is how the young Antonio describes what he feels:

> When she came the beauty of the llano unfolded before my eyes, and the gurgling waters of the river sang to the hum of the turning earth. The magical time of childhood stood still, and the pulse of the living earth pressed its mystery into my living blood. She took my hand, and the silent, magic powers she possessed made beauty from the raw, sun-baked llano, the green river valley, and the blue bowl which was the white sun's home. My bare feet felt the throbbing earth, and my body trembled with excitement. Time stood still . . .

Vocabulary Development: permeate (pʉr´ mē āt) *v.* spread or flow throughout

---

6. **fiestas** (fē es´ təz) celebrations; feasts.
7. **llano** (yä´ nō) plain.
8. **pueblo** (pweb´ lō) village or town.
9. *curandera* (koo rän dä´ rä) medicine woman.

◆ **Reading Check**

What does the author mean in the first underlined sentence when he calls the lives of the elders "authentic"? Review the text from the top of the page to help you explain.

_____

_____

_____

_____

◆ **Stop to Reflect**

In this section, Anaya portrays time moving slowly as something positive. Do you agree or disagree with this point of view? Explain.

_____

_____

_____

_____

◆ **Reading Check**

What is Anaya attempting to show by including the passage from his first novel?

_____

_____

_____

_____

◆ Literary Analysis

1. Where was Anaya when he felt a strength that was similar to that which the old ones draw on?

Underline the words that show what he felt.

_____

_____

_____

2. What was he doing?

_____

_____

_____

◆ Reading Strategy

What is Anaya's **attitude** toward his grandfather? Give two examples from the text to support your opinion.

_____

_____

_____

_____

_____

◆ Reading Check

Briefly describe Anaya's grandfather. Include details about his appearance, personality, and manner of speaking.

_____

_____

_____

_____

_____

At other times, in other places, when I have been privileged to be with the old ones, to learn, I have felt this inner reserve of strength upon which they draw. I have been held motionless and speechless by the power of curanderas. I have felt the same power when I hunted with Cruz, high on the Taos[10] mountain, where it was more than the incredible beauty of the mountain bathed in morning light, more than the shining of the quivering aspen, but a connection with life, as if a shining strand of light connected the particular and the cosmic. That feeling is an <u>epiphany</u> of time, a standing still of time.

But not all of our old ones are curanderos or hunters on the mountain. My grandfather was a plain man, a farmer from Puerto de Luna[11] on the Pecos River. He was probably a descendent of those people who spilled over the mountain from Taos, following the Pecos River in search of farmland. There in that river valley he settled and raised a large family.

Bearded and walrus-mustached, he stood five feet tall, but to me as a child he was a giant. I remember him most for his silence. In the summers my parents sent me to live with him on his farm, for I was to learn the ways of a farmer. My uncles also lived in that valley, the valley called Puerto de Luna, there where only the flow of the river and the whispering of the wind marked time. For me it was a magical place.

I remember once, while out hoeing the fields, I came upon an anthill and before I knew it I was badly bitten. After he had covered my welts with the cool mud from the irrigation ditch, my grandfather calmly said: "Know where you stand." That is the way he spoke, in short phrases, to the point.

One very dry summer, the river dried to a trickle, there was no water for the fields. The young plants withered and died. In my sadness and with the impulses of youth I said, "I wish it would rain!" My grandfather touched me, looked up in the sky and whispered, "Pray for rain." In his language there was a difference. He felt connected to the cycles that brought the rain or kept it from us. His prayer was a meaningful action, because he was a participant with the forces that filled our world, he was not a bystander.

A young man died at the village one summer. A very tragic death. He was dragged by his horse. When he was found I cried, for the boy was my friend. I did not understand why death had come to one so young. My grandfather took me aside and said: "Think of the death of the trees and the

---

Vocabulary Development: epiphany (ē pif′ ə nē) *n.* moment of sudden understanding

---

10. **Taos** (tä′ ōs)
11. **Puerto de Luna** (pwer′ tō dä loo′ nə) port of the Moon, the name of a town.

fields in the fall. The leaves fall, and everything rests, as if dead. But they bloom again in the spring. Death is only this small transformation in life."

These are the things I remember, these fleeting images, few words.

I remember him driving his horse-drawn wagon into Santa Rosa in the fall when he brought his harvest produce to sell in the town. What a tower of strength seemed to come in that small man huddled on the seat of the giant wagon. One click of his tongue and the horses obeyed, stopped or turned as he wished. He never raised his whip. How unlike today when so much teaching is done with loud words and threatening hands.

I would run to greet the wagon, and the wagon would stop. "Buenos días le de Dios, abuelo," I would say. This was the prescribed greeting of esteem and respect. Only after the greeting was given could we approach these venerable old people. "Buenos días le de Dios, mi hijo,"[12] he would answer and smile, and then I could jump up on the wagon and sit at his side. Then I, too, became a king as I rode next to the old man who smelled of earth and sweat and the other deep aromas from the orchards and fields of Puerto de Luna.

We were all sons and daughters to him. But today the sons and daughters are breaking with the past, putting aside los abuelitos. The old values are threatened, and threatened most where it comes to these relationships with the old people. If we don't take the time to watch and feel the years of their final transformation, a part of our humanity will be lessened.

I grew up speaking Spanish, and oh! how difficult it was to learn English. Sometimes I would give up and cry out that I couldn't learn. Then he would say, "Ten paciencia."[13] Have patience. *Paciencia*, a word with the strength of centuries, a word that said that someday we would overcome. *Paciencia*, how soothing a word coming from this old man who could still sling hundred-pound bags over his shoulder, chop wood for hours on end, and hitch up his own horses and ride to town and back in one day.

"You have to learn the language of the Americanos,"[14] he said. "Me, I will live my last days in my valley. You will live in a new time, the time of the gringos."[15]

A new time did come, a new time is here. How will we form it so it is fruitful? We need to know where we stand.

---

12. **mi hijo** (mē ē´ hō) my son.
13. **Ten paciencia** (ten pä sē en´ sē ä)
14. **Americanos** (ä mer´ ē kä´ nōs) Americans.
15. **gringos** (griŋ´ gōs) foreigners; North Americans.

◆ Reading Check

1. How did Anaya's grandfather control his horses?

_____

_____

_____

_____

2. How does this differ from today's teaching?

_____

_____

_____

_____

◆ Literary Analysis

In the bracketed passage, what is Anaya saying about the lives of older people?

_____

_____

_____

_____

_____

_____

◆ Reading Check

Why does his grandfather urge Anaya to "Have patience"?

_____

_____

_____

What is the **author's attitude** toward his grandfather's advice?

_____

_____

_____

_____

How have the roles of grandfather and grandson been reversed?

_____

_____

_____

_____

_____

_____

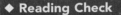

We need to speak softly and respect others, and to share what we have. We need to pray not for material gain, but for rain for the fields, for the sun to nurture growth, for nights in which we can sleep in peace, and for a harvest in which everyone can share. Simple lessons from a simple man. These lessons he learned from his past which was deep and strong as the currents of the river of life, a life which could be stronger than death.

He was a man; he died. Not in his valley, but nevertheless cared for by his sons and daughters and flocks of grandchildren. At the end, I would enter his room which carried the smell of medications and Vicks, the faint pungent odor of urine, and cigarette smoke. Gone were the aroma of the fields, the strength of his young manhood. Gone also was his patience in the face of crippling old age. Small things bothered him; he shouted or turned sour when his expectations were not met. It was because he could not care for himself, because he was returning to that state of childhood, and all those wishes and desires were now wrapped in a crumbling old body.

"Ten paciencia," I once said to him, and he smiled. "I didn't know I would grow this old," he said. "Now, I can't even roll my own cigarettes." I rolled a cigarette for him, placed it in his mouth and lit it. I asked him why he smoked, the doctor had said it was bad for him. "I like to see the smoke rise," he said. He would smoke and doze, and his quilt was spotted with little burns where the cigarettes dropped. One of us had to sit and watch to make sure a fire didn't start.

I would sit and look at him and remember what was said of him when he was a young man. He could mount a wild horse and break it, and he could ride as far as any man. He could dance all night at a dance, then work the acequia the following day. He helped neighbors, they helped him. He married, raised children. Small legends, the kind that make up everyman's life.

He was 94 when he died. Family, neighbors, and friends gathered; they all agreed he had led a rich life. I remembered the last years, the years he spent in bed. And as I remember now, I am reminded that it is too easy to romanticize old age. Sometimes we forget the pain of the transformation into old age, we forget the natural breaking down of the body. Not all go gentle into the last years, some go crying and cursing, forgetting the names of those they loved the most, withdrawing into an internal anguish few of us can know. May we be granted the patience and care to deal with our ancianos.

For some time we haven't looked at these changes and needs of the old ones. The American image created by the mass media is an image of youth, not of old age. It is the beautiful and the young who are praised in this society. If analyzed carefully, we see that same damaging thought has crept into the way society views the old. In response to the old, the mass media have just created old people who act like the young. It is only the healthy, pink-cheeked, outgoing, older persons we are shown in the media. And they are always selling something, as if an entire generation of old people were salesmen in their lives. Commercials show very lively old men, who must always be in excellent health according to the new myth, selling insurance policies or real estate as they are out golfing; older women selling coffee or toilet paper to those just married. That image does not illustrate the real life of the old ones.

Real life takes into account the natural cycle of growth and change. My grandfather pointed to the leaves falling from the tree. So time brings with its transformation the often painful, wearing-down process. Vision blurs, health wanes; even the act of walking carries with it the painful reminder of the autumn of life. But this process is something to be faced, not something to be hidden away by false images. Yes, the old can be young at heart, but in their own way, with their own dignity. They do not have to copy the always young image of the Hollywood star.

My grandfather wanted to return to his valley to die. But by then the families of the valley had left in search of a better future. It is only now that there seems to be a return to the valley, a revival. The new generation seeks its roots, that value of love for the land moves us to return to the place where our ancianos formed the culture.

I returned to Puerto de Luna last summer, to join the community in a celebration of the founding of the church. I drove by my grandfather's home, my uncles' ranches, the neglected adobe[16] washing down into the earth from whence it came. And I wondered, how might the values of my grandfather's generation live in our own? What can we retain to see us through these hard times? I was to become a farmer, and I became a writer. As I plow and plant my words, do I nurture as my grandfather did in his fields and orchards? The answers are not simple.

"They don't make men like that anymore," is a phrase we hear when one does honor to a man. I am glad I knew my grandfather. I am glad there are still times when I can see him in my dreams, hear him in my reverie. Sometimes I

---

16. **adobe** (ä dō´ bē) sun-dried clay brick.

◆ **Stop to Reflect**

Do you agree with Anaya's criticism of the way old people are portrayed in the media? Explain why or why not.

_____

_____

_____

_____

_____

◆ **Reading Strategy**

Summarize the **author's attitude** toward aging, based on the bracketed paragraph.

_____

_____

_____

_____

_____

◆ **Reading Check**

What new trend does the author notice in the new generation?

_____

_____

_____

_____

_____

Why does the author urge us to adopt his attitude toward the "old ones"?

_____

_____

_____

_____

_____

_____

_____

_____

think I catch a whiff of that earthy aroma that was his smell, just as in lonely times sometimes I catch the fragrance of Ultima's herbs. Then I smile. How strong these people were to leave such a lasting impression.

So, as I would greet my abuelo long ago, it would help us all to greet the old ones we know with this kind and respectful greeting: "Buenos días le de Dios."

Reader's Response: How do the "old ones" in Anaya's life compare with the "old ones" in your own life?

_____

_____

_____

_____

_____

_____

_____

Thinking About the Skill: Anaya's attitude comes from his heritage and his own experience. Do you think he could convince others who do not have the same background to adopt his attitude? Why or why not?

_____

_____

_____

_____

_____

_____

The Tragedy of Romeo and Juliet, *Act II, Scene ii*

William Shakespeare

Summary

In this scene, Romeo visits Juliet under cover of darkness. He calls to Juliet from below her window and speaks of his love for her. Juliet says it is dangerous for Romeo to visit her, since their families are bitter enemies. If any member of her family spots him, he will be killed. They both agree that their love is stronger than their families' hatred. Juliet wants proof that Romeo's love will last. Romeo leaves her with the promise that he will send word the next day about his plans to marry her. The nurse calls Juliet, but she and Romeo find it hard to say good night. Finally, they separate. Juliet goes inside, and Romeo goes to find the friar to ask for his help in arranging the marriage.

Visual Summary

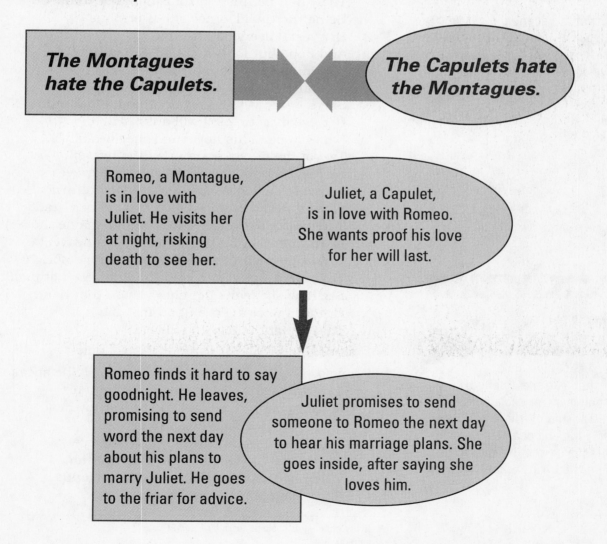

The Montagues hate the Capulets.

The Capulets hate the Montagues.

Romeo, a Montague, is in love with Juliet. He visits her at night, risking death to see her.

Juliet, a Capulet, is in love with Romeo. She wants proof his love for her will last.

Romeo finds it hard to say goodnight. He leaves, promising to send word the next day about his plans to marry Juliet. He goes to the friar for advice.

Juliet promises to send someone to Romeo the next day to hear his marriage plans. She goes inside, after saying she loves him.

◆ Activate Prior Knowledge

This scene is taken from a famous play. What do you know about the characters Romeo and Juliet?

_____

_____

_____

_____

_____

_____

_____

◆ Literary Analysis

In most of this scene the characters speak in blank verse. **Blank verse** consists of unrhymed lines with ten syllables per line. Draw a vertical line between the syllables in the bracketed lines.

◆ Reading Strategy

The key to **reading blank verse** lies in knowing when a sentence ends. A sentence ends *only* when you see a period, question mark, or exclamation point. The end of a line is not necessarily the end of a sentence. In the bracketed section, circle the beginning and end of the sentence.

The Tragedy of Romeo and Juliet
Act II, Scene ii
William Shakespeare

A feud is a bitter hatred between two families. Romeo and Juliet may come from feuding families, but they are determined to be together. In the previous act, Romeo met Juliet in disguise at a costume ball and they fell in love. In this scene he makes the risky journey in the dark of night to proclaim his love for Juliet.

Scene ii. CAPULET'S *orchard.*

ROMEO. [*Coming forward*] He jests at scars that never felt a wound.

[*Enters* JULIET *at a window.*]

But soft! What light through yonder window breaks?
It is the East, and Juliet is the sun!
Arise, fair sun, and kill the envious moon,
5 Who is already sick and pale with grief
That thou her maid art far more fair than she.
Be not her maid, since she is envious.
Her vestal livery[1] is but sick and green,
And none but fools do wear it. Cast it off.
10 It is my lady! O, it is my love!
O, that she knew she were!
She speaks, yet she says nothing. What of that?
Her eye discourses; I will answer it.
I am too bold; 'tis not to me she speaks.
15 Two of the fairest stars in all the heaven,
Having some business, do entreat her eyes
To twinkle in their spheres[2] till they return.
What if her eyes were there, they in her head?
The brightness of her cheek would shame those stars
20 As daylight doth a lamp; her eyes in heaven
Would through the airy region stream so bright
That birds would sing and think it were not night.
See how she leans her cheek upon that hand,
O, that I were a glove upon that hand,
That I might touch that cheek!

JULIET.   Ay me!

25 ROMEO.   She speaks.
O, speak again, bright angel, for thou art
As glorious to this night, being o'er my head,
As is a wingèd messenger of heaven
Unto the white-upturnèd wond'ring eyes
30 Of mortals that fall back to gaze on him
When he bestrides the lazy puffing clouds
And sails upon the bosom of the air.

---

1. **livery** clothing or costume worn by a servant.
2. **spheres** orbits.

JULIET. O Romeo, Romeo! Wherefore art thou Romeo?[3]
Deny thy father and refuse thy name;

35   Or, if thou wilt not, be but sworn my love,
And I'll no longer be a Capulet.

ROMEO. [*Aside*] Shall I hear more, or shall I speak
at this?

JULIET. 'Tis but thy name that is my enemy.
Thou art thyself, though not[4] a Montague.

40   What's Montague? It is nor hand, nor foot,
Nor arm, nor face, nor any other part
Belonging to a man. O, be some other name!
What's in a name? That which we call a rose
By any other name would smell as sweet.

45   So Romeo would, were he not Romeo called,
Retain that dear perfection which he owes[5]
Without that title. Romeo, doff[6] thy name;
And for thy name, which is no part of thee,
Take all myself.

ROMEO.   I take thee at thy word.

50   Call me but love, and I'll be new baptized;
Henceforth I never will be Romeo.

JULIET. What man art thou, thus bescreened in night,
So stumblest on my counsel?[7]

ROMEO.   By a name
I know not how to tell thee who I am.

55   My name, dear saint, is hateful to myself
Because it is an enemy to thee.
Had I it written, I would tear the word.

JULIET. My ears have yet not drunk a hundred words
Of thy tongue's uttering, yet I know the sound.

60   Art thou not Romeo, and a Montague?

ROMEO. Neither, fair maid, if either thee dislike.

JULIET. How camest thou hither, tell me, and
wherefore?
The orchard walls are high and hard to climb,
And the place death, considering who thou art,

65   If any of my kinsmen find thee here.

ROMEO. With love's light wings did I o'erperch[8] these
walls;
For stony limits cannot hold love out,
And what love can do, that dares love attempt.
Therefore thy kinsmen are no stop to me.

---

3. **Wherefore . . . Romeo?** Why are you Romeo—a Montague?
4. **though not** even if you were not.
5. **owes** owns; possesses.
6. **doff** remove.
7. **counsel** secret thoughts.
8. **o'erperch** fly over.

◆ **Reading Check**

Why are Romeo and Juliet making
such a fuss over their families'
names?

_____

_____

_____

_____

◆ **Reading Strategy**

In lines 63–65, mark the beginning
and end of the sentence with a
vertical line. Then, draw arrows to
show where the sen-
tence continues onto
the next line. Now,
reread the sentence.

◆ **Reading Check**

Juliet is afraid that Romeo will be
murdered. By whom?

_____

JULIET. If they do see thee, they will murder thee.

ROMEO. Alack, there lies more peril in thine eye
  Than twenty of their swords! Look thou but sweet,
  And I am proof⁹ against their enmity.

JULIET. I would not for the world they saw thee here.

75 **ROMEO.** I have night's cloak to hide me from their
    eyes;
  And but¹⁰ thou love me, let them find me here.
  My life were better ended by their hate
  Than death proroguèd,¹¹ wanting of thy love.

JULIET. By whose direction found'st thou out this
    place?

80 **ROMEO.** By love, that first did prompt me to inquire.
  He lent me counsel, and I lent him eyes.
  I am no pilot; yet, wert thou as far
  As that vast shore washed with the farthest sea,
  I should adventure¹² for such merchandise.

85 **JULIET.** Thou knowest the mask of night is on my face;
  Else would a maiden blush bepaint my cheek
  For that which thou hast heard me speak tonight.
  Fain would I dwell on form¹³—fain, fain deny
  What I have spoke; but farewell compliment!¹⁴
90 Dost thou love me? I know thou wilt say "Ay";
  And I will take thy word. Yet, if thou swear'st,
  Thou mayst prove false. At lovers' perjuries,
  They say Jove laughs. O gentle Romeo,
  If thou dost love, pronounce it faithfully.
95 Or if thou thinkest I am too quickly won,
  I'll frown and be perverse¹⁵ and say thee nay,
  So thou wilt woo; but else, not for the world.
  In truth, fair Montague, I am too fond,¹⁶
  And therefore thou mayst think my havior light;¹⁷
100 But trust me, gentleman, I'll prove more true
  Than those that have more cunning to be strange.¹⁸
  I should have been more strange, I must confess,
  But that thou overheard'st, ere I was ware,
  My truelove passion. Therefore pardon me,
105 And not impute this yielding to light love,

Vocabulary Development: cunning (kun´ iŋ) *n.* cleverness; slyness

---

9. **proof** protected, as by armor.
10. **And but** unless.
11. **proroguèd** postponed.
12. **adventure** risk a long journey, like a sea adventurer.
13. **Fain . . . form** eagerly would I follow convention (by acting reserved).
14. **compliment** conventional behavior.
15. **be perverse** act contrary to my true feelings.
16. **fond** affectionate.
17. **my havior light** my behavior immodest or unserious.
18. **strange** distant and cold.

◆ **Literary Analysis**

Read lines 80–85, stressing every second syllable. Place an accent mark (´) above each stressed syllable. **Blank verse** has a formal, impressive sound. Why do you think Shakespeare uses this type of verse for important, noble characters?

_____

_____

_____

◆ **Reading Check**

What doubt is Juliet expressing in lines 90–93?

_____

_____

_____

_____

◆ **Stop to Reflect**

Is Juliet's concern about how Romeo thinks of her similar to concerns voiced by couples today? Explain.

_____

_____

_____

_____

Which the dark night hath so discoverèd.[19]

ROMEO. Lady, by yonder blessèd moon I vow,
    That tips with silver all these fruit-tree tops—

JULIET. O, swear not by the moon, th' inconstant
    moon,
110   That monthly changes in her circle orb,
    Lest that thy love prove likewise variable.

ROMEO. What shall I swear by?

JULIET.   Do not swear at all;
    Or if thou wilt, swear by thy gracious self,
    Which is the god of my idolatry,
    And I'll believe thee.

115 ROMEO.   If my heart's dear love—

JULIET. Well, do not swear. Although I joy in thee,
    I have no joy of this contract[20] tonight.
    It is too rash, too unadvised, too sudden;
    Too like the lightning, which doth cease to be
120   Ere one can say it lightens. Sweet, good night!
    This bud of love, by summer's ripening breath,
    May prove a beauteous flow'r when next we meet.
    Good night, good night! As sweet repose and rest
    Come to thy heart as that within my breast!

125 ROMEO. O, wilt thou leave me so unsatisfied?

JULIET. What satisfaction canst thou have tonight?

ROMEO. Th' exchange of thy love's faithful vow for
    mine.

JULIET. I gave thee mine before thou didst request it;
    And yet I would it were to give again.

130 ROMEO. Wouldst thou withdraw it? For what purpose,
    love?

JULIET. But to be frank[21] and give it thee again.
    And yet I wish but for the thing I have.
    My bounty[22] is as boundless as the sea,
    My love as deep; the more I give to thee,
135   The more I have, for both are infinite,
    I hear some noise within. Dear love, adieu!

[NURSE calls within.]

    Anon, good nurse! Sweet Montague, be true.
    Stay but a little, I will come again.   [Exit.]

ROMEO. O blessèd, blessèd night! I am afeard,
140   Being in night, all this is but a dream,
    Too flattering-sweet to be substantial.[23]

---

19. **discoverèd** revealed.
20. **contract** betrothal.
21. **frank** generous.
22. **bounty** what I have to give.
23. **substantial** real.

◆ Reading Strategy

Mark the Text

Read the bracketed lines, pausing at the commas and semicolon, and stopping only at the end of the sentence. Underline the groups of words that you emphasize.

◆ Reading Check

Why does Juliet say she can take no joy from Romeo's promise of marriage in line 117?

_____

_____

_____

_____

◆ Reading Check

In lines 120–141, what are the two lovers delaying?

_____

_____

_____

_____

◆ Stop to Reflect

Juliet is expressing her love for Romeo in lines 158–163. What expressions do modern lovers use to show love for one another?

_____

_____

_____

_____

◆ Reading Check

What do Romeo and Juliet agree to do in the bracketed section?

_____

_____

_____

_____

[*Enter* JULIET *again.*]

JULIET. Three words, dear Romeo, and good night indeed.
   If that thy bent[24] of love be honorable,
   Thy purpose marriage, send me word tomorrow,
145 By one that I'll procure to come to thee,
   Where and what time thou wilt perform the rite;
   And all my fortunes at thy foot I'll lay
   And follow thee my lord throughout the world.

NURSE. [*Within*] Madam!

150 JULIET. I come anon.—But if thou meanest not well,
   I do beseech thee—

NURSE.   [*Within*] Madam!

JULIET.   By and by[25] I come.—
   To cease thy strife[26] and leave me to my grief.
   Tomorrow will I send.

ROMEO.   So thrive my soul—

JULIET. A thousand times good night!   [*Exit.*]

155 ROMEO. A thousand times the worse, to want thy light!
   Love goes toward love as schoolboys from their books;
   But love from love, toward school with heavy looks.

[*Enter* JULIET *again.*]

JULIET. Hist! Romeo, hist! O for a falc'ner's voice
   To lure this tassel gentle[27] back again!
160 Bondage is hoarse[28] and may not speak aloud,
   Else would I tear the cave where Echo[29] lies
   And make her airy tongue more hoarse than mine
   With repetition of "My Romeo!"

ROMEO. It is my soul that calls upon my name.
165 How silver-sweet sound lovers' tongues by night,
   Like softest music to attending ears!

JULIET. Romeo!

ROMEO.   My sweet?

JULIET.   What o'clock tomorrow
   Shall I send to thee?

ROMEO.   By the hour of nine.

JULIET. I will not fail. 'Tis twenty year till then.
170 I have forgot why I did call thee back.

---

24. **bent** purpose; intention.
25. **By and by** at once.
26. **strife** efforts.
27. **tassel gentle** male falcon.
28. **Bondage is hoarse** being bound in by my family restricts my speech.
29. **Echo** in classical mythology, the nymph Echo, unable to win the love of Narcissus, wasted away in a cave until nothing was left of her but her voice.

ROMEO. Let me stand here till thou remember it.

JULIET. I shall forget, to have thee still stand there,
Rememb'ring how I love thy company.

ROMEO. And I'll stay, to have thee still forget,
175   Forgetting any other home but this.

JULIET. 'Tis almost morning. I would have thee gone—
And yet no farther than a wanton's[30] bird,
That lets it hop a little from his hand,
Like a poor prisoner in his twisted gyves,[31]
180   And with a silken thread plucks it back again,
So loving-jealous of his liberty.

ROMEO. I would I were thy bird.

JULIET.   Sweet, so would I.
Yet I should kill thee with much cherishing.
Good night, good night! Parting is such sweet sorrow
185   That I shall say good night till it be morrow.   [*Exit.*]

ROMEO. Sleep dwell upon thine eyes, peace in thy
breast!
Would I were sleep and peace, so sweet to rest!
Hence will I to my ghostly friar's[32] close cell,[33]
His help to crave and my dear hap[34] to tell.   [*Exit.*]

---

30. **wanton's** spoiled, playful child's.
31. **gyves** (jivz) chains.
32. **ghostly friar's** spiritual father's.
33. **close cell** small room.
34. **dear hap** good fortune.

◆ **Reading Strategy**

 Read the bracketed lines aloud. Underline the words that you stress.

◆ **Reading Check**

Where is Romeo going at the end of the scene? Why?

_____

_____

_____

_____

Reader's Response: Did you like the characters of Romeo and Juliet? Why or why not?

_____

_____

_____

Thinking About the Skill: How did the blank verse in this scene affect the way you read?

_____

_____

_____

Memory
Margaret Walker

Summary

In this poem, Margaret Walker describes a certain type of rainy day in the city. She presents images of cold, windy, rainy days that depress people's spirits. The weather brings out the worst in people, who appear hurt, confused, and angry because of the rain. These are the same miserable people the poet sees alone at work or in their apartment buildings.

Visual Summary

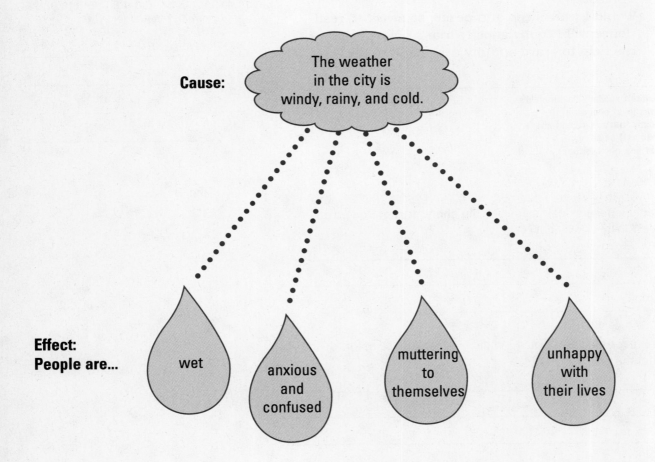

Memory
Margaret Walker

Margaret Walker describes the feeling of cold, rainy days in the city. These are days that not only affect the body but also the spirit.

I can remember wind-swept streets of cities
on cold and blustery nights, on rainy days;
heads under shabby felts[1] and parasols
and shoulders hunched against a sharp concern;
5   seeing hurt bewilderment on poor faces,
smelling a deep and <u>sinister</u> unrest
these brooding people cautiously caress;
hearing ghostly marching on pavement stones
and closing fast around their squares of hate.
10 I can remember seeing them alone,
at work, and in their tenements at home.
I can remember hearing all they said:
their muttering protests, their whispered oaths,
and all that spells their living in distress.

Vocabulary Development: sinister (sin´ is tər) *adj.* threatening harm, evil or misfortune

---

1. **felts** felt hats.

Reader's Response: What emotions does "Memory" bring out in you? Why?

_____

_____

_____

Thinking About the Skill: How did picturing the images contribute to your appreciation of this poem?

_____

_____

_____

◆ **Activate Prior Knowledge**

Think about how you feel on cold, rainy days. How does the bad weather affect your mood?

_____

_____

_____

_____

◆ **Reading Strategy**

Mark the Text Circle the details in this poem that help you **picture the image** of isolated people in line 10.

◆ **Literary Analysis**

Images in a poem are the pictures the poet creates through words. Which line presents an image of people walking against the wind?

_____

_____

List two other images in lines 1–5.

1. _____

_____

2. _____

_____

Woman's Work
Julia Alvarez

Summary

The speaker of this poem recalls helping her mother with the housework as a child. She resented having to do the housework while her friends played. In the end, though, she realizes she is similar to her mother, with one small difference. Instead of putting her heart into her housework, she puts it into her writing.

Visual Summary

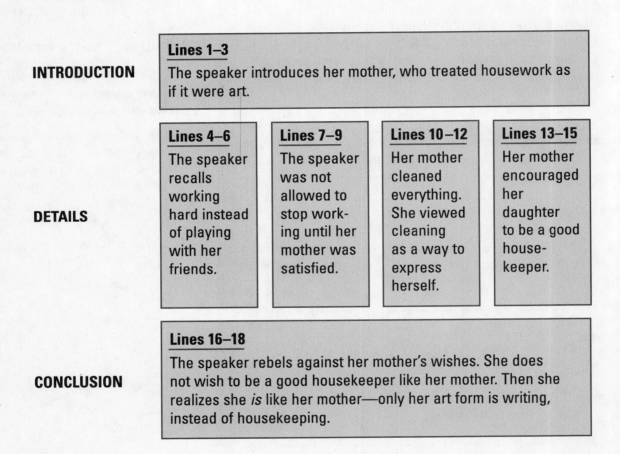

INTRODUCTION

Lines 1–3
The speaker introduces her mother, who treated housework as if it were art.

DETAILS

Lines 4–6
The speaker recalls working hard instead of playing with her friends.

Lines 7–9
The speaker was not allowed to stop working until her mother was satisfied.

Lines 10–12
Her mother cleaned everything. She viewed cleaning as a way to express herself.

Lines 13–15
Her mother encouraged her daughter to be a good house-keeper.

CONCLUSION

Lines 16–18
The speaker rebels against her mother's wishes. She does not wish to be a good housekeeper like her mother. Then she realizes she *is* like her mother—only her art form is writing, instead of housekeeping.

Woman's Work
Julia Alvarez

We do not ordinarily think of housework as art. The speaker shows us why she views her mother's painstaking housecleaning as a form of art.

Who says a woman's work isn't high art?
She'd challenge as she scrubbed the bathroom tiles.
Keep house as if the address were your heart.

We'd clean the whole upstairs before we'd start
5   downstairs. I'd sigh, hearing my friends outside.
Doing her woman's work was a hard art

to practice when the summer sun would bar
the floor I swept till she was satisfied.
She kept me prisoner in her housebound heart.

10   She'd shine the tines of forks, the wheels of carts,
cut lacy lattices[1] for all her pies.
Her woman's work was nothing less than art.

And, I, her masterpiece since I was smart,
was primed, praised, polished, scolded and advised
15   to keep a house much better than my heart.

I did not want to be her counterpart!
I struck out . . . but became my mother's child:
a woman working at home on her art,
housekeeping paper as if it were her heart.

Vocabulary Development: primed (prīmd) *v.* made ready; prepared

---

1. lattices (lat´ is əz) narrow strips of pastry laid on the pie in a crisscross pattern.

Reader's Response: How do you feel about the mother in this poem? Why?

_____

_____

Thinking About the Skill: How did picturing the images in this poem help you understand what the author was saying?

_____

_____

◆ **Activate Prior Knowledge**

What activity do you put your heart into or find meaningful?

_____

As you read this poem, consider how your activity compares with those of the women in this poem.

_____

_____

◆ **Literary Analysis**

Images in a poem are the pictures the poet creates through words. What image does the poet present in lines 1–3 to show how hard the speaker's mother worked?

_____

_____

◆ **Reading Strategy**

In lines 10–12, Alvarez presents images of housework. Underline the words that enable you to **picture these images**.

◆ **Reading Check**

Daughters sometimes find that they are similar to their mothers, even though they were determined to be different as children. In what way did Alvarez become "her mother's child"?

_____

_____

The Raven
Edgar Allan Poe

Summary

"The Raven" opens with the speaker describing a night alone with his books. He is reading to forget his lost love, Lenore. Suddenly, the speaker hears someone tapping at the door. When he opens the door, no one is there. The tapping continues. Then he opens the window, and a raven flies into the room. The bird perches on a sculpture of a Greek goddess. Asked its name, the raven replies, "Nevermore." This is all the bird can say. At first, the speaker is amused. But by the end of the poem, the speaker believes the raven is mocking him and his loneliness. The speaker does not succeed in driving the raven from the room, however, and this only intensifies his gloom.

Visual Summary

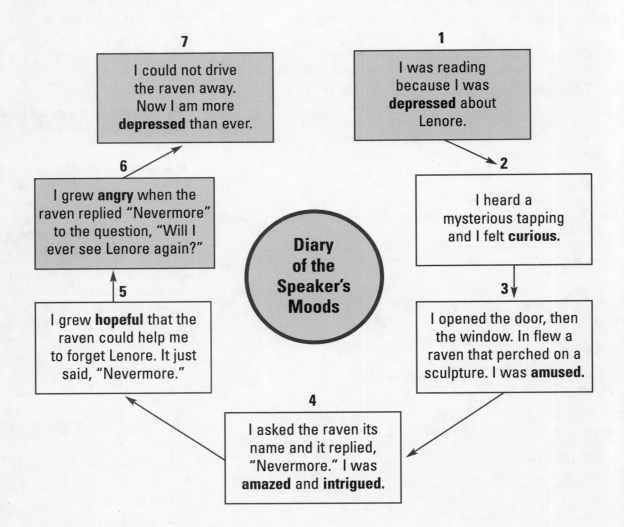

7 I could not drive the raven away. Now I am more **depressed** than ever.

1 I was reading because I was **depressed** about Lenore.

6 I grew **angry** when the raven replied "Nevermore" to the question, "Will I ever see Lenore again?"

Diary of the Speaker's Moods

2 I heard a mysterious tapping and I felt **curious**.

5 I grew **hopeful** that the raven could help me to forget Lenore. It just said, "Nevermore."

3 I opened the door, then the window. In flew a raven that perched on a sculpture. I was **amused**.

4 I asked the raven its name and it replied, "Nevermore." I was **amazed** and **intrigued**.

The Raven
Edgar Allan Poe

The speaker begins the poem by describing the night that strange tapping interrupted his reading.

Once upon a midnight dreary, while I pondered, weak
    and weary,
Over many a <u>quaint</u> and curious volume of forgotten
    lore,[1]
While I nodded, nearly napping, suddenly there came
    a tapping,
As of someone gently rapping, rapping at my chamber
    door.
5 "Tis some visitor," I muttered, "tapping at my chamber
    door—
        Only this, and nothing more."

Ah, distinctly I remember it was in the bleak
    December,
And each separate dying ember wrought its ghost
    upon the floor.
Eagerly I wished the morrow—vainly I had tried to
    borrow
10 From my books surcease[2] of sorrow—sorrow for the
    lost Lenore—
For the rare and radiant maiden whom the angels
    name Lenore—
        Nameless here for evermore.

And the silken, sad, uncertain rustling of each purple
    curtain
Thrilled me—filled me with fantastic terrors never felt
    before;
15 So that now, to still the beating of my heart, I stood
    repeating
"'Tis some visitor entreating entrance at my chamber
    door—
Some late visitor entreating entrance at my chamber
    door—
        This it is and nothing more."

Vocabulary Development: quaint (kwānt) *adj.* strange; unusual

---

1. **quaint . . . lore** strange book of ancient learning.
2. **surcease** (sɐr sēs´) *n.* end.

◆ **Activate Prior Knowledge**

Sudden, mysterious events can affect the way you feel. Have you ever been alone at night when something out of the ordinary happened? Explain.

_____

_____

_____

_____

_____

◆ **Reading Strategy**

From lines 9–14, you can **draw the inference** that the speaker of this poem is in a gloomy mood. Circle the words that support this inference.

◆ **Reading Check**

What is scaring the speaker?

_____

_____

_____

Presently my soul grew stronger; hesitating then no longer,
20 "Sir," said I, "or Madam, truly your forgiveness I implore;
But the fact is I was napping, and so gently you came rapping,
And so faintly you came tapping, tapping at my chamber door,
That I scarce was sure I heard you"—here I opened wide the door—
    Darkness there, and nothing more.

25 Deep into that darkness peering, long I stood there wondering, fearing,
Doubting, dreaming dreams no mortal ever dared to dream before;
But the silence was unbroken, and the darkness gave no token,[3]
And the only word there spoken was the whispered word, "Lenore!"
This I whispered, and an echo murmured back the word, "Lenore!"
30   Merely this, and nothing more.

Then into the chamber turning, all my soul within me burning,
Soon I heard again a tapping somewhat louder than before.
"Surely," said I, "surely that is something at my window lattice;[4]
Let me see, then, what thereat[5] is, and this mystery explore—
35 Let my heart be still a moment and this mystery explore—
    "Tis the wind, and nothing more!"

Open here I flung the shutter, when, with many a flirt[6] and flutter,
In there stepped a stately raven of the saintly days of yore;
Not the least obeisance[7] made he; not an instant stopped or stayed he;
40 But, with mien[8] of lord or lady, perched above my chamber door—

---

3. **token** (tō´ kən) *n.* sign.
4. **lattice** (lat´ is) *n.* framework of wood or metal.
5. **thereat** (*th*er at´) *adv.* there.
6. **flirt** (flu̇rt) *n.* quick, uneven movement.
7. **obeisance** (ō bā´ səns) *n.* bow or another sign of respect.
8. **mien** (mēn) *n.* manner.

Perched upon a bust of Pallas[9] just above my chamber door—
　　　Perched, and sat, and nothing more.

Then this ebony bird beguiling my sad fancy[10] into smiling,
By the grave and stern decorum of the countenance[11] it wore,
45　"Though thy crest be shorn and shaven, thou," I said, "art sure no craven,[12]
Ghastly grim and ancient raven wandering from the Nightly shore—
Tell me what thy lordly name is on the Night's Plutonian[13] shore!"
　　　Quoth[14] the raven, "Nevermore."

Much I marveled this ungainly fowl to hear discourse so plainly,
50　Though its answer little meaning—little relevancy bore;
For we cannot help agreeing that no sublunary[15] being
Ever yet was blessed with seeing bird above his chamber door—
Bird or beast upon the sculptured bust above his chamber door,
　　　With such name as "Nevermore."

55　But the raven, sitting lonely on the placid bust, spoke only
That one word, as if his soul in that one word he did outpour.
Nothing farther then he uttered—not a feather then he fluttered—
Till I scarcely more than muttered, "Other friends have flown before—
On the morrow *he* will leave me, as my hopes have flown before."
60　　　Quoth the raven, "Nevermore."

Wondering at the stillness broken by reply so aptly spoken,
"Doubtless," said I, "what it utters is its only stock and store,

---

9. **bust of Pallas** (paľ əs) sculpture of the head and shoulders of Pallas Athena (ə thē´ nə), the ancient Greek goddess of wisdom.
10. **fancy** (fan´ sē) *n.* imagination.
11. **countenance** (koun´ tə nəns) *n.* facial appearance.
12. **craven** (krā´ vən) *n.* coward (usually an adjective).
13. **Plutonian** (plo͞o tō´ nē ən) *adj.* like the underworld, ruled over by the ancient Roman god Pluto.
14. **quoth** (kwōth) *v.* said.
15. **sublunary** (sub lo͞on´ ər ē) *adj.* earthly.

◆ **Reading Strategy**

From the bracketed passage, you could **draw the inference** that the speaker's mood has changed. What word might lead you to draw this inference?

_____

_____

_____

_____

◆ **Stop to Reflect**

Why do you think the raven replies "Nevermore" to the speaker's question?

_____

_____

_____

_____

◆ **Literary Analysis**

A **narrative poem** has the same elements as a story—including a problem. What is the problem facing the speaker in this poem?

_____

_____

_____

◆ **Reading Check**

In the underlined passage, what is the speaker wondering about the raven?

_____

_____

_____

_____

_____

_____

_____

_____

_____

◆ Stop to Reflect

How can something as ordinary as a couch cushion remind someone of lost love?

_____

_____

_____

_____

_____

◆ Reading Check

The speaker thinks the raven may help him forget his sorrow. What is the cause of the speaker's sorrow?

_____

_____

_____

Caught from some unhappy master whom unmerciful Disaster
Followed fast and followed faster—so, when Hope he would adjure,[16]
65   Stern Despair returned, instead of the sweet Hope he dared adjure—
      That sad answer, 'Nevermore.'"

But the raven still <u>beguiling</u> all my sad soul into smiling,
Straight I wheeled a cushioned seat in front of bird, and bust, and door;
Then upon the velvet sinking, I betook myself to linking
70   Fancy unto fancy, thinking what this ominous bird of yore—
What this grim, ungainly, ghastly, gaunt, and ominous bird of yore
      Meant in croaking "Nevermore."

This I sat engaged in guessing, but no syllable expressing
To the fowl whose fiery eyes now burned into my bosom's core;
75   This and more I sat divining,[17] with my head at ease reclining
On the cushion's velvet lining that the lamplight gloated o'er,
But whose velvet violet lining with the lamplight gloating o'er,
      She shall press, ah, nevermore!

Then, methought, the air grew denser, perfumed from an unseen censer[18]
80   Swung by angels whose faint footfalls tinkled on the tufted floor.
"Wretch," I cried, "thy God hath lent thee—by these angels he hath sent thee
Respite—respite and Nepenthe[19] from thy memories of Lenore!

Vocabulary Development: beguiling (bi gīl´ iŋ) *adj.* tricking; charming
respite (res´ pit) *n.* rest; relief

---

16. **adjure** (ə joor´) *v.* appeal to.
17. **divining** (də vīn´ iŋ) *v.* guessing.
18. **censer** (sen´ sər) *n.* container for burning incense.
19. **Nepenthe** (nē pen´ thē) *n.* drug used in ancient times to cause forgetfulness of sorrow.

Let me quaff[20] this kind Nepenthe and forget this lost
Lenore!"
    Quoth the raven, "Nevermore."

85   "Prophet!" said I, "thing of evil!—prophet still, if bird or
      devil!—
      Whether Tempter[21] sent, or whether tempest tossed
      thee here ashore,
      <u>Desolate</u>, yet all undaunted, on this desert land
      enchanted—
      On this home by Horror haunted—tell me truly, I
      implore—
      Is there—is there balm in Gilead?[22]—tell me—tell me,
      I implore!"
90   Quoth the raven, "Nevermore."

    "Prophet!" said I, "thing of evil!—prophet still, if bird
    or devil!
    By that Heaven that bends above us—by that God we
    both adore—
    Tell this soul with sorrow laden if, within the distant
    Aidenn,[23]
    It shall clasp a sainted maiden whom the angels
    name Lenore—
95 Clasp a rare and radiant maiden whom the angels
    name Lenore."
        Quoth the raven, "Nevermore."

    "Be that word our sign of parting, bird or fiend!" I
    shrieked, upstarting—
    "Get thee back into the tempest and the Night's
    Plutonian shore!
    Leave no black plume as a token of that lie thy soul
    hath spoken!
100 Leave my loneliness unbroken!—quit the bust above
    my door!
    Take thy beak from out my heart, and take thy form
    from off my door!"
        Quoth the raven, "Nevermore."

Vocabulary Development: desolate (des′ ə lit) *adj.* deserted;
                              abandoned

---

20. **quaff** (kwäf) *v.* drink.
21. **Tempter** devil.
22. **balm** (bäm) **in Gilead** (gil′ ē əd) cure for suffering; the Bible refers to a medicinal ointment, or balm, made in a region called Gilead.
23. **Aidenn** name meant to suggest Eden or paradise.

◆ **Literary Analysis**

Circle the words and phrases in the bracketed section that build tension in the poem.

◆ **Reading Strategy**

From lines 91–96 you could safely **draw the inference** that Lenore is no longer alive. Circle words and phrases in those lines that might lead you to draw this inference.

◆ **Literary Analysis**

A **narrative poem** has a climax where the action reaches the highest point of tension. Explain why lines 97–102 can be seen as the climax of this poem.

_____

_____

_____

◆ **Reading Check**

What does the speaker want the raven to do?

_____

_____

_____

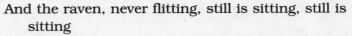

What can you **infer** about the narrator's state of mind by the end of the poem? Underline the words and phrases that lead you to this inference.

_____

_____

_____

_____

And the raven, never flitting, still is sitting, still is sitting
   On the <u>pallid</u> bust of Pallas just above my chamber door;
105 And his eyes have all the seeming of a demon that is dreaming,
   And the lamplight o'er him streaming throws his shadow on the floor;
   And my soul from out that shadow that lies floating on the floor
      Shall be lifted—nevermore!

Vocabulary Development: pallid (pal′ id) *adj.* pale

Reader's Response: Did you sympathize with the speaker in this story? Why or why not?

_____

_____

_____

Thinking About the Skill: How did drawing inferences about the speaker increase your understanding of the poem?

_____

_____

_____

The Seven Ages of Man
William Shakespeare

Summary

The speaker in this poem notes that we all have our time in the world and then we die. Then he traces the journey of all people from the cradle to the grave. The stages he mentions are the infant, the schoolboy, the lover, the soldier, the judge, the old man, and finally, the dying man. In each stage, a person grows older, but not necessarily any wiser. In the end, according to the speaker, the entire journey proves meaningless.

Visual Summary

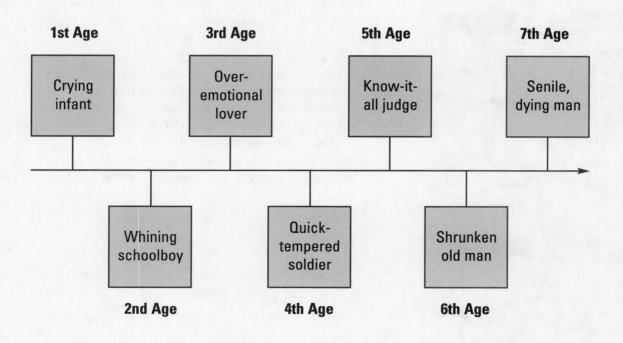

1st Age

Crying infant

3rd Age

Over-emotional lover

5th Age

Know-it-all judge

7th Age

Senile, dying man

Whining schoolboy

2nd Age

Quick-tempered soldier

4th Age

Shrunken old man

6th Age

The Seven Ages of Man
William Shakespeare

◆ Activate Prior Knowledge

Write an adjective or a phrase that you think describes the following:

An infant

_____

A young child

_____

A teenager

_____

A middle-aged person

_____

An old person

_____

◆ Stop to Reflect

Compare Shakespeare's descriptions of the first three ages to the descriptions you wrote above. How are they similar or different in attitude?

_____

_____

_____

◆ Reading Check

Circle the words the speaker uses to describe the soldier and the justice. Does the speaker view these ages positively or negatively?

_____

_____

_____

_____

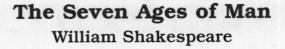

"The Seven Ages of Man" is a speech from William Shakespeare's comedy As You Like It. *The play is about a duke who has been deprived of his rights and exiled to the forest by his own brother. The duke's attendant, Jacques, delivers this speech to his master that reveals a cold and bitter outlook on life.*

All the world's a stage,
And all the men and women merely players:[1]
They have their exits and their entrances;
And one man in his time plays many parts,
5   His acts being seven ages.[2] At first the infant,
Mewling[3] and puking in the nurse's arms.
And then the whining schoolboy, with his satchel,
And shining morning face, creeping like snail
Unwillingly to school. And then the lover,
10   Sighing like furnace, with a <u>woeful</u> ballad
Made to his mistress' eyebrow. Then a soldier,
Full of strange oaths, and bearded like the pard,[4]
Jealous in honor,[5] sudden and quick in quarrel,
Seeking the bubble reputation
15   Even in the cannon's mouth. And then the justice,[6]
In fair round belly with good capon[7] lined,
With eyes severe and beard of formal cut,
Full of wise saws and modern instances;[8]
And so he plays his part. The sixth age shifts
20   Into the lean and slippered pantaloon,[9]
With spectacles on nose and pouch on side,
His youthful hose[10] well saved, a world too wide

Vocabulary Development: woeful (wō´ fəl) *adj.* full of sorrow

---

1. **players** actors.
2. **ages** periods of life.
3. **mewling** (myōōl´ in) *adj.* whimpering; crying like a baby.
4. **pard** (pärd) *n.* leopard or panther.
5. **Jealous in honor** very concerned about his honor.
6. **justice** judge.
7. **capon** (kā´ pän) *n.* roasted chicken.
8. **wise saws and modern instances** wise sayings and modern examples that show the truth of the sayings.
9. **pantaloon** (pan´ tə lōōn´) *n.* thin, foolish old man—originally a character in old comedies.
10. **hose** (hōz) *n.* stockings.

For his shrunk shank;[11] and his big manly voice,
Turning again toward childish <u>treble</u>, pipes
25 And whistles in his sound. Last scene of all,
That ends this strange eventful history,
Is second childishness, and mere oblivion,
Sans[12] teeth, sans eyes, sans taste, sans everything.

Vocabulary Development: treble (treb´ əl) *n.* high-pitched voice

---

11. **shank** (shank) *n.* leg.
12. **sans** (sanz) *prep.* without; lacking.

Reader's Response: Do you agree or disagree with the speaker's descriptions of the stages of life? Explain.

_____

_____

_____

_____

Thinking About the Skill: How did identifying the attitude of the speaker give you insight into the poem?

_____

_____

_____

_____

© Pearson Education, Inc.

◆ **Reading Strategy**

The speaker has already given you his view of several ages of man. From the lines you have read, what type of person do you think the speaker is?

_____

_____

_____

_____

◆ **Literary Analysis**

This **dramatic poem** is part of a play. It is meant to be spoken. In what tone of voice do you think the speaker should read the last four lines of the poem?

_____

_____

_____

_____

from the Odyssey

Homer (Translated by Robert Fitzgerald)

Summary

This epic tells the story of the Greek hero Odysseus, who is trying to return home to Ithaca after the Trojan War. Odysseus and his men arrive at the land of the Cyclopes, a race of one-eyed giants. Odysseus decides to wait for one of them. The Cyclops finds them in his cave and eats two men. Odysseus finds a large club and uses part of it to make a spike. He gives the giant some brandy, and the Cyclops—Polyphemus—gets drunk. Odysseus and his men blind the giant by ramming the spike into his eye. Polyphemus calls for help from the other Cyclopes but is foiled by the fact that Odysseus gave him a false name: Nohbdy. Odysseus ties the Cyclops' sheep together and hides his men under them. When Polyphemus lets the sheep out, Odysseus and his men escape. Odysseus taunts the giant from his ship, and Polyphemus realizes that he was warned about Odysseus long ago. He asks the god Poseidon to curse Odysseus.

Visual Summary

Setting	Land of the Cyclopes

Characters	Odysseus	Odysseus' men	Polyphemus, a Cyclops

Problem	Odysseus and his men must escape from the Cyclops before he kills them all.

Events	1. Odysseus and his men arrive at the land of the Cyclopes.
	2. Odysseus decides to wait for one of the Cyclopes.
	3. Polyphemus, a Cyclops, finds them and eats two men.
	4. Odysseus finds an enormous club and turns it into a spike.
	5. Odysseus gives the Cyclops wine to get him drunk.
	6. Odysseus tells Polyphemus his name is *Nohbdy*.
	7. Odysseus and his men blind Polyphemus with a spiked club.
	8. Polyphemus calls for help but is foiled by Odysseus' false name.
	9. Odysseus ties the sheep together and hides his men under them.

Outcome	When the Cyclops lets the sheep out, Odysseus and his men escape. Odysseus taunts the giant from his ship, and Polyphemus realizes that he was warned about Odysseus long ago. He asks Poseidon to curse Odysseus.

from the Odyssey
The Cyclops

Homer (Translated by Robert Fitzgerald)

"The Cyclops" is part of a much longer work, written in the Greek language long ago. After the Trojan War, Odysseus spends years wandering around the Mediterranean, trying to return home. A ruler offers him a ship for the return voyage, in exchange for hearing about his adventures. This story is one of those adventures.

◆ Activate Prior Knowledge

Think of adventure stories you have read or seen. What kinds of characters do you usually find in these stories?

_____

_____

_____

In the next land we found were Cyclopes,[1]
110   giants, louts, without a law to bless them.
In ignorance leaving the fruitage of the earth in
       mystery
to the immortal gods, they neither plow
nor sow by hand, nor till the ground, though
       grain—
wild wheat and barley—grows untended, and
115   wine grapes, in clusters, ripen in heaven's rains.
Cyclopes have no muster and no meeting,
no consultation or old tribal ways,
but each one dwells in his own mountain cave
dealing out rough justice to wife and child,
120   indifferent to what the others do. . . .

◆ Reading Check

Using lines 109–120 as a reference, list three reasons why the Greeks thought the Cyclopes were uncivilized.

1. _____

2. _____

3. _____

As we rowed on, and nearer to the mainland,
at one end of the bay, we saw a cavern
yawning above the water, screened with laurel,
and many rams and goats about the place
125   inside a sheepfold—made from slabs of stone
earthfast between tall trunks of pine and rugged
towering oak trees.

                          A prodigious[2] man
slept in this cave alone, and took his flocks
to graze afield—remote from all companions,
130   knowing none but savage ways, a brute
so huge, he seemed no man at all of those
who eat good wheaten bread; but he seemed rather
a shaggy mountain reared in solitude.
We beached there, and I told the crew
135   to stand by and keep watch over the ship:
as for myself I took my twelve best fighters

◆ Reading Strategy

In an epic poem like the *Odyssey*, it is easier to follow the story if you **read in complete sentences.** In the bracketed section, mark where each sentence ends. After you have marked the ends of sentences, read the section aloud, ignoring the ends of lines and stopping only at periods, questions marks, and exclamation points.

◆ Reading Check

With whom did Odysseus go ashore?

_____

_____

---

1. **Cyclopes** (sī klō´ pēz) *n.* plural form of Cyclops (sī´ kläps), a race of giants with one eye in the middle of the forehead.
2. **prodigious** (prə dij´ əs) *adj.* enormous.

_____

_____

_____

_____

_____

In a Greek **epic,** the **hero** always has a flaw, or fault, that gets him into trouble. In lines 157–175, what possible flaw can you identify in Odysseus' character?

_____

_____

_____

_____

Why does Odysseus decide to ignore the advice of his men?

_____

_____

_____

_____

and went ahead. I had a goatskin full
of that sweet liquor that Euanthes' son,
Maron, had given me. He kept Apollo's[3]
140 holy grove at Ismarus; for kindness
we showed him there, and showed his wife and child,
he gave me seven shining golden talents[4]
perfectly formed, a solid silver winebowl,
and then this liquor—twelve two-handled jars
145 of brandy, pure and fiery. Not a slave
in Maron's household knew this drink; only
he, his wife and the storeroom mistress knew;
and they would put one cupful—ruby-colored
honey—smooth—in twenty more of water,
150 but still the sweet scent hovered like a fume
over the winebowl. No man turned away
when cups of this came round.

                A wineskin full
I brought along, and victuals[5] in a bag,
for in my bones I knew some towering brute
155 would be upon us soon—all outward power,
a wild man, ignorant of civility.

We climbed, then, briskly to the cave. But Cyclops
had gone afield, to pasture his fat sheep,
so we looked round at everything inside:
160 a drying rack that sagged with cheeses, pens
crowded with lambs and kids,[6] each in its class:
firstlings apart from middlings, and the 'dewdrops,'
or newborn lambkins, penned apart from both.
And vessels full of whey[7] were brimming there—
165 bowls of earthenware and pails for milking.
My men came pressing round me, pleading:

                      'Why not
take these cheeses, get them stowed, come back,
throw open all the pens, and make a run for it?
We'll drive the kids and lambs aboard. We say
170 put out again on good salt water!'

                        Ah,
how sound that was! Yet I refused. I wished
to see the cave man, what he had to offer—
no pretty sight, it turned out, for my friends.
We lit a fire, burnt an offering,

---

3. Apollo (ə päl´ ō) god of music, poetry, prophecy, and medicine.
4. talents units of money in ancient Greece.
5. victuals (vit´ əls) *n.* food or other provisions.
6. kids (kids) *n.* young goats.
7. whey (hwā) *n.* thin, watery part of milk separated from the thicker curds.

175 and took some cheese to eat: then sat in silence
around the embers, waiting. When he came
he had a load of dry boughs[8] on his shoulder
to stoke his fire at suppertime. He dumped it
with a great crash into that hollow cave,
180 and we all scattered fast to the far wall.
Then over the broad cavern floor he ushered
the ewes he meant to milk. He left his rams
and he-goats in the yard outside, and swung
high overhead a slab of solid rock
185 to close the cave. Two dozen four-wheeled wagons,
with heaving wagon teams, could not have stirred
the tonnage of that rock from where he wedged it
over the doorsill. Next he took his seat
and milked his bleating ewes. A practiced job
190 he made of it, giving each ewe her suckling;
thickened his milk, then, into curds and whey,
sieved out the curds to drip in withy[9] baskets,
and poured the whey to stand in bowls
cooling until he drank it for his supper.
195 When all these chores were done, he poked the fire,
heaping on brushwood. In the glare he saw us.

'Strangers,' he said, 'who are you? And where from?
What brings you here by seaways—a fair traffic?
Or are you wandering rogues, who cast your lives
200 like dice, and ravage other folk by sea?'

We felt a pressure on our hearts, in dread
of that deep rumble and that mighty man.
But all the same I spoke up in reply:

'We are from Troy, Achaeans, blown off course
205 by shifting gales on the Great South Sea;
homeward bound, but taking routes and ways
uncommon; so the will of Zeus would have it.
We served under Agamemnon,[10] son of Atreus—
the whole world knows what city
210 he laid waste, what armies he destroyed.
It was our luck to come here; here we stand,
beholden for your help, or any gifts
you give—as custom is to honor strangers.
We would entreat you, great Sir, have a care
215 for the gods' courtesy; Zeus will avenge
the unoffending guest.'

8. **boughs** (bouz) n. tree branches.
9. **withy** (with´ ē) adj. tough, flexible twigs.
10. **Agamemnon** (ag´ ə mem´ nän) king who led the Greek army during the Trojan War.

© Pearson Education, Inc.

◆ Literary Analysis

Epic heroes like Odysseus face dangerous situations where escape seems unlikely, if not impossible. What does the Cyclops do that puts Odysseus and his men in grave danger?

_____

_____

_____

◆ Stop to Reflect

Judging from his first speech on lines 197–200, do you think the Cyclops wishes to harm Odysseus and his men? Explain.

_____

_____

_____

_____

◆ Reading Check

Mark the Text

In the bracketed speech, Odysseus uses a combination of threats and pleas to influence the Cyclops. Circle the threats and place a P next to any passage where Odysseus pleas for mercy.

from his brute chest, unmoved:

'You are a ninny,
or else you come from the other end of nowhere,
telling me, mind the gods! We Cyclopes
220 care not a whistle for your thundering Zeus
or all the gods in bliss; we have more force by far.
I would not let you go for fear of Zeus—
you or your friends—unless I had a whim[11] to.
Tell me, where was it, now, you left your ship—
225 around the point, or down the shore, I wonder?'

He thought he'd find out, but I saw through this,
and answered with a ready lie:

'My ship?
Poseidon[12] Lord, who sets the earth a-tremble,
broke it up on the rocks at your land's end.
230 A wind from seaward served him, drove us there.
We are survivors, these good men and I.'

Neither reply nor pity came from him,
but in one stride he clutched at my companions
and caught two in his hands like squirming puppies
235 to beat their brains out, spattering the floor.
Then he dismembered them and made his meal,
gaping and crunching like a mountain lion—
everything: innards, flesh, and marrow bones.
We cried aloud, lifting our hands to Zeus,
240 powerless, looking on at this, appalled;
but Cyclops went on filling up his belly
with manflesh and great gulps of whey,
then lay down like a mast among his sheep.
My heart beat high now at the chance of action,
245 and drawing the sharp sword from my hip I went
along his flank to stab him where the midriff
holds the liver. I had touched the spot
when sudden fear stayed me: if I killed him
we perished there as well, for we could never
250 move his ponderous doorway slab aside.
So we were left to groan and wait for morning.

When the young Dawn with fingertips of rose
lit up the world, the Cyclops built a fire

◆ Stop to Reflect

Why do you think Odysseus lies in lines 227–231?

_____

_____

_____

_____

◆ Reading Strategy

Read lines 244–250 in **complete sentences,** ignoring the end of lines. What do you notice about where sentences end?

_____

_____

_____

◆ Literary Analysis

An **epic hero** shows qualities that are admired by that society. Underline the part of the bracketed passage that shows Odysseus' wisdom. Why does Odysseus decide not to attack the Cyclops?

_____

_____

_____

_____

---

11. **whim** (hwim) *n.* sudden thought or wish to do something.
12. **Poseidon** (pō sī´ dən) god of the sea and of earthquakes.

and milked his handsome ewes, all in due order,
255 putting the sucklings to the mothers. Then,
his chores being all <u>dispatched</u>, he caught
another brace[13] of men to make his breakfast,
and whisked away his great door slab
to let his sheep go through—but he, behind,
260 reset the stone as one would cap a quiver.[14]
There was a din[15] of whistling as the Cyclops
rounded his flock to higher ground, then stillness.
And now I pondered how to hurt him worst,
if but Athena[16] granted what I prayed for.
265 Here are the means I thought would serve my turn:

a club, or staff, lay there along the fold—
an olive tree, felled green and left to season[17]
for Cyclops' hand. And it was like a mast
a lugger[18] of twenty oars, broad in the beam—
270 a deep-sea-going craft—might carry:
so long, so big around, it seemed. Now I
chopped out a six foot section of this pole
and set it down before my men, who scraped it;
and when they had it smooth, I hewed again
275 to make a stake with pointed end. I held this
in the fire's heart and turned it, toughening it,
then hid it, well back in the cavern, under
one of the dung piles in profusion there.
Now came the time to toss for it: who ventured
280 along with me? whose hand could bear to thrust
and grind that spike in Cyclops' eye, when mild
sleep had mastered him? As luck would have it,
the men I would have chosen won the toss—
four strong men, and I made five as captain.

285 At evening came the shepherd with his flock,
his woolly flock. The rams as well this time,
entered the cave: by some sheepherding whim—
or a god's bidding—none were left outside.
He hefted his great boulder into place
290 and sat him down to milk the bleating ewes
in proper order, put the lambs to suck,
and swiftly ran through all his evening chores.
Then he caught two more men and feasted on them.

Vocabulary Development: dispatched (dis pacht´) *v.* finished quickly

---

13. **brace** (brās) *n.* pair.
14. **cap** (kap) **a quiver** (kwiv´ ər) close a case holding arrows.
15. **din** (din) *n.* loud, continuous noise; uproar.
16. **Athena** (ə thē´ nə) goddess of wisdom, skills, and warfare.
17. **felled green and left to season** chopped down and exposed to the weather to age the wood.
18. **lugger** (lug´ ər) *n.* small sailing vessel.

◆ **Reading Check**

Underline the passage that explains how the Cyclops makes sure that the men will not escape.

◆ **Literary Analysis**

What heroic qualities does Odysseus show as he prepares to fight the Cyclops?

_____

_____

_____

_____

_____

_____

◆ **Reading Check**

What does Odysseus find to use as a weapon against the Cyclops?

_____

_____

_____

_____

_____

_____

_____

_____

We usually do not think of dishonesty as a heroic quality. Defend Odysseus' actions in the bracketed section. What reasons can you offer for the hero to lie in this situation?

_____

_____

_____

_____

_____

_____

_____

What is the gift that the Cyclops promises to give Odysseus?

_____

_____

_____

_____

295   My moment was at hand, and I went forward
holding an ivy bowl of my dark drink,
looking up, saying:

                    'Cyclops, try some wine.
Here's liquor to wash down your scraps of men.
Taste it, and see the kind of drink we carried
300   under our planks. I meant it for an offering
if you would help us home. But you are mad,
unbearable, a bloody monster! After this,
will any other traveler come to see you?'

He seized and drained the bowl, and it went down
so fiery and smooth he called for more:

305   'Give me another, thank you kindly. Tell me,
how are you called? I'll make a gift will please you.
Even Cyclopes know the wine grapes grow
out of grassland and loam in heaven's rain,
but here's a bit of nectar and ambrosia!'[19]

310   Three bowls I brought him, and he poured them
   down.
I saw the fuddle and flush come over him,
then I sang out in cordial tones:

                    'Cyclops,
you ask my honorable name? Remember
the gift you promised me, and I shall tell you.
315   My name is Nohbdy: mother, father, and friends,
everyone calls me Nohbdy.'

                    And he said:
"Nohbdy's my meat, then, after I eat his friends.
Others come first. There's a noble gift, now.'

Even as he spoke, he reeled and tumbled backward,
320   his great head lolling to one side; and sleep
took him like any creature. Drunk, hiccuping,
he dribbled streams of liquor and bits of men.

Now, by the gods, I drove my big hand spike
deep in the embers, charring it again,
325   and cheered my men along with battle talk
to keep their courage up; no quitting now.
The pike of olive, green though it had been,

---

19. **nectar** (nek´ tər) **and ambrosia** (am brō´ zhə) drink and food of the gods.

reddened and glowed as if about to catch.
I drew it from the coals and my four fellows

330   gave me a hand, lugging it near the Cyclops
as more than natural force nerved them; straight
forward they sprinted, lefted it, and rammed it
deep in his crater eye, and leaned on it
turning it as a shipwright turns a drill

335   in planking, having men below to swing
the two-handled strap that spins it in the groove.
So with our brand we bored[20] that great eye socket
while blood ran out around the red-hot bar.
Eyelid and lash were seared; the pierced ball

340   hissed broiling, and the roots popped.

                     In a smithy
one sees a white-hot axhead or an adze
plunged and wrung in a cold tub, screeching steam—
the way they make soft iron hale and hard—:
just so that eyeball hissed around the spike.

345   The Cyclops bellowed and the rock roared round him,
and we fell back in fear. Clawing his face
he tugged the bloody spike out of his eye,
threw it away, and his wild hands went groping;
then he set up a howl for Cyclopes

350   who lived in caves on windy peaks nearby.
Some heard him; and they came by divers[21] ways
to clump around outside and call:

                     'What ails you,
Polyphemus?[22] Why do you cry so sore
in the starry night? You will not let us sleep.

355   Sure no man's driving off your flock? No man
has tricked you, ruined you?'

                     Out of the cave
the mammoth Polyphemus roared in answer:
'Nohbdy, Nohbdy's tricked me, Nohbdy's ruined me!'

To this rough shout they made a sage[23] reply:

360   'Ah well, if nobody has played you foul
there in your lonely bed, we are no use in pain
given by great Zeus. Let it be your father,
Poseidon Lord, to whom you pray.'

Vocabulary Development: mammoth (mam´ əth) *adj.* enormous

---

20. **bored** (bôrd) *v.* made a hole in.
21. **divers** (dī´ vərz) *adj.* several; various.
22. **Polyphemus** (päl´ ə fē´ məs)
23. **sage** (sāj) *adj.* wise.

◆ **Reading Strategy**

Circle the place in the text where the sentence that begins on line 329 is complete.

Mark THE Text

◆ **Reading Check**

What does Odysseus do to blind Polyphemus?

_____

_____

_____

_____

◆ **Reading Check**

1. In the first underlined passage, what does Polyphemus mean?

_____

_____

_____

2. What do the other Cyclopes understand in the second underlined passage?

_____

_____

_____

they trailed away. And I was filled with laughter

365 to see how like a charm the name deceived them.
Now Cyclops, wheezing as the pain came on him,
fumbled to wrench away the great doorstone
and squatted in the breach with arms thrown wide
for any silly beast or man who bolted—

370 hoping somehow I might be such a fool.
But I kept thinking how to win the game:
death sat there huge; how could we slip away?
I drew on all my wits, and ran through tactics,
reasoning as a man will for dear life,

375 until a trick came—and it pleased me well.
The Cyclops' rams were handsome, fat, with heavy
fleeces, a dark violet.

Three abreast

I tied them silently together, twining
cords of willow from the ogre's bed

380 then slung a man under each middle one
to ride there safely, shielded left and right.
So three sheep could convey each man. I took
the woolliest ram, the choicest of the flock,
and hung myself under his kinky belly,

385 pulled up tight, with fingers twisted deep
in sheepskin ringlets for an iron grip.
So, breathing hard, we waited until morning.

When Dawn spread out her fingertips of rose
the rams began to stir, moving for pasture,

390 and peals of bleating echoed round the pens
where dams with udders full called for a milking.
Blinded, and sick with pain from his head wound,
the master stroked each ram, then let it pass,
but my men riding on the pectoral[24] fleece

395 the giant's blind hands blundering never found.
Last of them all my ram, the leader, came,
weighted by wool and me with my meditations.
The Cyclops patted him, and then he said:

'Sweet cousin ram, why lag behind the rest

400 in the night cave? You never linger so,
but graze before them all, and go afar
to crop sweet grass, and take your stately way
leading along the streams, until at evening
you run to be the first one in the fold.

405 Why, now, so far behind? Can you be grieving
over your Master's eye? That carrion rogue[25]

Reading Check

What is Odysseus' plan for escaping from the Cyclops?

_____

_____

_____

_____

Literary Analysis

Which important heroic qualities does Odysseus show by coming up with his plan?

_____

_____

_____

_____

Reading Strategy

Read the bracketed passage aloud with the vocal expression you imagine the giant might use. Draw a vertical line wherever you pause. How did **reading in complete sentences** help you to imagine the way the Cyclops talks?

_____

_____

_____

---

24. **pectoral** (pek´ tər əl) *adj.* located on the chest.
25. **carrion** (kar´ ē ən) **rogue** (rōg) repulsive scoundrel.

and his accurst companions burnt it out
when he had conquered all my wits with wine.
Nohbdy will not get out alive, I swear.
410 Oh, had you brain and voice to tell
where he may be now, dodging all my fury!
Bashed by this hand and bashed on this rock wall
his brains would strew the floor, and I should have
rest from the outrage Nohbdy worked upon me.'

415 He sent us into the open, then. Close by,
I dropped and rolled clear of the ram's belly,
going this way and that to untie the men.
With many glances back, we rounded up
his fat, stiff-legged sheep to take aboard,
420 and drove them down to where the good ship lay.
We saw, as we came near, our fellows' faces
shining; then we saw them turn to grief
tallying those who had not fled from death.
I hushed them, jerking head and eyebrows up,
425 and in a low voice told them: 'Load this herd;
move fast, and put the ship's head toward the
    breakers.'
They all pitched in at loading, then embarked
and struck their oars into the sea. Far out,
as far offshore as shouted words would carry,
430 I sent a few back to the adversary:

'O Cyclops! Would you feast on my companions?
Puny, am I, in a cave man's hands?
How do you like the beating that we gave you,
you damned cannibal? Eater of guests
435 under your roof! Zeus and the gods have paid you!'

The blind thing in his doubled fury broke
a hilltop in his hands and heaved it after us.
Ahead of our black prow it struck and sank
whelmed in a spuming geyser, a giant wave
440 that washed the ship stern foremost back to shore.
I got the longest boathook out and stood
fending us off, with furious nods to all
to put their backs into a racing stroke—
row, row, or perish. So the long oars bent
445 kicking the foam sternward, making head
until we drew away, and twice as far.
Now when I cupped my hands I heard the crew
in low voices protesting:

                                'Godsake, Captain!
Why bait the beast again? Let him alone!'

◆ Reading Check

How do Odysseus and his companions escape from the Cyclops?

_____

_____

_____

_____

_____

◆ Literary Analysis

An **epic hero** is larger than life
but usually also has some human
failings.

1. What is Odysseus doing in the
bracketed passage?

_____

_____

_____

2. What human weakness does
Odysseus' behavior reveal?

_____

_____

_____

◆ Reading Check

How are Odysseus' actions putting
his entire crew at risk?

_____

_____

_____

'That tidal wave he made on the first throw
all but beached us.'

'All but stove us in!'
'Give him our bearing with your trumpeting,
he'll get the range and lob a boulder.'

'Aye
He'll smash our timbers and our heads together!'
455 I would not heed them in my glorying spirit,
but let my anger flare and yelled:

'Cyclops,
if ever mortal man inquire
how you were put to shame and blinded, tell him
Odysseus, raider of cities, took your eye:
460 Laertes' son, whose home's on Ithaca!'

At this he gave a mighty sob and rumbled:
'Now comes the weird[26] upon me, spoken of old.
A wizard, grand and wondrous, lived here—Telemus,[27]
a son of Eurymus;[28] great length of days
465 he had in wizardry among the Cyclopes,
and these things he foretold for time to come:
my great eye lost, and at Odysseus' hands.
Always I had in mind some giant, armed
in giant force, would come against me here.
470 But this, but you—small, pitiful and twiggy—
you put me down with wine, you blinded me.
Come back, Odysseus, and I'll treat you well,
praying the god of earthquake[29] to befriend you—
his son I am, for he by his avowal
475 fathered me, and, if he will, he may
heal me of this black wound—he and no other
of all the happy gods or mortal men.'

Few words I shouted in reply to him:

'If I could take your life I would and take
480 your time away, and hurl you down to hell!
The god of earthquake could not heal you there!'

At this he stretched his hands out in the darkness
toward the sky of stars, and prayed Poseidon:

---

26. **weird** (wird) *n.* fate or destiny.
27. **Telemus** (tel e´ məs)
28. **Eurymus** (yōo rim´ əs)
29. **god of earthquake** Poseidon.

Literary Analysis

In the bracketed section, underline the word that shows the emotion that is causing Odysseus to risk the safety of his men.

Stop to Reflect

How do you think Polyphemus feels?

_____

_____

_____

_____

Reading Check

Underline the passage that tells the prophecy that has come to pass. What surprised Polyphemus about how events happened?

_____

_____

_____

_____

_____

_____

'O hear me, lord, blue girdler of the islands,
485   if I am thine indeed, and thou art father:
grant that Odysseus, raider of cities, never
see his home: Laertes' son, I mean,
who kept his hall on Ithaca. Should destiny
intend that he shall see his roof again
490   among his family in his father land,
far be that day, and dark the years between.
Let him lose all companions, and return
under strange sail to bitter days at home.'

In these words he prayed, and the god heard him.
495   Now he laid hands upon a bigger stone
and wheeled around, titanic for the cast,
to let it fly in the black-prowed vessel's track.
But it fell short, just aft the steering oar,
and whelming seas rose giant above the stone
500   to bear us onward toward the island.

There
as we ran in we saw the squadron waiting,
the trim ships drawn up side by side, and all
our troubled friends who waited, looking seaward.
We beached her, grinding keel in the soft sand,
505   and waded in, ourselves, on the sandy beach.
Then we unloaded all of Cyclops' flock
to make division, share and share alike.
Only my fighters voted that my ram,
the prize of all, should go to me. I slew him
510   by the seaside and burnt his long thighbones
to Zeus beyond the stormcloud, Cronus'[30] son,
who rules the world. But Zeus disdained my
    offering:
destruction for my ships he had in store
and death for those who sailed them, my
    companions.
515   Now all day long until the sun went down
we made our feast on mutton and sweet wine,
till after sunset in the gathering dark
we went to sleep above the wash of ripples.

Vocabulary Development: titanic (ti tan´ ik) *adj.* of great size or strength

---

30. **Cronus** (krō´ nəs) Titan who was ruler of the universe until he was overthrown by his son Zeus.

◆ Stop to Reflect

Beginning on line 484, Polyphemus calls on Poseidon to curse Odysseus. What do you think will happen as a result of the underlined passage?

_____
_____
_____
_____
_____
_____

◆ Literary Analysis

What admirable qualities does Odysseus show in what he does with the stolen sheep?

_____
_____
_____
_____
_____

◆ Reading Check

Underline the words that tell what the future holds for Odysseus' ship and his companions.

Think about what you know of Odysseus.

1. What are his strengths?

_____

_____

_____

_____

2. What are his weaknesses?

_____

_____

_____

_____

3. Why does he make a good **epic hero**?

_____

_____

_____

_____

When the young Dawn with fingertips of rose
520   touched the world, I roused the men, gave orders
      to man the ships, cast off the mooring lines:
      and filing in to sit beside the rowlocks
      oarsmen in line dipped oars in the gray sea.
      So we moved out, sad in the vast offing,[31]
525   having our precious lives, but not our friends.

_____

31. offing (ôf´ əin) *n.* distant part of the sea visible from the shore.

Reader's Response: What part of the story did you find most exciting? Explain.

_____

_____

_____

Thinking About the Skill: Why is reading in sentences useful when you read an epic poem?

_____

_____

_____

_____

Part 2

Selection Summaries With Alternative Reading Strategies

Part 2 contains summaries of all selections in *Prentice Hall Literature: Timeless Voices, Timeless Themes*. An alternative reading strategy follows each summary.

- Use the selection summaries in Part 2 to preview what you will read in *Prentice Hall Literature: Timeless Voices, Timeless Themes*.

- Read the selection in *Prentice Hall Literature: Timeless Voices, Timeless Themes*.

- Use the alternative reading strategies in Part 2 to guide your reading or to check your understanding of the selection.

"The Cask of Amontillado" by Edgar Allan Poe

Summary This spine-tingling tale of vengeance is set in Italy during carnival season. Montresor, a man from an old aristocratic family, seeks revenge against his one-time friend Fortunato. Knowing that Fortunato prides himself on his ability to judge fine wine, Montresor lures his victim to the family palace to judge a cask of Amontillado sherry. The men descend twisted stairways to an underground tunnel, past burial caves, to a room in which the wine is supposedly stored. Once inside, Montresor chains Fortunato to the wall and then walls up the entrance from the outside. As the entrance wall rises, Fortunato moans, protests, and finally suggests that the whole incident is a joke. Montresor ignores the pleas. When he places the last stone in the wall, he hears only the bells jingling on Fortunato's holiday costume.

Resumen Este escalofriante relato ocurre en Italia, durante el Carnaval. Montresor, un aristócrata, busca vengarse de Fortunato, quien había sido su amigo. Montresor sabe que Fortunato se enorgullece de poder reconocer buenos vinos y lo invita a su palacio para que pruebe un jerez Amontillado. Los hombres descienden por una escalera en espiral hasta un túnel, pasan frente a tumbas, y llegan a un cuarto, donde supuestamente está el vino. Una vez adentro, Montresor encadena a Fortunato a la pared y comienza a tapiar la entrada del cuarto. Fortunato se queja, protesta y finalmente cree que todo es una broma. Montresor no le hace caso y continúa tapiando la entrada. Cuando finalmente coloca la última piedra, sólo escucha los cascabeles del disfraz de Fortunato.

Form a Mental Picture Good readers picture in their mind's eye what an author describes. Listen to the audiocassette recording of the story as you read. Picture each scene as you listen. Use this page to jot down notes to describe what you picture in your mind. Then work with a partner to draw sketches of what Poe describes in each of the following five scenes.

1. Fortunato's costume in the street
2. The passage through the vaults
3. The prison chamber
4. Fortunato chained to the wall
5. Montresor building the wall

_____

_____

_____

_____

_____

_____

_____

_____

_____

_____

_____

_____

"The Most Dangerous Game" by Richard Connell

Summary This spine-tingler is set on an island in the Caribbean Sea. Rainsford, an expert hunter, is traveling by boat in search of big game. He accidentally falls overboard and is forced to swim to a nearby mysterious island. There, he comes upon a palace owned by a General Zaroff. Over dinner, Zaroff explains that since hunting animals is no longer a challenge, he now stocks the island with more interesting game—shipwrecked sailors. Shocked, Rainsford refuses to join the hunt. He quickly learns, however, that *he* will be the hunted and can leave only if he stays alive for three days. Cornered on the third evening, Rainsford jumps into the sea. Confident that Rainsford has drowned, Zaroff returns to his room. Rainsford, however, is already there. Zaroff is killed by his prey.

Resumen Este espeluznante relato ocurre en una isla del mar Caribe. Rainsford, un experto cazador, viaja en bote en busca de caza mayor, cuando accidentalmente cae al agua. Rainsford nada hasta una misteriosa isla, donde encuentra un palacio que es propiedad de un tal general Zaroff. En la cena, Zaroff le explica que para él la caza mayor ya no es un reto y que por eso, ahora se dedica a cazar náufragos. Sorprendido, Rainsford se rehusa a cazar seres humanos. Pronto, Rainsford se da cuenta de que él será la presa y que sólo podrá dejar la isla si consigue eludir a Zaroff por tres días. En la tarde del tercer día, Rainsford está acorralado y se arroja al mar. Creyendo que su presa se ha ahogado, Zaroff vuelve a su cuarto. Allí lo espera Rainsford y Zaroff es muerto por su presa.

Identify Chain of Events Part of the fun of a good story is finding out what happens next and what happens in the end. As you read a story or as you watch a movie, you probably anticipate, or think about, what will happen next. As you read "The Most Dangerous Game," use a Chain of Events organizer like the one below to keep track of what happens.

Begin with the conversation between Whitney and Rainsford on board the boat. Then draw boxes joined by arrows to mark each event in the story. The first two boxes have been modeled for you.

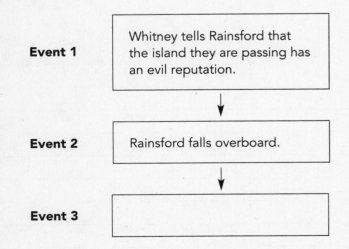

Event 1 — Whitney tells Rainsford that the island they are passing has an evil reputation.

Event 2 — Rainsford falls overboard.

Event 3

Name _____ Date _____

"Casey at the Bat" by Ernest Lawrence Thayer

Summary A classic narrative poem about baseball, "Casey at the Bat" captures the sights, sounds, and excitement of a game in only a few lines of verse. With the score two to four in the bottom of the ninth, the Mudville baseball team seems sure to lose. Two men are out; then two batters get on base. That brings star player Casey to bat as the crowd cheers. A cocky Casey entertains the fans and sneers at the pitcher. Casey lets the first two pitches go by, and the fans object to the umpire calling them strikes. At the third pitch, Casey finally makes a mighty swing—and strikes out.

Resumen Éste clásico poema de béisbol, *Casey at the Bat,* captura en unos pocos versos el espectáculo, los sonidos y la emoción de un partido de béisbol. El anotador está dos a cuatro, es el fin de la novena entrada y parece casi seguro que el equipo de Mudville va a perder. Hay dos hombres afuera y dos bateadores en base. Es entonces cuando Casey, la estrella del equipo, va a batear, en medio de la ovación de la multitud. Muy seguro de sí mismo, Casey entretiene a los aficionados y se burla del lanzador. Casey deja pasar las dos primeras bolas, y los aficionados protestan la decisión del árbitro que las considera *strikes.* Cuando lanzan la tercera bola, Casey batea con toda su fuera, y no conecta.

Translate Baseball Phrases This poem uses many words and phrases in unusual, colorful expressions that characterize the language of baseball. In order to understand what is happening, you need to "translate" these expressions into plain English. Sometimes a dictionary will tell you what these words mean. Sometimes you may need to ask someone familiar with the language of baseball to explain the phrases to you.

Look for these colorful words and phrases in the poem. Figure out what the underlined words mean, and write a translation in the second column. Add more words and phrases to the first column as you read.

Baseball Phrases	Translation
1. It looked rocky for the Mudville nine.	Rough, difficult—as it would be to travel on a road covered with rocks
2. Cooney died at second.	_____ _____
3. Blakey tore the cover off the ball.	_____ _____
4. Flynn was a-huggin' third.	_____ _____
5. Five thousand tongues applauded.	_____ _____
6. The pitcher ground the ball into his hip.	_____ _____

"The Birds" by Daphne du Maurier

Summary In a terrifying tale of the random violence of nature, the peace and beauty of an isolated English farm are shattered by hundreds of murderous birds. Nat Hocke, his wife, and their two children first notice that the birds seem restless. That night a small flock bangs against the outside of the cottage. As Nat rushes to bolt the windows, dozens of birds attack his eyes and arms. He then charges upstairs to discover fifty birds in his children's bedroom. In daylight, the birds grow quiet; Nat prepares to protect his family from another attack. After another night of terror, Nat and his family awake to find their neighbors pecked to death and carcasses of dead birds strewn across the farm. The story ends with Nat shoring up the cottage as still larger birds splinter the doors.

Resumen Este relato muestra un aspecto siniestro de la naturaleza cuando cientos de pájaros homicidas destruyen la paz y belleza de un remota granja inglesa. Nat Hocke, su esposa y sus dos niños, notan primero un nerviosismo en los pájaros. Luego, una pequeña bandada se arroja contra las ventanas de la casa. Nat corre a cerrarlas y los pájaros lo picotean en los ojos y brazos. Nat luego corre al piso alto, donde descubre cincuenta pájaros en el cuarto de los niños. En el día, los pájaros se calman y Nat se prepara para proteger a su familia de otro ataque. Después de otra noche de terror, Nat y su familia descubren a sus vecinos muertos a picotazos, y a pájaros muertos por toda la granja. El relato termina con Nat reforzando la casa mientras los pájaros más grandes comienzan a astillar las puertas.

Use a Timeline This story builds in suspense from day to day. Work with a partner to divide the story into days. Use a chart like the one below to record the events of each day in the order in which they happen.

Timeline

Day 1 Events	Day 2 Events	Day 3 Events

Name _____ Date _____

"The Red-headed League" by Sir Arthur Conan Doyle

Summary In this spine-tingler, Sherlock Holmes uses his powers of observation and deductive reasoning to solve the mystery of an elaborate deception. Jabez Wilson, the red-haired owner of a small pawnshop, was employed by a group called "The Red-headed League" for four hours a day for eight weeks, after which his job was mysteriously eliminated. Wilson had learned of the job from his assistant, who volunteered to watch the pawnshop while the owner was away. Piecing the clues together, Holmes quickly suspects that the assistant is a notorious thief named John Clay who, Holmes surmises, set Wilson up with the phony job so that he could dig a tunnel from the shop cellar to a nearby bank. That night, Holmes and his trusted colleague Dr. Watson catch the criminals red-handed.

Resumen En esta selección, Sherlock Holmes usa sus poderes de observación y de deducción para resolver el misterio de un engaño. Jabez Wilson, un pelirrojo dueño de una casa de empeños, trabajaba cuatro horas por día para el grupo *The Red-headed League*, cuando su trabajo es misteriosamente eliminado. Wilson se había enterado del trabajo por su asistente, quien había ofrecido encargarse del negocio cuando Wilson estuviera trabajando. Usando las pistas, Holmes sospecha que el asistente es John Clay, un ladrón famoso, y que éste había engañado a Wilson con un trabajo falso, y así poder hacer un túnel desde el sótano del negocio hasta un banco vecino. Esa noche, Holmes y su colega, el Dr. Watson, capturan a los criminales *in fraganti*.

Break Down Sentences Many of the sentences in this story are four or five lines long—or even longer. To help you understand the long sentences, break them down into parts. For example:

Sentence: I had called upon my friend, Mr. Sherlock Holmes, one day in the autumn of last year and found him in deep conversation with a very stout, florid-faced, elderly gentleman with fiery red hair.

Sentence broken into parts: Last autumn I had called upon my friend, Mr. Sherlock Holmes. I found him in deep conversation with an elderly gentleman. The elderly gentleman was very stout and florid-faced. He had fiery red hair.

Find at least four more sentences that are four or more lines long. Break them into parts. Compare your sentences with those of your classmates.

1. _____
   _____
   _____

2. _____
   _____
   _____

3. _____
   _____
   _____

4. _____
   _____
   _____

Name _____ Date _____

"The Listeners" by Walter de la Mare
"Beware: Do Not Read This Poem" by Ishmael Reed
"Echo" by Henriqueta Lisboa

Summary These three poems begin and end in mystery, with images that hint at possibilities, not solutions. In "The Listeners," a man knocks on the moonlit door of a house. Inside, phantoms hear his voice but they do not answer. He senses their presence, shouts that he has kept his word, and then rides off on his horse. "Beware: Do Not Read This Poem" tells two stories. In the first story, a woman and other people disappear into a mirror. The second story is the tale of what happens to the reader who disappears into the poem. "Echo" describes parrots screaming in the jungle, their screams echoing off the rocks, but concludes that despite the blood-chilling sound, "no one died."

Resumen Éstos tres poemas comienzan y terminan en un misterio, y sus imágenes sugieren posibilidades, no soluciones. En *The Listeners*, un hombre llama a la puerta de una casa, iluminada por la luna. Adentro, fantasmas escuchan su voz pero no le responden. El hombre siente la presencia de los fantasmas, les grita que él ha mantenido su palabra y se aleja galopando. *Beware: Do Not Read This Poem*, trata de dos historias. Primero, una mujer y otras personas desaparecen en un espejo. Segundo, el poema cuenta qué le sucede al lector que desaparece en el poema. *Echo*, describe a loros gritando en la selva, el eco de sus gritos que rebota en las rocas y termina diciendo que, a pesar del escalofriante sonido, "nadie murió."

Restate Poetry as Prose Some poets write without punctuation or capital letters and use unusual symbols and spellings. Only the lines and their placement on the page help you follow the meaning. "Beware: Do Not Read This Poem" is written this way. In order to understand the poem better, you could rewrite the text of the poem as if it were prose. For each stanza of the poem, add capital letters, punctuation, and standard spelling to help you follow the meaning. For example, the first stanza would look like this:

> Tonight, *Thriller* was about an old woman, so vain she surrounded herself with many mirrors. It got so bad that finally she locked herself indoors and her whole life became the mirrors.

Choose one poem to rewrite as prose. If you choose "Echo," rewrite the entire poem. If you choose "Beware: Do Not Read This Poem," rewrite a stanza. If you choose "The Listeners," Rewrite from lines 8–10.

_____

_____

_____

_____

_____

_____

_____

_____

_____

Name _____ Date _____

"Caucasian Mummies Mystify Chinese" by Keay Davidson

Summary What's mysterious about mummies? This news article reports the discovery of more than 100 mummified bodies in a desert in northwestern China—Caucasian, not Asian, mummies. With their blond hair and white skin, these 4,000-year-old mummies alter the traditional view of Chinese history and suggest that China has been influenced by other civilizations throughout its long history. Remarkably, these bodies are preserved well enough to allow scientists to conduct DNA testing to discover who the mummies were and where they came from. The article reports that the discovery so baffled Chinese scholars that they kept the news to themselves for several years. According to the report, "It just didn't make sense to them."

Resumen ¿Cuál es el misterio de las momias? Este artículo nos estremece con la noticia de que, en un desierto del noroeste de China se han descubierto 100 cuerpos momificados. Las momias no son de asiáticos, sino de caucásicos. Con su pelo rubio y piel blanca, estas momias de 4,000 años cambian completamente la interpretación tradicional de la historia de China y sugieren la influencia de otras civilizaciones. Las momias están suficientemente bien preservadas como para que se puedan realizar pruebas de ADN y establecer quiénes eran y de dónde venían. El artículo afirma que el descubrimiento desconcertó tanto a los estudiosos chinos que por años fue un secreto. Según el artículo, "Simplemente, no tenía sentido para ellos."

Analyze Sources Newspaper reporters write about many subjects, but they're not experts on all of them. Reporters rely on authorities whom they interview for information. "Caucasian Mummies Mystify Chinese" refers to many such authorities. The one most often quoted is Victor Mair. As you read the article, look for the reporter's use of Mair's exact words—those words inside quotation marks with Mair's name before or after. Make a list of at least five important details provided by Mair or other authorities in the article.

Quotation	Details

Name _____ Date _____

from *A Lincoln Preface* by Carl Sandburg

Summary This selection reflects the admiration Sandburg felt for the president who led the nation through the Civil War and afterward was assassinated. The author brings Abraham Lincoln's contradictory character to life through stories, recollections, and quotations. During the war, Lincoln held near dictatorial powers and brought about tremendous social and economic changes. When he died in April 1865, the nation, which had been reluctant to reelect him, mourned deeply. Sandburg shows Lincoln to be a man of contrasts—possessing a great sense of humor and insight into people, sometimes cunning and manipulative, often gracious and merciful. Sandburg crafts a portrait of a man determined to save the Union at all costs.

Resumen Esta selección refleja la admiración que Sandburg sintió por el presidente que condujo a la nación durante la Guerra Civil y que murió asesinado. El autor muestra el complejo carácter de Lincoln a través de historias, recuerdos y citas. Durante la guerra, Abraham Lincoln tuvo poderes casi dictatoriales e introdujo tremendos cambios sociales y económicos. Cuando murió, en abril de 1865, la nación que se había mostrado reacia a reelegirlo, sintió un dolor profundo. Sandburg muestra a Lincoln como a un hombre de contrastes, con gran sentido del humor y una gran intuición, a veces astuto y manipulador, con frecuencia cortés y misericordioso. Sandburg crea el retrato de un hombre determinado a salvar la Unión a toda costa.

Summarize This excerpt from *A Lincoln Preface* is made up of many little stories, or anecdotes. Most (but not all) paragraphs begin a new story. Choose ten of the anecdotes and write a one-sentence summary of each. Two have been modeled for you. When you finish, compare your summaries to those of your classmates.

1. A guard left his watch at the door, and Lincoln was shot and killed.

2. During Lincoln's presidency, the bloody Civil War brought much loss of property.

3. _____

4. _____

5. _____

6. _____

7. _____

8. _____

9. _____

10. _____

Name _____ Date _____

"I Have a Dream" by Martin Luther King, Jr.
from *Rosa Parks: My Story* by Rosa Parks with Jim Haskins
"There Is a Longing . . ." by Chief Dan George
"I Hear America Singing" by Walt Whitman

Summary Persuasive, exhilarating, and inspiring, these four selections describe the struggle for civil rights and the authors' visions of the United States. Martin Luther King, Jr., dreams that blacks and whites will join in brotherhood, with equal opportunity for all. Rosa Parks tells firsthand about her refusal to move to the back of a bus to allow white people to sit down. Her act sparked the civil rights movement of the 1960's. Chief Dan George longs to see his fellow Native Americans freed from the hardships and mistakes of the past, and living in dignity with a sense of worth and purpose. Walt Whitman captures the spirit of the United States by celebrating the diversity of voices in the workplace—from the mechanic to the mason.

Resumen Persuasivas, vívidas e inspiradoras, éstas selecciones describen la lucha por los derechos civiles y la visión de Estados Únidos de cada autor. Martin Luther King, Jr. sueña con negros y blancos unidos como hermanos, y con igualdad de oportunidades para todos. Rosa Parks cuenta de cuando se rehusó a ceder su asiento e ir a la parte posterior de un autobús. Esta acción inició el Movimiento por los derechos civiles de la década 1960–1970. El Jefe Dan George anhela ver a sus hermanos, los indígenas americanos, libres de las penurias y errores del pasado, viviendo con dignidad, con autoestima y propósito en sus vidas. Walt Whitman captura el espíritu de Estados Únidos al celebrar la diversidad de voces en el lugar de trabajo, desde el mecánico hasta el albañil.

Identify Key Ideas The writers of these selections talk about civil rights and their vision of the United States. In a small group, take turns reading the selections aloud. Read each prose selection one paragraph at a time, and each poem one stanza at a time. As you read, make a list of the rights or dreams each writer names or suggests. When you are finished, compare your list with those of your classmates. The first entry has been done for you.

"I Have a Dream"

1. All created equal

2. Brotherhood

3. Freedom

4. Justice

5. Judge people by character, not color

6. Walk as equals

7. Land of liberty

from *Rosa Parks: My Story*

"There Is a Longing"

"I Hear America Singing"

"The Golden Kite, the Silver Wind" by Ray Bradbury

Summary In this fable, two cities are locked in a rivalry. Messengers bring word to each ruler, or Mandarin, about the wall of the rival town. Each time the Mandarin of one city changes his wall, the Mandarin of the other city changes his. One wall is shaped like a pig; the other, an orange. Since pigs eat oranges, the orange-shaped wall is changed to a club. Clubs beat pigs, so another wall is changed. And so it goes until the effort to alter the walls makes the people of both cities exhausted and sick. The two leaders finally meet and agree to make one wall in the shape of the wind, the other in the shape of a kite. Without wind, kites cannot fly; without kites, the sky is dull. The message is clear: Cooperation helps everyone involved.

Resumen En esta fábula hay dos ciudades rivales. Los mensajeros llevan noticias a los gobernantes, o mandarines, acerca de las murallas de la ciudad rival. Cada vez que un mandarín cambia sus murallas, el otro cambia las suyas. Una muralla tiene forma de cerdo; la otra de naranja. Como los cerdos comen naranjas, la muralla en forma de naranja es cambiada por la de un garrote. Los garrotes golpean a los cerdos. Y así continúa todo hasta que el trabajo de cambiar las murallas hace que la gente de ambas ciudades se enferme y empiece a morir. Los dos líderes se encuentran y acuerdan hacer una muralla en forma de viento y la otra en forma de cometa. Sin viento las cometas no pueden volar, sin cometas el cielo es aburrido. El mensaje es claro: la cooperación es mejor para todos.

Recognize Cause and Effect Listen to the audiocassette recording of the story. Make a cause-and-effect chart like the one below to show how each city wall changes as a result of the change in the other city's wall. The first line of the chart has been done for you.

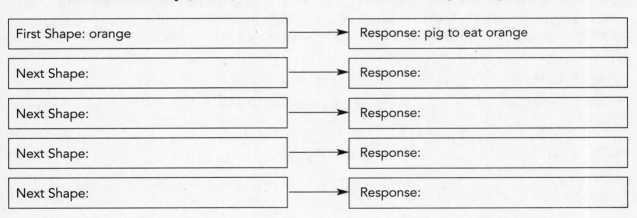

Walls of First City (Cause)   **Other City's Response (Effect)**

First Shape: orange → Response: pig to eat orange

Next Shape: _____ → Response: _____

Next Shape: _____ → Response: _____

Next Shape: _____ → Response: _____

Next Shape: _____ → Response: _____

Name _____ Date _____

"The Road Not Taken" by Robert Frost
"New Directions" by Maya Angelou
"To Be of Use" by Marge Piercy

Summary These three selections celebrate the strength of the human spirit, as characters make choices at decisive points in their lives. In "The Road Not Taken," the speaker chooses a road that few people have traveled and reflects on how that choice has affected his life. In "New Directions," a poor woman left alone to take care of her small children is offered few opportunities. She decides to start a business of her own. With hard work and commitment, she turns the business into a success and finds the fulfillment she is seeking. In "To Be of Use," the speaker celebrates people who work hard, find meaning in their work, and give themselves wholly to the task at hand.

Resumen Éstos tres poemas celebran la fuerza del espíritu humano representado por tres personajes que toman decisiones en momentos determinados de sus vidas. En *The Road Not Taken,* el narrador elige un camino que poca gente recorre y reflexiona sobre cómo esa decisión ha afectado su vida. En *New Directions,* a una mujer pobre, que debe criar sola a sus niños, se le presentan muy pocas oportunidades. Ella decide empezar su propio negocio. Con dedicación, y mucho trabajo, la mujer logra que su negocio sea un éxito y halla la satisfacción que buscaba. En *To Be of Use,* la narradora elogia a la gente que trabaja duro, halla satisfacción en su trabajo y se entrega por completo a lo que hace.

Paraphrase Sometimes poetry seems hard to understand, the ideas hard to find. Sometimes, the best way to tackle poetry is to read it a sentence, or phrase, at a time, pausing at punctuation marks rather than at the end of each line. In a small group, take turns reading aloud "The Road Not Taken" and "To Be of Use." When you get to the end of a sentence—that is, to a period or semicolon—restate, or paraphrase, that part in your own words. For example, the first sentence in "The Road Not Taken" is the first five lines, up to the semicolon. Your paraphrase of that sentence might be something like this:

> When I came to a fork in the road, I knew I couldn't go both ways, so I just looked down one way as far as I could see.

Take turns reading one of the poems and writing the sentences in your own words. When you finish, compare your sentences with those of your classmates.

_____
_____
_____
_____
_____
_____
_____
_____
_____
_____
_____

Name _____ Date _____

"Old Man of the Temple" by R. K. Narayan

Summary In this fantasy tale set in India, the reader must decide what is fantasy and what is real. The story opens with a man and his driver on a lonely rural road at night. Doss, the driver, suddenly swerves the car, shouting at an old man. The narrator, however, sees no one. Doss claims to see the old man at the temple door, then in the car. The narrator, wondering about Doss's condition, sees Doss pass out. When awakened, Doss assumes an old man's personality. As he talks with the narrator, Doss claims to be Krishna Battar, a temple builder. The narrator tells Battar that he is dead and that he should join his deceased wife, Seetha. Battar falls, and Doss awakens as his old self. They learn that a strange knocking at the temple door had for years disturbed neighbors and animals. It occurred no more.

Resumen En este cuento fantástico que ocurre en la India, el lector debe decidir qué es fantasía y qué es real. Empieza con el narrador y Doss, su chófer, viajando de noche por una carretera rural. Doss repentinamente desvía el coche, y grita a un hombre viejo. El narrador no ve a nadie. Doss dice ver al viejo en la puerta de un templo y después en el coche. Luego, Doss pierde el conocimiento y cuando se recupera, tiene la personalidad del viejo. Doss le dice al narrador que su nombre es Krishna Battar, constructor de templos. El narrador le dice a Battar que está muerto, que debería reunirse con Sheeta, su mujer, también muerta. Cuando Battar se cae, Doss se despierta con su antigua personalidad. El narrador y Doss se enteran de que, por años, extraños golpes en la puerta del templo habían inquietado a los vecinos. Los golpes no ocurrieron más.

Prepare a Readers Theater This story contains narration and dialogue. With three classmates, plan a Readers Theater presentation of this story. Assign the four parts as follows:

  One of you should read the narrator's thoughts.
  Another should read the narrator's spoken words.
  The third should be Doss.
  The fourth should be Krishna Battar.

  Practice reading your parts as a group. Battar should sound like an old man with "a thin, piping voice." The narrator and Doss should sound younger but mature. When you have practiced, present your Readers Theater to the class, or tape it to play for the class. Then ask your classmates to evaluate your performances.

  Use the lines below to assign roles and jot down ideas about your performance.

Role	Student
1. Narrator's thoughts	_____
2. Narrator's spoken words	_____
3. Doss	_____
4. Krishna Battar	_____

Performance Ideas _____

_____

_____

_____

"Perseus" by Edith Hamilton

Summary This Greek myth is a tale of adventure. It begins with a god telling King Acrisius that his grandson will kill him. Alarmed, the king casts his daughter Danaë and her son, Perseus, into the sea. They are rescued by Dictys. They live with him and his wife for many years until Polydectes, the ruler of the island, plots to marry Danaë and get rid of Perseus. Unaware of the ruler's intentions, Perseus promises the head of the monster Medusa as a wedding gift. After years of travel, and help from the gods, Perseus returns with Medusa's head. He kills Polydectes. Then he and his mother search for the old king. They find him quite by accident at an athletic contest. When Perseus throws a discus, he hits a spectator—the old king. The king dies. The prophecy comes true.

Resumen En este mito griego, un dios le dice al viejo rey Acrisius que su nieto lo matará. Alarmado, el rey abandona a su hija Danaë y a su nieto Perseus en el mar. Danaë y Perseus son rescatados por Dictys, y viven con él y su mujer varios años hasta que Polydectes, el gobernante de la isla, planea casarse con Danaë y deshacerse de Perseus. Sin conocer los planes del gobernante, Perseus le promete la cabeza de Medusa como regalo de bodas. Luego de viajar por años, y con la ayuda de los dioses, Perseus regresa con la cabeza de Medusa. Mata a Polydectes y luego, él y su madre buscan al viejo rey. Lo encuentran por accidente en un torneo deportivo. Cuando Perseus lanza el disco, éste golpea a un espectador: el viejo rey Acrisius. El rey muere, y se cumple así la profecía.

Identify Characters Keeping track of who's who in a story like "Perseus" aids understanding. Make your own "Who's Who" chart like the one below. First, name a character. Then, define the relationship between that character and other characters. Finally, list an important idea to identify him or her. The character Medusa has been done for you as an example.
Include these characters in your "Who's Who" list:

Acrisius	Polydectes	Athena	Cepheus
Danaë	Gorgons	Gray Women	Apollo
Zeus	Medusa	Hyperboreans	Electryon
Perseus	Selli	Andromeda	Hercules
Dictys	Hermes	Cassiopeia	

Character	Relationship to Other Characters	Important Idea About Character
Medusa	one of the three ugly Gorgons	turned to stone anyone who looked at her

"Slam, Dunk, & Hook" by Yusef Komunyakaa
"The Spearthrower" by Lillian Morrison
"Shoulders" by Naomi Shihab Nye

Summary In these three poems, the characters face physical challenges. In "Slam, Dunk, & Hook," basketball players use their strength and skill in stiff competition. "The Spearthrower" honors women who compete in track with crowds cheering the heroines. "Shoulders" reminds readers that we must look out for one another in the same way that a man protectively carries his son asleep on his shoulder. Not all challenges are found in sports contests; everyday life has its challenges as well.

Resumen Los personajes de éstos tres poemas se enfrentan a desafíos físicos. En *Slam, Dunk, & Hook,* unos basquetbolistas se exigen al extremo usando fuerza física y habilidad en reñida competición. *The Spearthrower,* honra a las mujeres que compiten en eventos de pista, con multitudes que las alientan. *Shoulders,* nos recuerda que debemos protegernos unos a otros, de la misma manera en que un padre protege a su hijo cuando lo lleva dormido sobre sus hombros. Porque el exigirse al extremo no ocurre sólo en los deportes; la vida diaria es también un desafío.

Explain Poetic Phrases Some groups of words in these poems may be confusing. One way to understand unfamiliar phrases is to explain or restate the words and phrases in everyday language. Get together with two or three of your classmates, and determine how the following excerpts from "Slam, Dunk, & Hook," might be restated in everyday language. Two explanations have been given. Restate other lines from the poem at the end of the list.

Confusing Phrases	Translation
1. Mercury's insignia on our sneakers	1. Mercury was a winged messenger; the sneakers are so marked by their manufacturer to make the players feel that they're flying.
2. Hot swish of strings	2. Sound of the ball going fast through the net; "hot" suggests the friction generated by the speed of the shot.
3. Roundhouse labyrinth our bodies created	3. _____
4. High note hung there a long second	4. _____
5. Corkscrew up	5. _____
6. Metaphysical when girls cheered	6. _____
7. Muscles were a bright motor	7. _____
8. Metal hoop nailed to our oak	8. _____
9. _____	9. _____
10. _____	10. _____

"Children in the Woods" by Barry Lopez

Summary In this poetic work of nonfiction, the author shares his thoughts on how to help children make the discoveries that enable them to understand their world. On a walk in the Cascade Mountain forest that surrounds his house, he and a group of children find a fragment of a raccoon's jaw. With this find, the children learn how different aspects of the natural world fit together. The author learns the importance of fostering the process of discovery rather than teaching the technical names for skeletal parts, plants, and animals. Understanding the relationships among parts of the whole in nature becomes a metaphor for how we can understand our own place in the world.

Resumen En este poético ensayo, el autor comparte sus pensamientos sobre cómo ayudar a los niños a hacer descubrimientos que los ayuden a entender su mundo. Durante una caminata por los bosques que rodean su casa, el autor y un grupo de niños encuentran un fragmento de la mandíbula de un mapache. Con este hallazgo, los niños aprenden cómo están relacionados distintos aspectos de la naturaleza. Por su parte, el autor aprende la importancia de alentar el proceso de descubrimiento en vez de simplemente enseñar los nombres de las partes del esqueleto, de las plantas y los animales. Entender las relaciones entre las partes de un todo en la naturaleza se convierte así en una metáfora sobre cómo entender nuestro propio lugar en el mundo.

Outline Author's Argument "Children in the Woods" is a nonfiction essay in which the author presents his ideas about how children should be taught to appreciate and understand the natural world. To help you follow the author's reasoning, make an outline that lists the main ideas and supporting details for each paragraph. Use the lines below to make notes on the main ideas and supporting details as you read.

_____

_____

_____

_____

_____

_____

_____

_____

_____

_____

_____

_____

_____

_____

_____

_____

Name _____ Date _____

"Rules of the Game" by Amy Tan

Summary In this story set in San Francisco's Chinatown, a generational tug-of-war is complicated by a conflict between Chinese and American cultures. As a young person of Chinese parentage who is growing up in the United States, nine-year-old Waverly is learning the unwritten and often unspoken rules of life while she learns the rules of chess. After her brother Vincent gets a used chess set, Waverly's fascination with the game blossoms. She challenges her brothers, the men at the park, and finally tournament players, eventually beating them all. Frustrated by her mother's tendency to "show her off," Waverly rebels and faces the toughest game of her life: how to deal with generational and cultural differences.

Resumen En este cuento ambientado en el barrio chino de San Francisco, las tensiones entre generaciones se complican aún más por el conflicto entre las culturas china y estadounidense. Waverly, una niña estadounidense de nueve años e hija de padres chinos, está aprendiendo las reglas no escritas, y muchas veces no mencionadas de la vida, al mismo tiempo que aprende las reglas del ajedrez. Después de que su hermano obtiene un juego usado de ajedrez, su fascinación por este juego florece. Waverly desafía a sus hermanos, a los hombres del parque y hasta a jugadores expertos, derrotando a todos. Frustrada por la tendencia de su madre a "exhibirla", Waverly se rebela y enfrenta el juego más difícil de su vida: cómo resolver las diferencias entre generaciones y culturas.

Respond to Characters' Actions In "Rules of the Game," the narrator explains how her actions conflict with her mother's wishes. As you read, you may agree or disagree with what the narrator says and does. To record your responses to her actions and those of other characters, make a chart like the one below. In the first column, list the character's name. In the second, tell what the character does. In the third, tell what you think about each character's actions. Share your chart with your classmates. The first example has been modeled for you.

Character	What the Character Does	Your Reaction to What He/She Does
Mrs. Jong	She tells Waverly not to nag her to buy plums.	She sounds like a typical mother.

"Checkouts" by Cynthia Rylant
"Fifteen" by William Stafford

Summary In these two selections, characters learn something about themselves as they experience lost opportunities. In "Checkouts," a teenage girl and a bag boy in the supermarket are attracted to each other, and yet they never act on those feelings. In "Fifteen," a boy chances upon a riderless motorcycle with the engine still running. Although he thinks about how thrilling it would be to take the motorcycle for a spin, the boy instead helps the injured owner. In both of these selections, the authors use irony, or a discrepancy between what the reader expects and what really happens, to capture the contradictory impulses of young people.

Resumen En éstas dos selecciones, los personajes pierden oportunidades pero aprenden algo sobre sí mismos. En *Checkouts*, una adolescente y un muchacho que trabaja en un supermercado se sienten atraídos pero nunca hacen nada para investigar esos sentimientos. En *Fifteen*, un muchacho encuentra una motocicleta con el motor en marcha y sin conductor. El muchacho admira la motocicleta e imagina lo apasionante que sería montarse en ella y andar por las rutas, pero en vez de hacerlo ayuda al conductor que está herido. En ambas selecciones, los autores usan la ironía, o una discrepancia entre lo que el lector espera que ocurra y lo que en realidad sucede, para capturar los impulsos contradictorios de los jóvenes.

Analyze Characters' Behavior Read "Checkouts" with a partner, one or two paragraphs at a time. As you read, make a character analysis chart like the one below. In the first column of the chart, write what the girl in the story does. In the second column, write why she does what she does. Then add the checkout boy to the chart, and list his actions and why he does what he does. The first entry has been done for you.

Use the same kind of character analysis chart for "Fifteen." Compare your explanations with those of your classmates.

"Checkouts"

Character	What the Character Does	Why the Character Does It
The girl	She spends days going through old pictures.	She misses her old life.

"Sympathy" by Paul Laurence Dunbar
"Caged Bird" by Maya Angelou
"We never know how high we are" by Emily Dickinson
from *In My Place* by Charlayne Hunter-Gault

Summary These four selections tell about the way that dreams drive our secret lives, and suggest that a dream is part of our identity. In "Sympathy," the poet sympathizes with a caged bird that so wants to escape that it beats its wings bloody against the bars. It sings a plea for freedom. In "Caged Bird," the poet compares the caged bird with the free bird, lyrically describing how the caged bird sings for freedom. "We never know how high we are" celebrates people's accomplishments and our ability to rise to an occasion. In the excerpt from *In My Place*, the author shares her experience in 1961 of being the first African American to enroll at the University of Georgia. She and a fellow student suffered threats and physical danger, but their dreams held fast.

Resumen Estas cuatro selecciones sugieren que nuestros sueños manejan nuestros anhelos más secretos y son parte de nuestra identidad. En *Sympathy*, el poeta sabe qué siente un pájaro enjaulado que anhela tanto escapar que golpea sus alas contra las rejas hasta ensangrentarlas. En *Caged Bird*, la autora compara al pájaro enjaulado con el pájaro libre, describiendo líricamente su canto por la libertad. *We never know how high we are*, elogia los logros de la gente y su habilidad para hacer frente a todo. En el pasaje de *In My Place*, la autora describe su experiencia como la primera estudiante afroamericana matriculada en la Universidad de Georgia en 1961. Ella y otro estudiante recibieron amenazas y corrieron peligro físico, pero mantuvieron sus sueños con firmeza.

Compare and Contrast Images One way to compare themes in different works of literature is to compare and contrast the images that writers use to express their theme. The poets of "Sympathy" and "Caged Bird" both use the same image—a bird in a cage. Using a Venn Diagram like the one below, compare and contrast the image in these poems. Write the differences in the outer sections of the circles. Write the similarities in the overlapping part of the circles.

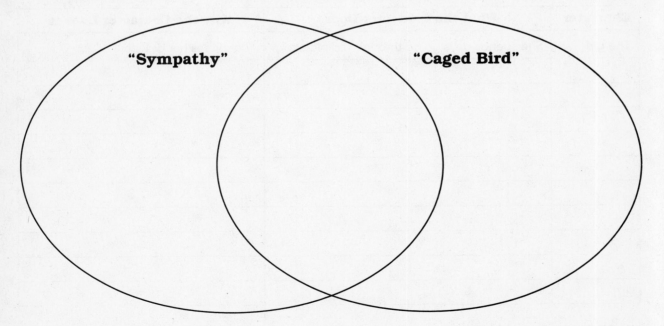

Name _____ Date _____

"The Interlopers" by Saki (H. H. Munro)

Summary In this story, a catastrophe helps people discover what's truly important in life. Two men meet in a forest, prepared to kill each other because of a long-standing dispute over a piece of land. Before they can act, however, a storm knocks down a tree, pinning the pair to the ground. Badly hurt and unable to move, they continue to quarrel, vowing to fight until death. After threatening one another, they lie silently waiting to be rescued. One man, Ulrich, manages to open his flask, and he offers the other, Georg, a sip of wine. Georg refuses, but Ulrich makes an effort to end the feud. Georg agrees. Together they shout for help and soon hear the sound of movement in the woods. Ulrich can make out nine or ten figures approaching. Unfortunately, the figures are not men but wolves.

Resumen En este cuento una catástrofe ayuda a dos hombres a descubrir qué es realmente importante en la vida. Los hombres se encuentran en un bosque para matarse uno al otro de por una antigua disputa sobre tierras. Sin embargo, antes de que puedan hacerlo, un árbol cae sobre ellos y los inmoviliza. Malheridos y sin poder moverse, continúan peleando, y prometen hacerlo hasta la muerte. Luego se callan y esperan por ayuda. Uno de ellos, Ulrich, le ofrece al otro, Georg, un trago de vino. Georg lo rehusa, pero Ulrich continúa su esfuerzo para terminar la disputa. Al fin, Georg acepta. Juntos gritan para lograr socorro y pronto escuchan movimientos en el bosque. Ulrich ve nueve o diez figuras que se acercan. Desgraciadamente, no son hombres sino lobos.

Follow Dialogue Most of this story consists of dialogue between the two characters, Georg, the poacher, and Ulrich von Gradwitz, the landowner. Play the audiocassette recording of the story as you follow along in your book. Listen carefully to the dialogue between Ulrich and Georg. Then make a dialogue flow chart like the one below to follow the conversation between the two characters. The first few bits of conversation have been charted for you. When you finish, compare your flow chart with those of your classmates.

Poacher Georg	Landowner Ulrich
"So you're not killed . . . but you're caught, anyway. . . . there's real justice for you!"	"I'm caught in my own forest land. . . . you will wish, perhaps, you weren't caught poaching on a neighbor's land."

"The Rug Merchant" by James A. Michener

Summary In this nonfiction work, the author makes discoveries about other people that help him see himself in a new way. The setting is a hotel in the Middle East. A thin, toothy man with an irresistible smile rides up on a camel, walks into a room, and throws dozens of beautiful carpets on the floor. The author protests that he doesn't have any money. For four days, the rug merchant persists. Finally, he persuades the author to make a purchase by offering to ship four rugs to the United States and accepting only a hand-written check as payment. It takes five years before the author's check clears and the rugs arrive. Why? As it turns out, the rug merchant used the author's improvised check (and his good name) as an advertisement to customers around the world.

Resumen El autor de este relato de no ficción descubre cosas sobre otra gente que lo ayudan a verse a sí mismo desde una nueva perspectiva. Un hombre delgado, de dientes grandes y sonrisa irresistible llega a un hotel del Medio Oriente montado en un camello, entra en un cuarto y arroja al suelo docenas de hermosas alfombras. El autor dice que no tiene dinero pero el vendedor de alfombras insiste por cuatro días. Finalmente, persuade al autor de hacer una compra con la asombrosa oferta de enviar cuatro alfombras a Estados Unidos y aceptando un cheque como pago. Toma cinco años para que el cheque se cobre y lleguen las alfombras. ¿Por qué? Resulta que el vendedor de alfombras usó el cheque del autor como un anuncio para otros clientes en otras partes del mundo.

Question Author's Purpose As you read a nonfiction work you should ask yourself why the writer gives you the information in the way that he or she does. Make a record of "The Rug Merchant" by asking a question for each paragraph and writing an answer to your question. A sample question and answer for the first three paragraphs have been modeled below.

1. **Q:** Why does Michener tell about the mosque and the man with the rugs?

   A: Michener introduces the reader to his subject with the story of how he first met the rug merchant.

2. **Q:** Who is this man with the rugs?

   A: He is a salesman.

3. **Q:** What does the man want Michener to do?

   A: He wants him to examine the rugs.

Name _____ Date _____

"Combing" by Gladys Cardiff
"Women" by Alice Walker
"maggie and milly and molly and may" by E. E. Cummings
"Astonishment" by Wisława Szymborska

Summary In these four poems, the speakers explore their identities through family connections, nature, and an appreciation of the world around us. "Combing" describes how women in different generations discover who they are as they fix each other's hair. "Women" addresses the strength of the women who paved the way for future generations. In "maggie and milly and molly and may," four girls identify with the treasures of the sea—shells, starfish, crabs, and stones. In "Astonishment," the poet explores some fundamental questions about life: why she is here at this particular time in this particular place.

Resumen Las mujeres en estos cuatro poemas exploran sus identidades a través de conexiones familiares, la naturaleza y una apreciación del mundo que nos rodea. *Combing* describe cómo mujeres de distintas generaciones descubren quiénes son mientras se ayudan a peinarse. *Women* se refiere la fortaleza de las mujeres que abrieron senderos para futuras generaciones. En *maggie and milly and molly and may*, cuatro niñas se identifican con los tesoros del mar: caracolas, estrellas de mar, cangrejos y piedras. En *Astonishment*, la poeta explora algunas preguntas fundamentales sobre la vida: ¿por qué está aquí, en este momento y lugar específicos?

Connect In these poems, the characters explore their identities by making connections to family, other generations, nature, or their place in the universe. For each poem, list a character, whom or what that character connects with, and what is discovered through this connection. The first one has been modeled for you.

Character	Connects with Whom or What?	What is discovered?
Speaker in "Combing"	other generations of women in her family	Combing hair is something that connects the generations of women in her family.

Name _____ Date _____

"The Secret Life of Walter Mitty" by James Thurber

Summary In this story, Walter Mitty, an ordinary man, leaves his tiresome day-to-day existence behind as he imagines himself a hero in a number of bold and exciting situations. His daydreams are triggered by common events on a shopping trip with his wife. Driving to town, he sees himself as a navy officer leading his ship through a hurricane. Passing a hospital, he imagines himself as a world-famous surgeon saving the life of a multimillionaire. Intermittently, events bring him back to reality—his wife nags him about his driving and, later, he nearly has an accident in the parking lot. As Mitty continues his shopping expedition, each errand triggers another daydream. The contrast between his secret life and his real life provides some genuinely comic moments.

Resumen En esta historia, Walter Mitty, un hombre común, escapa de su aburrida vida diaria imaginándose que es el héroe de situaciones emocionantes y audaces. Sus sueños son activados por sucesos comunes mientras va de compras con su mujer. Conduciendo hacia la ciudad, Mitty imagina que es un capitán navegando su barco durante un huracán. Al pasar frente a un hospital, Mitty imagina que es un cirujano de fama mundial, salvándole la vida a un multimillonario. Por momentos, distintos sucesos lo vuelven a la realidad: su mujer critica su manera de conducir y, más tarde, está a punto de tener un accidente en el estacionamiento. Y así, cada situación produce otro sueño. El contraste entre su vida secreta y su vida real ofrece algunos momentos verdaderamente cómicos.

Distinguish Between Fantasy and Reality In order to understand this story, you need to recognize when Mitty is daydreaming and when he is not. To help you distinguish between reality and the character's daydream fantasies, look for signals in the story that mark the shifts. Pause at the end of each page and fill in a chart like the following. For each page of the story, list examples of fantasy in the first column and examples of reality in the other. The first entry has been done for you.

Fantasy	Reality
Mitty is a Commander in full-dress uniform.	Mrs. Mitty complains he is driving too fast.

Name _____ Date _____

"The Inspector-General" by Anton Chekhov

Summary In this play, set in Russia in the nineteenth century, a traveler begins asking his driver questions about the newly-appointed inspector-general, a government official appointed by the ruling czar to keep an eye on local affairs. The driver responds with detailed information provided, he says, by gossip from the inspector-general's servants. He tells of the inspector-general's failed attempts to disguise himself, his strange wheezing when he talks, and even his drinking habits. By the end of the story, the reader realizes that the traveler is, in fact, the inspector-general. Although the traveler feels humiliated when his charade backfires, the situation is humorous because he seems to be getting what he deserves.

Resumen Esta obra tiene lugar en Rusia, en el siglo XIX. Un viajero le hace preguntas a su conductor acerca del inspector general, un nuevo funcionario del gobierno designado por el zar para supervisar los asuntos locales. El conductor responde con información detallada, que proviene según él, de los mismos sirvientes del inspector general. El conductor cuenta los fallidos intentos del funcionario para hacerse pasar por otra persona, de su respiración dificultosa al hablar, y hasta de su costumbre de beber. Hacia el fin del cuento, el lector se da cuenta de que el viajero es en realidad el inspector general. Si bien el viajero se siente humillado cuando su estratagema le sale mal, la situación es cómica porque parece ser que él recibe lo que se merece.

Prepare a Readers Theater Plays are written to be performed. Reading a play aloud is more rewarding than reading it silently. With two other classmates, plan a Readers Theater presentation of this play. Each should take one of these three parts:

The Storyteller
The Traveler
The Driver

Practice reading your parts as a group. When you have practiced, present your Readers Theater to the class or record it to play for the class. Then ask your classmates to evaluate your performances.

Use the lines below to assign roles and to jot down ideas about your performance.

Role	Student
1. Storyteller	_____
2. Traveler	_____
3. Driver	_____

Performance Ideas _____

_____

_____

_____

_____

_____

_____

_____

"Go Deep to the Sewer" by Bill Cosby
"Fly Away" by Ralph Helfer

Summary These two selections focus on finding the humor in difficult personal situations. In "Go Deep to the Sewer," comedian Bill Cosby uses sports jargon to describe how he and his boyhood friends used the city streets as ball fields. Sewer covers served as stickball bases. Parked cars made good linebackers. With his humor, Cosby draws parallels between the obstacles on the urban playing fields and the obstacles in life. In "Fly Away," a famous animal trainer, known for his work with dangerous beasts, tells about one of his greatest challenges. He trained 5,000 flies to sit, stay, and then fly away on command for the glory of a Hollywood film. In this humorous remembrance, the author tells his secret early on to allow the reader to sit back and watch the fun.

Resumen Estas selecciones muestran cómo la gente halla humor aun en situaciones difíciles. En *Go Deep to the Sewer*, Bill Cosby cuenta cómo él y sus amigos usaban las calles de la ciudad como campos de béisbol, las tapas del alcantarillado servían como bases de *stickball* y los carros estacionados eran buenas líneas de defensas. Cosby traza paralelos entre los obstáculos de los campos de juego urbanos y los de la vida. En *Fly Away*, un famoso adiestrador de animales cuenta uno de sus mayores retos. Adiestró a 5,000 moscas para que aterrizaran, se quedaran quietas y luego, siguieran volando bajo sus órdenes, en una película de Hollywood. En esta humorística remembranza, el autor revela su secreto al comienzo para permitir que el lector disfrute más de la lectura.

Translate Jargon Much of the humor in these selections comes from the vocabulary. For instance, Cosby uses professional sports jargon to describe street games. To understand unfamiliar jargon from sports or elsewhere, work with a partner to examine the meaning of words or phrases individually. Then translate the jargon into plain English. Practice this strategy on the following phrases. The first two have been done for you. When you finish, add other examples from the stories and translate them as well.

1. Asphalt fields These are the city streets where they played.

2. Allowed almost no lateral movement They couldn't run to either side on the narrow streets.

3. Taking a handoff and sweeping to glory _____

4. Quarterback could diagram plays with trash _____

5. You can hit me at the fender. _____

6. Zig out to the bakery _____

7. You fake goin' in deep and then buttonhook at the DeSoto. _____

8. _____

9. _____

10. _____

"An Entomological Study of Apartment 4A" by Patricia Volk

Summary In this feature article, natural curiosity drives the author to collect the bugs found in her apartment and to take them to an expert for identification. Entomologist Louis Sorkin not only identifies each bug but also explains their habits. As the author and the expert trade humorous remarks, the reader learns a lot about these creatures. By making light of the problem of insects in her home, the author is able to pass on new and interesting details about these unwelcome guests.

Resumen La curiosidad de la autora de este ensayo, la impulsa a coleccionar los insectos que encuentra en su departamento y llevarlos a un experto para que los identifique. El entomólogo Louis Sorkin no sólo identifica cada insecto sino que también explica sus costumbres. Mientras la autora y el experto intercambian bromas, el lector aprende mucho sobre estos seres. Al tratar con humor el problema de tener insectos en su casa, la autora logra hacer conocer nuevos e interesantes detalles sobre estos inoportunos visitantes.

Recognize Puns and Word Play Much of the humor in this selection comes from the clever way the writer uses language. For example, describing the entomologist Louis Sorkin as if he were a bug—"has a prominent forehead, gently rounded abdomen and powerful bandy legs"—sets the tone of amusement for the article. Figure out what is amusing about each of the following phrases from the article, and write your explanation on the back of this page. The first has been modeled for you. Add other words and phrases to your list.

1. A black crawly thing with more legs than the Rockettes The Rockettes are a dancing group that perform at Radio City Music Hall in New York. Their routine is famous for its chorus line of perfectly timed high kicks.

2. We scuttle into a room crammed with journals, papers and boxes of stoppered vials.

3. On the wall, a sign reads, "Feeling Lousy?"

4. Sorkin is the 911 of insect emergencies.

5. Maybe moisturizer kills [certain follicle mites around the nose and forehead].

6. I head home thinking about the high drama that goes on behind the kitchen pegboard.

7. When I put in the chili powder it started to move.

8. Sorkin's personal favorite is grubs over easy.

9. Sorkin is encyclopedic.

10. Sorkin and I nod goodbye and shake hands, a Homo sapiens-specific ritual.

"Macavity: The Mystery Cat" by T. S. Eliot
"Problems With Hurricanes" by Victor Hernández Cruz
"Jabberwocky" by Lewis Carroll

Summary In these poems, the clever use of language and the depiction of amusing characters and events make you laugh out loud. In "Macavity: The Mystery Cat," a criminal cat breaks human laws and laws of gravity. He is suspected of many crimes but is never caught. In "Problems With Hurricanes," the poet combines the serious with the ridiculous for comic effect. An out-of-the-ordinary description of death by flying fruit makes this image of hurricanes hilarious. In "Jabberwocky," the poet uses made-up words to describe a hero battling fearsome beasts. The reader needs to guess at the meaning of these made-up words, which contrast humorously with this tale of daring.

Resumen El ingenioso uso del lenguaje y la descripción de personajes y sucesos cómicos de estos poemas logran despertar las carcajadas del lector. En *Macavity: The Mystery Cat*, un gato criminal rompe no sólo las leyes humanas sino también las de la gravedad. Lo sospechan culpable de muchos delitos pero no lo atrapan nunca. En *Problems with Hurricanes*, el poeta combina lo serio con lo ridículo para lograr un efecto cómico. La descripción de un hecho extraordinario: la muerte causada por fruta que vuela pinta una imagen absurda de los huracanes. En *Jabberwocky*, el autor inventa palabras para describir a un héroe en batalla con bestias terroríficas. El lector necesita adivinar el significado de estas palabras, lo que contrasta humorísticamente con esta historia de valor.

Identify Incongruity Often, the basis for humor is incongruity—the difference between what is expected and what is being described. For example, in "Problems With Hurricanes," the poet describes a serious topic—death—but uses unexpected comical details—death from flying fruit. Read or listen to audiocassette recordings of "Macavity: The Mystery Cat" and "Problems With Hurricanes" and list two or three places in each where the humor comes from the difference between what is expected and what is actually described.

"Macavity: The Mystery Cat" _____

_____

_____

_____

_____

_____

"Problems With Hurricanes" _____

_____

_____

_____

_____

_____

_____

"Talk" by Harold Courlander

Summary A strange and funny folk tale, "Talk" tells about people's reactions when objects speak out, revealing minds of their own. The tale, set in western Africa, begins as a farmer is digging yams. One yam, which has felt neglected all year, tells the farmer to go away and leave him alone. Next, the dog speaks up, the palm tree responds, and a stone talks. Frightened, the farmer runs toward the village. As he meets others along the way, they, too, hear objects talking: a fish trap, a bundle of cloth, the river, and finally the chief's stool. The last line of the story, spoken to the chief by the stool, adds the final bit of humor: "Imagine, a talking yam."

Resumen Esta original y divertido cuento popular, *Talk*, trata de las reacciones de la gente cuando los objetos comienzan a hablar y demuestran tener su propia personalidad. El cuento, ambientado en el oeste de África, comienza con una familia escarbando la tierra en busca de batatas. Una batata, que se ha sentido abandonada todo el año, le dice al granjero que se vaya y la deje tranquila. Luego, el perro comienza a hablar, la palmera le responde y una piedra también habla. Asustado, el granjero sale corriendo hacia el pueblo. A medida que encuentra a otra gente en su camino, ellos también escuchan hablar a las cosas: una trampa para peces, un atado de tela, el río y finalmente, el asiento del jefe. El cuento con un toque de humor: el jefe dice, "Imaginense, una batata que habla."

Read Aloud Folk tales are usually stories that are handed down from generation to generation by being told and retold. In "Talk," the read-aloud quality is particularly strong. Prepare to read the tale aloud. Make a list of the objects that speak, beginning with the yam. Then, with your classmates, choose parts and read the selection aloud. One person should be the narrator. Others should read the parts of the farmer, fisherman, weaver, bather, and chief. Still others should read the parts of the objects that speak. Use this page to assign roles and to jot down ideas about what kind of voice you might use to bring your character to life.

"One Ordinary Day, With Peanuts" by Shirley Jackson

Summary An out-of-the-ordinary man, Mr. John Philip Johnson, seems to have as his goal helping people enjoy life. He entertains the child of a frustrated woman who is busy moving out of her apartment. He helps two people to enjoy a day off together. He gives a man money for lunch. He even gives birds and dogs peanuts. When he arrives home and talks about his work day with his wife, however, she tells about opposite experiences. She has caused people misery by filing complaints and having them arrested. The surprise comes when they agree that the next day they will trade jobs.

Resumen Mr. Philip Johnson parece ser una persona especial, cuya meta es ayudar a la gente a disfrutar de la vida. Entretiene al hijo de una mujer que se está mudando de su departamento. Ayuda a dos personas a disfrutar juntas de un día libre. Da dinero a un hombre para su almuerzo. Hasta le da cacahuates a los perros y los pájaros. Sin embargo, cuando Mr. Johnson llega a su casa y habla con su mujer sobre cómo les fue en el trabajo, ella le cuenta experiencias opuestas. Ella creó problemas a la gente presentando demandas contra ellos y haciéndolos arrestar. La sorpresa llega cuando los esposos acuerdan intercambiar trabajos al día siguiente.

Use a Chain-of-Events Organizer To appreciate a good story, readers should anticipate the events of a story as they unfold. Sometimes a storyteller will intentionally put a twist into a story that the reader could not anticipate.

Use a Chain-of-Events organizer like the following to list the events of the plot in the story as they unfold. Then label each event as predictable or not predictable. For example, it is *not* predictable that Mr. Johnson will give a carnation to the small child in the carriage.

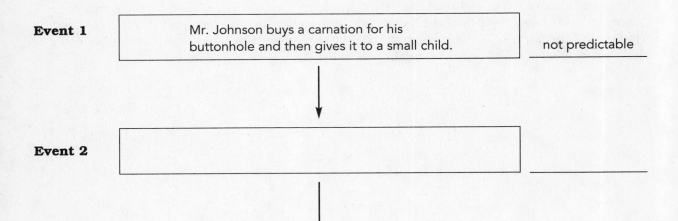

Event 1   Mr. Johnson buys a carnation for his buttonhole and then gives it to a small child.   not predictable

Event 2

Name _____ Date _____

from *The Road Ahead* by Bill Gates

Summary A nonfiction vision of the future, this excerpt from *The Road Ahead* tells about the direction Bill Gates sees for technology in the home. As a child, Gates remembers the frustration of missing a television show on the day and time it was broadcast. Today, video tape recorders (VCRs) allow viewing whenever one wishes, although there is the inconvenience of timers and tapes. In the future, however, movies, television shows, and other kinds of digital information will be stored on servers. Computers will then access video-on-demand for home televisions connected to the broadband network. It will become the money-making venture of the near future.

Resumen Este pasaje de *The Road Ahead*, un ensayo futurista, presenta la visión de Bill Gates sobre la función de la tecnología en el hogar. Gates recuerda la frustración que sufría de niño cuando no podía ver un programa de televisión en el día y hora en que se transmitía. Hoy en día, las videograbadoras (VCR's) permiten ver cualquier programa cuando uno lo desea, si bien todavía tenemos que lidiar con cintas y programadores. Sin embargo, en el futuro, los programas de televisión, y otros tipos de información digitalizada, estarán almacenados en bases de datos. Las computadoras tendrán acceso en todo momento a los videos que se verán en los televisores del hogar conectados a una amplia red de programación. Éste será el negocio más lucrativo del futuro inmediato.

Outline Main Idea and Supporting Details To understand nonfiction, you must find the main ideas and study the details that tell about them. Working with a partner, list the main ideas and supporting details in this excerpt from *The Road Ahead*. Name the main idea for each paragraph. Then list the details that tell about it. The first paragraph has been modeled for you.

Main Idea: When Gates was a child, the only way to see *The Ed Sullivan Show* was to tune in on Sunday night at 8:00.

Details about the Main Idea:

1. Could see famous musicians and other acts

2. If away from TV, too bad

3. If missed show, not part of conversation later

Name _____ Date _____

"The Machine That Won the War" by Isaac Asimov

Summary In this futuristic story, a giant computer named Multivac is credited with winning a war against a rival planet named Deneb. As the three main characters discuss the victory, they reveal their own wartime activities. Henderson admits that he was forced to "correct" computer data that had become meaningless. Jablonsky admits that he knew Multivac was unreliable but did nothing about it. To protect his job, he, too, adjusted data until it looked right. Finally, Swift admits that he hadn't taken the data seriously anyway. In fact, he used the oldest computer available to make his war decisions: the flip of a coin.

Resumen En este cuento sobre el futuro, se dice que la victoria contra Deneb, un planeta rival, ha sido posible gracias a una supercomputadora llamada Multivac. Mientras los tres personajes principales hablan sobre la victoria, cada uno revela lo que hizo durante la guerra. Henderson admite que se vio forzado a "corregir" información que no tenía sentido. Jablonsky admite que él sabía que Multivac no era fiable pero que no había hecho nada al respecto. Para proteger su trabajo, él también había corregido información. Finalmente, Swift admite que él no había creído en la información de cualquier manera. De hecho, él había usado el método más antiguo que existe para tomar decisiones durante la guerra: tirar una moneda.

Paraphrase Conversations Some of the conversations in this story are hard to read because they seem to have so many ideas. One way to make them clear is to paraphrase, or restate, the main idea of the conversation. Choose one sentence spoken by each character—Henderson, Jablonsky, and Swift—and restate the idea of their conversation. Use the example as a guide.

Example:

Henderson: "Do you know to what extent data concerning our production capacity, our resource potential, our trained manpower—everything of importance to the war effort, in fact—had become unreliable and untrustworthy during the last half of the war?"

Paraphrase: Do you realize how inaccurate our information had become in recent years?

Sentence 1 Paraphrase

_____

_____

_____

Sentence 2 Paraphrase

_____

_____

_____

Sentence 3 Paraphrase

_____

_____

_____

"Fire and Ice" by Robert Frost
"All Watched Over by Machines of Loving Grace" by Richard Brautigan
"There Will Come Soft Rains" by Sara Teasdale
"The Horses" by Edwin Muir

Summary In each of these selections, the poets warn readers to consider the possible impact of present events and developments on the future. In "Fire and Ice," the poet considers how the world may be destroyed by either desire or hate, as he considers death by fire or ice. In "All Watched Over by Machines of Loving Grace," the poet believes that machines will free us from labor, improve the quality of our lives, and allow us to appreciate the natural world. In "There Will Come Soft Rains," the poet warns that nothing in the natural world will know or care if people wipe themselves out through war. In "The Horses," a seven days' war brings silence to the earth. The arrival of a herd of horses signals rebirth and renewal as the powerful animals help people cultivate the fields.

Resumen Estos poemas tratan del posible impacto que sucesos y adelantos actuales téndrán en el futuro. En *Fire and Ice*, el poeta considera cómo el mundo podría ser destruido por el deseo o el odio, así como él considera la muerte por fuego o hielo. En *All Watched Over by Machines of Loving Grace*, el autor cree que las máquinas nos librarán del trabajo, mejorarán la calidad de la vida y nos permitirán apreciar al mundo natural. En *There Will Come Soft Rains*, el poeta nos advierte que la naturaleza no se enterará, ni le importará, si la humanidad se autodestruye. Una guerra de siete días trae el silencio a la Tierra en *The Horses*. La llegada de una manada de caballos significa renacimiento y renovación: estos poderosos animales ayudan a la gente a cultivar los campos.

Interpret Poetic Images Poets use images or word pictures to express ideas and feelings. In order to understand what these images express, you must first form a mental picture of them and then decide how that picture makes you feel.

Following are some of the images, or word pictures, from the poems. On the back of this paper, describe the picture that forms in your mind when you read each of these images, and then tell how it makes you feel. The first one has been modeled for you.

"All Watched Over by Machines of Loving Grace"

1. cybernetic meadow
   a grassy field with computers scattered among the flowers—feels like an advertisement for the benefit of computers
2. all watched over/by machines of loving grace

"There Will Come Soft Rains"

1. wild plum trees in tremulous white
2. Robins will wear their feathery fire

"The Horses"

1. old bad world that swallowed its children quick/At one great gulp
2. nations lying asleep/Curled blindly in impenetrable sorrow

"If I Forget Thee, Oh Earth . . ." by Arthur C. Clarke
from *Silent Spring* by Rachel Carson
"To the Residents of A.D. 2029" by Bryan Woolley

Summary These selections examine the future by studying the problems we face today. "If I Forget Thee, Oh Earth. . ." warns about the threat of nuclear destruction, as a small colony of survivors endure a bleak existence on the Moon. Their only hope is that distant descendants might one day return to Earth. In the excerpt from *Silent Spring*, the author warns that environmental disasters might one day destroy the world. In "To the Residents of A.D. 2029," the author writes for future readers about present-day wastefulness and a sense of decline. He remains optimistic, however, and wishes future generations four things: an understanding of history, a better relationship between man and nature, an appreciation of beauty, and a sense of humor.

Resumen Estas selecciones examinan el futuro estudiando los problemas actuales. *If I Forget Thee, Oh Earth* nos alerta sobre el peligro de destrucción nuclear relatando la historia de una pequeña colonia de sobrevivientes en la Luna. Su única esperanza es que un día sus descendientes puedan regresar a la Tierra. En el pasaje de *Silent Spring*, la autora dice que los desastres ecológicos podrían destruir el mundo. En *To the Residents of A.D. 2029*, el autor escribe para futuros lectores sobre el derroche y sentido de declinación actuales. Sin embargo, se mantiene optimista, y desea cuatro cosas para las futuras generaciones: comprensión de la historia, una mejor relación entre la gente y la naturaleza, apreciación de la belleza y sentido del humor.

Identify Predictions Each of the writers in these selections talks about what is happening in an imagined present time in order to show us what they predict will happen in the future. To keep track of the predictions, make a chart like the one below listing details for "Now" and "In the Future." (Remember that "Now" can be a past time or a future time; it need not be "today.")

Selection Title	Now	In the Future (Prediction)
"If I Forget Thee, Oh Earth . . ."	Marvin and father in dome; take vehicle through Outside to see the destroyed Earth.	

Name _____ Date _____

"Gifts" by Shu Ting
"Glory and Hope" by Nelson Mandela

Summary These two selections look to the future with hope for peace among the world's people. "Gifts" asserts that Earth's gifts are simple but profound: ponds, sky, plants, sunlight, children, birds, everything. "Glory and Hope" reflects the author's hope for the future of a beautiful, bountiful South Africa. In a speech delivered at his presidential inauguration, Mandela thanks all who helped, pledges the protection of freedom for all, and vows to work toward amnesty for those still in prison. He pleads for all to work together to prevent future oppression.

Resumen Éstas dos selecciones miran hacia el futuro con la esperanza de paz entre los pueblos del mundo. *Gifts* reflexiona sobre los regalos de la Tierra, que, de tan simples, son profundos: agua, cielo, plantas, sol, niños, pájaros, todo. *Glory and Hope* refleja la esperanza de su autor sobre el futuro de una hermosa y rica África del Sur. Éste es el discurso que Nelson Mandela pronunció el día en que asumió el poder y, en él, Mandela agradece a todos los que ayudaron, promete proteger la libertad para todos y se compromete a trabajar por la amnistía de todos aquéllos que todavía están en prisión. Mandela ruega a todos que trabajen juntos para evitar cualquier intento de opresión en el futuro.

Break Down Long Sentences Breaking sentences into their parts helps you understand long and complicated sentences. Listen to the audiocassette recording of Nelson Mandela's speech. Then work with a partner to break down any sentence that is more than five lines long. Use the example as a model.

Example:

Mandela's Sentence: That spiritual and physical oneness we all share with this common homeland explains the depth of the pain we all carried in our hearts as we saw our country tear itself apart in terrible conflict, and as we saw it spurned, outlawed and isolated by the peoples of the world, precisely because it has become the universal base of the pernicious ideology and practice of racism and racial oppression.

Sentence in Parts: We all share spiritual and physical oneness with this common homeland. That [shared oneness] explains the depth of the pain we all carried in our hearts as we saw our country tear itself apart in terrible conflict. That [shared oneness] also explains the depth of pain we carried as we saw our country spurned, outlawed and isolated by the peoples of the world. [Our country was spurned, outlawed and isolated by the people of the world] because it has become the universal base of the pernicious ideology and practice of racism and racial oppression.

"The Gift of the Magi" by O. Henry

Summary On Christmas Eve, Della realizes that she has only $1.87, a grossly inadequate sum, to buy a present for her husband Jim. Money is a problem for the couple, whose income has just been reduced from $30 to $20 per week. Impetuously, Della decides to sell her prize possession—her hair—in order to buy Jim a platinum fob chain for his prize possession—his watch. When Jim arrives home, he is shocked by Della's appearance, not only because her hair is gone, but also because he has just sold his watch in order to buy his Christmas present for Della—combs for her hair. Such sacrifices, the narrator concludes, are wise. They are the gifts of the magi.

Resumen Una Nochebuena, Della se da cuenta que sólo tiene $1.87, una suma realmente muy pequeña, para comprar un regalo a Jim, su esposo. El dinero es un problema para la pareja, cuyos ingresos se habían visto reducidos de $30 a $20 por semana. Impetuosamente, Della decide vender su más preciada posesión, su cabello, para comprar a Jim una cadena de platino para el reloj que él tanto quiere. Cuando Jim llega a casa, lo sorprende la apariencia de Della, no sólo porque ya no tiene su hermoso cabello, sino porque él acaba de vender su reloj para comprarle su regalo de Navidad, un juego de peines. Estos sacrificios, concluye el narrador, son sabios. Son regalos de los Reyes Magos.

Simplify Word Order Several of the sentences in "The Gift of the Magi" contain unusual words in an unexpected order. For each sentence or sentence part in the following paragraph, restate the sentence in a way that makes sense to you. Change the word order and use more familiar words. The first part of the paragraph has been done for you.

> In the vestibule below was a letter-box into which no letter would go, and an electric button from which no mortal finger could coax a ring. Also appertaining thereunto was a card bearing the name "Mr. James Dillingham Young."

1. In the vestibule below was a letter-box into which no letter would go.

   The mailbox in the hall below was too small for letters.

2. and an electric button from which no mortal finger could coax a ring.

   _____

3. Also appertaining thereunto was a card bearing the name "Mr. James Dillingham Young."

   _____

Choose another paragraph from the story, and practice the strategy of simplifying the word order.

_____

_____

_____

_____

_____

_____

"Sonata for Harp and Bicycle" by Joan Aiken

Summary Jason wonders why employees must leave the office at 5:00 P.M., so he sneaks into the building at night. Inside he encounters a presence asking for Daisy. In the morning Berenice, a co-worker, explains that years ago, Heron, the night watchman, mistakenly thought Daisy had betrayed him when she failed to show up the night he planned to propose. However, she had simply overslept. Distraught, Heron jumped from the fire escape, and Daisy died soon after. Their ghosts have been searching for each other in the office every night since—he riding his bicycle, she playing the harp. That night Jason and Berenice reunite the ghosts by waking Daisy and summoning Heron. Jason and Berenice parachute to the ground and kiss in midair.

Resumen Jason se pregunta por qué los empleados deben salir de la oficina a las 5:00 P.M. Para averiguarlo, una noche se cuela en el edificio. Dentro, Jason encuentra una "presencia" preguntando por Daisy. Por la mañana, Berenice, otra empleada, le explica a Jason que años atrás, Heron, el sereno, pensó que Daisy lo había traicionado porque no había ido la noche que él iba a proponerle matrimonio. Pero Daisy simplemente se había quedado dormida. Enloquecido, Heron se había arrojado de la escalera de emergencia, y Daisy había muerto poco después. Desde entonces, sus espíritus se habían buscado por la oficina. Esa noche, Jason y Berenice reúnen a los espíritus despertando a Daisy y llamando a Heron. Jason y Berenice se arrojan en paracaídas y se besan en el aire.

Explain Comparisons The author of "Sonata for Harp and Bicycle" uses fresh and interesting comparisons to describe the people and places in the story. As you read this selection, write the comparisons you find and tell what you think the author intends by the comparison. Use a chart like the following. Two comparisons from the first few paragraphs of the story have been modeled for you.

Person or thing being described	It is compared to	This comparison suggests
a room	the inside of a parcel	It is a very small room.
darkness	a flight of bats	It is very dark and somewhat frightening.

"The Scarlet Ibis" by James Hurst

Summary The narrator remembers his boyhood with his brother, Doodle. Doodle was different from other children and a disappointment to his brother, who resented the responsibility of caring for him and was sometimes cruel to him. Still, a bond developed between them. Pride drove the narrator to teach Doodle to walk—a feat others had deemed impossible—and to set other physical goals for him. One day Doodle noticed a dying scarlet ibis that had been blown far from its normal range by a storm. Later that day, in the same storm, and only moments after the narrator had cruelly abandoned him, Doodle was struck by lightning and died.

Resumen El narrador recuerda la niñez, compartida con su hermano Doodle. Diferente de otros niños, Doodle fue una desilusión para su hermano, quién resintió tener la responsabilidad de cuidarlo y a veces fue cruel con él. Sin embargo, se formó un vínculo entre ellos. Una cuestión de orgullo hizo que el narrador enseñara a Doodle a caminar, una hazaña que otros creían imposible, y también a establecer otras metas físicas para él. Un día, Doodle halla un ibis carmesí moribundo, que había perdido su camino durante una tormenta. Más tarde, durante la misma tormenta, y sólo unos momentos después de haber sido cruelmente abandonado por su hermano, Doodle muere al ser alcanzado por un rayo.

Classify Descriptive Details "The Scarlet Ibis" is full of descriptive details that appeal to the senses. Read the following passage. Use the chart to tell what you see and hear. List movements, colors, positions, sounds, and other details. One example has been provided in each category. Complete this passage, and then practice the strategy by doing this exercise with another passage from the story.

At that moment the bird began to flutter, but the wings were uncoordinated, and amid much flapping and a spray of flying feathers, it tumbled down, bumping through the limbs of the bleeding tree and landing at our feet with a thud. Its long, graceful neck jerked twice into an S, then straightened out and the bird was still. A white veil came over the eyes and the long white beak unhinged. Its legs were crossed and its clawlike feet were delicately curved at rest.

Movements	fluttering, _____ _____
Colors	white, _____ _____
Positions	neck in S-shape, _____ _____
Sounds	flapping, _____ _____
Other Details	limbs of the bleeding tree, _____ _____

"Blues Ain't No Mockin Bird" by Toni Cade Bambara
"Uncle Marcos" by Isabel Allende

Summary These stories offer two views of memorable people and events from the authors' childhoods. In "Blues Ain't No Mockin Bird," the author recalls a day when two men from the county food-stamp program approached her Granny's home and began filming. Quietly, Granny refused them the right to film but was ignored. She then called for Granddaddy, who—with a show of his physical power—sent the men away. "Uncle Marcos" opens with Uncle Marcos lying in his coffin. A frequent visitor to his sister Nivea's home, Marcos had been a worldly adventurer and the first to bring an airplane to town. Most of all, he had been a friend and soulmate to his niece, Clara.

Resumen En esto relatos los autores recuerdan a gente y sucesos memorables de su niñez. La primera trata del día en que dos hombres del programa de cupones para comida se acercaron a la casa de Granny y comenzaron a filmar. Calmadamente, Granny les dijo que no podían filmar, pero los hombres no le prestaron atención. Granny llamó a Granddaddy, quien, haciendo muestra de su poder físico y mental, logró que los hombres se fueran. La segunda historia comienza con el tío Marcos en su ataúd. Marcos, quién visitaba a menudo la casa de su hermana Nivea, había sido un gran aventurero y el primero en traer un avión a la ciudad. Pero, por sobre todo, había sido el amigo y compañero del alma de su sobrina Clara.

Understand Dialect "Blues Ain't No Mockin Bird" is written in dialect, a way of speaking that is unique to certain people and places. Choose a passage that uses dialect and rewrite it the way you would state it, using your own words and sentences. An example from the story has been done for you. Complete this passage, and then practice the strategy by rewriting another passage from the story.

(1) I'm looking to Cathy to finish the story (2) cause she knows Granny's whole story before me even. (3) Like she knew how come we move so much and (4) Cathy ain't but a third cousin we picked up last Thanksgivin visitin. (5) But she knew it was on account of people driving Granny crazy (6) till she'd get up in the night and start packin. (7) Mumblin and packin and wakin everybody up (8) sayin, "Let's get on away from here before I kill me somebody."

1. I'm waiting for Cathy to finish the story. _____

2. _____

3. _____

4. _____

5. _____

6. _____

7. _____

8. _____

"The Man to Send Rain Clouds" by Leslie Marmon Silko
"The Invalid's Story" by Mark Twain

Summary In these two stories, setting is a key element; it affects the characters and the outcomes. In the first story, an old Indian dies in New Mexico. Leon, a relative, asks the Indian's spirit for much-needed rain. Then just before the burial, he asks the priest to sprinkle holy water on the body. Though upset that no Last Rites were performed, the priest agrees. Leon is happy; now that the spirit has water, perhaps rain will come. In "The Invalid's Story," the narrator tells of a time he accompanied a dead friend's body to Wisconsin. As the trip begins, however, he mistakenly loads the wrong box onto the train. Then someone leaves behind a smelly cheese. He and a train worker think the smell is from the decaying body. The smell grows so bad in the closed car that both men jump from the train into an icy storm. The experience has left the narrator's health ruined.

Resumen En estos dos cuentos, la ambientación es un elemento clave, que afecta tanto a los personajes como al desenlace. En el primero, un indio viejo muere en Nuev Mexico. Leon, un pariente, pide a su espíritu que envíe lluvia. Luego, Leon pide al cura que rocíe el cuerpo con agua bendita. El cura, aunque molesto porque el indio no recibió extremaunción, lo hace. Ahora que el espíritu tiene agua, tal vez llueva. En *The Invalid's Story*, el narrador cuenta de un viaje que hizo a Wisconsin llevando el cadáver de un amigo. Pero sube al tren una caja equivocada y alguien se olvida un queso muy oloroso. Tanta el como un ferroviario creen que el olor viene del muerto. El olor se hace tan fuerte que los dos saltan del tren, en una tormenta de hielo. La experiencia arruinó la salud del narrador.

Identify Cause and Effect In stories, one event often causes another, which in turns causes another event. Identifying these causes and effects will help you understand the story.

Ask yourself why characters do things. What causes them to act? What is the effect? Sometimes a word, such as *because*, signals a cause-and-effect relationship. At other times, you must infer the cause and effect from the facts you are given. Choose one story, find the causes and effects, and list them on a chart like the following. One example from "The Ivalid's Story" has been provided.

Cause	Effect
Hackett's death	the narrator's initial misery

"The Necklace" by Guy de Maupassant
"The Harvest" by Tomás Rivera

Summary These two stories are about people who make discoveries that profoundly affect their lives. In "The Necklace," Madame Loisel borrows a diamond necklace and loses it. Quietly, the Loisels buy a replacement for the necklace by taking a huge loan and sacrificing for ten years to repay it. When Madame Loisel finally admits to the owner what happened, she learns that the necklace did not contain real diamonds. In "The Harvest," Don Trine is seen taking mysterious walks alone at harvest time. Suspicious that money is involved, some youngsters follow him. When Don Trine is discovered "planting" his arms in the earth, everyone thinks he is crazy except one boy. The boy, who copies Don Trine's behavior, feels the power of the sleeping earth just as Don Trine does.

Resumen Los personajes de estos descubren algo que influye profundamente en sus vidas. En *The Necklace*, Madame Loisel toma prestado, y pierde, un collar de diamantes. Los Loisels se sacrifican económicamente por diez años y reemplazan el collar. Cuando Madame Loisel finalmente cuenta lo que ha ocurrido, descubre que los diamantes del collar eran falsos. En *The Harvest*, se ve a Don Trine haciendo solo misteriosas caminatas en época de cosecha. Sospechando que todo eso tiene que ver con dinero, unos jóvenes lo siguen. Cuando descubren a Don Trine "plantando" sus brazos en la tierra, todos creen que está loco. Todos, excepto un joven, quien hace lo mismo que había hecho Don Trine e, igual que Don, siente el poder de la tierra dormida.

Sequence Events Use the following sequence organizer to record the main events in "The Harvest." Some information has already been provided. When you are finished, make your own sequence organizer for "The Necklace."

↓

Rumors get started about Don Trine.

↓

↓

The boys investigate the ditch.

↓

The following Monday, the boys see Don Trine _____

↓

The next day, _____

↓

After that, the boy _____

Name _____ Date _____

"Single Room, Earth View" by Sally Ride

Summary In this selection, Sally Ride gives an account of her experiences and those of other astronauts in space. For example, astronauts are amazed that the Hawaiian islands look just as they do on maps. At orbiting speed, continents zip by, but geological features stand out. Although they are too low to view the entire globe at once, astronauts can see a surprising amount of detail. Signs of civilization are clear, including pollution, but especially, astronauts see the oceans, with intricate patterns from different currents and water colors. Among the most spectacular sights are lighting seen from above and a sunrise seen every ninety minutes.

Resumen Sally Ryde nos ofrece una descripción de sus experiencias y de las de otros astronautas, en el espacio. Por ejemplo, ellos se maravillan de que las islas de Hawai sean iguales a las de los mapas. A esa velocidad, los continentes no se ven bien, pero las formaciones geológicas se destacan. Si bien los astronautas no viajan a suficiente altura para ver toda la Tierra, sí pueden ver una sorprendente cantidad de detalles. Los signos de la civilización son claros, incluyendo la contaminación, pero más que nada, los astronautas pueden ver aguas azules, con intrincados diseños, causados por las diferentes corrientes y aguas de colores. Entre las vistas más espectaculares se encuentran los relámpagos vistos desde arriba y una salida de sol cada 90 minutos.

Identify Main Idea and Supporting Details Paragraphs contain one main idea and details that support that idea. When you read nonfiction, first identify the main idea of a paragraph, and then look for details that tell about the main idea.

The main idea and one detail in the following paragraph have been underlined and listed below. Add two more details that tell about the main idea. Then practice this strategy, using other paragraphs from the story.

Since the space shuttle flies fairly low (at least by orbital standards; it's more than 22,000 miles lower than a typical TV satellite), we can make out both natural and manmade features in surprising detail. Familiar geographic features like San Francisco Bay, Long Island, and Lake Michigan are easy to recognize, as are many cities, bridges, and airports. The Great Wall of China is *not* the only manmade object visible from space.

Main Idea: The space shuttle flies fairly low. _____

Detail: We can make out both natural and manmade features in surprising detail. _____

Detail: _____

Detail: _____

Main Idea: _____

Detail: _____

Detail: _____

Detail: _____

Name _____ Date _____

"The Washwoman" by Isaac Bashevis Singer
"On Summer" by Lorraine Hansberry
"A Celebration of Grandfathers" by Rudolfo A. Anaya

Summary Each of these first-person accounts tells how the author's view of the world was molded by one or more remarkable people. In "The Washwoman," the narrator recalls an old woman who washed his family's clothes when he was a boy. He remembers her hard work, her struggle to endure, and her last visits to his home. In "On Summer," the author explains that she once disliked summer but, over time, came to associate it with people of indomitable will and, therefore, with life lived fully. In "A Celebration of Grandfathers," the author remembers the quiet ways of the "old ones" of his grandfather's generation, who understood the seasons and appreciated the land in which they lived. He urges understanding of, and respect for, grandfathers.

Resumen En cada uno de estos relatos en primera persona, sus autores nos cuentan cómo su visión del mundo fue moldeada por una o más personas extraordinarias. En *The Washwoman*, el autor recuerda a una anciana, que no era judía que lavaba la ropa de su familia cuando él era un niño. Recuerda el duro trabajo de la mujer, su lucha y perseverancia, y sus últimas visitas a la casa del autor. En *On Summer*, la autora nos dice que en una época no le gustaba el verano, pero, con el tiempo, comenzó a asociarlo a gente de voluntad inquebrantable y, por consiguiente, con la vida vivida plenamente. En *A Celebration of Grandfathers*, el autor recuerda la manera tranquila y silenciosa en que los ancianos de la generación de su abuelo entendían las estaciones y el valle donde vivían. Finalmente, nos exorta a respetar y comprender a los abuelos.

Summarize Main Idea To follow the ideas of a nonfiction article, you should pause occasionally and summarize the main ideas you have read so far. For example, the paragraph below from "On Summer" can be summarized in one sentence.

It also seemed to me, esthetically speaking, that nature had got inexcusably carried away on the summer question and let the whole thing get to be rather much. By duration alone, for instance, a summer's day seemed maddeningly excessive; an utter overstatement. Except for those few hours at either end of it, objects always appeared too sharp a relief against backgrounds; shadows too pronounced and light too blinding. It always gave me a feeling of walking around in a motion picture which had been too artsily-craftsily exposed. Sound also had a way of coming to the ear without that muting influence, marvelously common to winter, across patios or beaches or through the woods. I suppose I found it too stark and yet too intimate a season.

Main Idea: <u>The author finds summer to be a very long, uncomfortable season.</u>

Supporting Details: <u>to be rather much, a summer's day seemed maddeningly excessive, objects appeared too sharp, light too blinding</u>

Apply this strategy to other paragraphs from "The Washwoman," "On Summer," or "A Celebration of Grandfathers." Summarize the main idea and list some supporting details.

Name _____ Date _____

from *A White House Diary* by Lady Bird Johnson
"Arthur Ashe Remembered" by John McPhee
"Georgia O'Keeffe" by Joan Didion

Summary These three selections offer insights into memorable people and events from three distinct points of view—a first-person account, a personal remembrance, and a biographical essay. In the first selection, Lady Bird Johnson relates in intimate, personal detail the tragic events of the day President Kennedy was assassinated and her husband assumed the presidency. In the second, John McPhee reveals the mixture of mental control and aggressive play that characterized the life and career of professional tennis player Arthur Ashe. The third selection is an essay paying tribute to artist Georgia O'Keeffe, whom the author describes as an independent woman who rejected convention and created astonishing paintings.

Resumen Estas tres selecciones, nos recuerdan gente y sucesos memorables desde tres puntos de vista distintos: un relato en primera persona, una remembranza y un ensayo autobiográfico. En la primera selección, Lady Bird Johnson ofrece detalles íntimos y personales del día en que el presidente Kennedy fue asesinado y su esposo, Lyndon Johnson, asumió la presidencia. En el segundo, John McPhee revela la mezcla de control mental y juego agresivo que caracterizaron la vida y carrera de Arthur Ashe. La tercera selección es un ensayo que rinde homenaje a la artista Georgia O'Keeffe, a quien el autor describe como a una mujer independiente y fuerte que rechazó las reglas convencionales para dar al mundo sus increíbles pinturas.

Interpret Direct Quotations The authors of these selections often quote the exact words someone spoke to give the reader some special insight into the person or the event. As you read these selections, write the quotations the author provides and interpret, or explain, the insights of each. Use a chart like the one below. Two entries have been made for you.

Quotation	Insight It Provides
Mr. Kilduff entered and said to Lyndon, "Mr. President."	This statement indicates that the burdens of the presidency have suddenly passed to Lyndon Johnson.
I heard a Secret Service man say . . . "We never lost a President in the Service."	Those responsible for guarding President Kennedy felt a deep sense of responsibility for his death.

Name _____ Date _____

"Understanding Comics" by Scott McCloud

Summary Artist Scott McCloud uses comics in this visual essay, in which he himself appears as a comic-book character. McCloud explains that he did not like comics at first, but later became obsessed with them and began making them himself. He says that many people look down on comics, thinking they are all bad art or stupid stories. Scott, though, thinks comics are exciting and powerful, and he feels we need a better definition for them. He illustrates the concept of sequential art and uses it to create this new definition. He and an imaginary audience decide that comics is a medium whose pictures and sequence can not only give information, but can also produce an aesthetic response in viewers.

Resumen El artista Scott McCloud presenta este ensayo como una tira cómica, en la que él mismo es un personaje. McCloud nos dice que al principio no le gustaban las tiras cómicas, pero que luego se obsesionó con ellas y comenzó a crearlas. Él sabe que mucha gente menosprecia a las tiras cómicas y las considera un arte inferior o historias estúpidas. Sin embargo, Scott piensa que las tiras cómicas son apasionantes y poderosas y que necesitamos una mejor definición para ellas. Scott explica el concepto de arte secuencial y lo usa para crear esta nueva definición. Él, y una audiencia imaginaria, deciden que las tiras cómicas son un medio en el que las ilustraciones y la secuencia no sólo dan información, sino que también pueden producir una reacción estética en los lectores.

Translate Cartoon Images If a picture is worth a thousand words, how many words is a cartoon image worth? Work with a partner to restate in words the ideas expressed in the cartoon boxes. Use a chart like the one below. An example has been provided to get you started.

Cartoon Image	Ideas Expressed
First frame: writer/cartoonist at his drawing board	The narrator of the cartoon is the writer himself; his work is done at an easel with lots of helpful equipment around him—a globe, pictures, posters, paints, reference books, and so on.

"Earhart Redux" by Alex Chadwick

In These Girls, Hope Is a Muscle by Madeleine Blais,
a book review by Steve Gietschier

In These Girls, Hope Is a Muscle by Madeleine Blais,
book jacket

Summary These examples of workplace writing reflect three distinct purposes. In "Earhart Redux," the author mixes references of sound effects and skillfully framed questions to capture the inside story of Linda Finch's re-creation of Amelia Earhart's attempt in 1937 to fly around the world. His interview covers Finch's motives, the flight's technical and mechanical similarity to the original flight, and Earhart's legacy. In the book review of *In These Girls, Hope Is a Muscle*, the reviewer applauds Blais's heartfelt, yet gently humorous account of the championship season of a girl's basketball team. Finally, the book jacket promotes the book by quoting reviews, presenting an overview of the story, and commenting on the story's broader significance for the women's movement.

Resumen Cada uno de estos trabajos cumple un propósito diferente. En *Earhart Redux*, el autor combina sonidos, películas y preguntas para capturar la historia verídica del vuelo en que Linda Finch siguió la misma ruta tomada por Amelia Earhart en su intento de volar alrededor del mundo en 1937. Su entrevista considera los motivos de Finch para hacer esto, las similitudes técnicas entre ambos vuelos y el legado histórico de Earhart. En *In These Girls, Hope Is a Muscle*, el autor aplaude el sentido y el humor del relato de Blais sobre la temporada de un equipo femenino de básquetbol. Finalmente, la cubierta del libro promociona al libro citando reseñas y presentando una vista panorámica de la historia y comentando sobre su más amplio significado para el movimiento feminista.

Propose Headlines Newspapers generate interest in their articles with headlines. A good headline states the main idea of the article in as few words as possible. Writing a headline requires a solid understanding of the information in the article.

Check your understanding of these three selections by writing one or more headlines for each selection. Each headline should pinpoint a key idea in the article. Several good headlines are possible for each story. A sample headline has been provided.

Story	Headline
"Earhart Redux"	Earhart's Flight: Can It Really Be Duplicated?
In These Girls, Hope Is a Muscle Book Review	_____ _____
In These Girls, Hope Is a Muscle Book Jacket	_____ _____

Name _____ Date _____

The Dancers by Horton Foote

Summary In this play, set in the 1950's, the characters face some common interpersonal problems: conflicts between a mother and a daughter, friends, and acquaintances. The conflicts begin when Elizabeth Crews arranges a date for her daughter, Emily, with a boy from out of town—without consulting her. A popular girl with a steady boyfriend, Emily is furious about it and refuses to leave her room when Horace comes to pick her up. Dejected, Horace wanders downtown for something to eat. There, he meets a friend of Emily's who agrees to be his date for the dance. Mother and daughter make up, friends reunite, and Horace gains new self-confidence.

Resumen Los personajes de esta obra, que tiene lugar durante la década de 1950, se enfrentan a problemas de relaciones muy comunes: conflictos entre madre e hija, amigos y conocidos. Los conflictos comienzan cuando Elizabeth Crews hace una cita, sin consultarla, entre su hija Emily y un muchacho que no es del pueblo. Emily una chica muy popular, y que ya tiene novio, se enoja y rehusa salir de su cuarto cuando Horace, el muchacho, pasa a buscarla para ir al baile. Descorazonado, Horace camina sin rumbo en busca de un lugar para comer. Allí, se encuentra con una amiga de Emily, que acepta acompañarlo al baile. Madre e hija hacen las paces, los amigos se juntan y Horace gana confianza en sí mismo.

Prepare a Readers Theater With your classmates, plan a reading of the play. Divide the play into scenes, and assign parts for each scene. Students may play more than one part. If you play more than one part, be sure the voice you use for each character is different. Practice your role, listening to the audiocassette recording as you follow your part in your book. Rehearse your part, giving your character an identifiable voice. Then, with your classmates, do a Readers Theater reading of the play. After the presentation, ask your classmates to evaluate your performances.

Use the lines below to assign roles and to jot down ideas about your performance.

Role	Student
Emily	_____
Horace	_____
Mrs. Crews	_____
_____	_____
_____	_____
_____	_____

Performance Ideas: _____

_____

_____

_____

_____

_____

The Tragedy of Romeo and Juliet, Act I, by William Shakespeare

Summary	**Resumen**
The Prologue informs the audience of the tragedy to come.	**El Prólogo** informa al público sobre la tragedia que va a ocurrir.
Scene i A fight between the supporters of rival families, the Capulets and the Montagues, angers the Prince of Verona, who vows to execute Capulet and Montague if it happens again. Romeo, a Montague, is told by a friend to give up his love for a woman we learn is named Rosaline.	**Escena 1** Una pelea entre partidarios de dos familias rivales, los Capulets y los Montagues, enoja al Prince of Verona, que jura hacer ejecutar Capulets y Montagues si hay más peleas. Un amigo le dice a Romeo, un Montague, que renuncie a su amor por Rosaline.
Scene ii Paris wants to marry Capulet's daughter, Juliet. Capulet says that this will happen only if she agrees. He invites Paris to a feast. Seeing that Rosaline is invited, Romeo decides to go as an uninvited masked guest.	**Escena 2** Paris quiere casarse con la hija de Capulet, Juliet, y el padre dice que sí sólo si Juliet consiente. Capulet invita a Paris a una fiesta. Al enterarse que Roseline está invitada, Romeo decide ir a la fiesta enmascarado.
Scene iii Juliet agrees to *consider* marrying Paris to please her mother.	**Escena 3** Juliet acepta *considerar* casarse con Paris para alegrar a su madre.
Scene iv Romeo predicts something terrible will happen.	**Escena 4** Romeo predice que algo terrible va a suceder.
Scene v Romeo and Juliet fall in love. Each learns the other's identity from the nurse.	**Escena 5** Romeo y Juliet se enamoran y se enteran quiénes son a través de la nana.

Summarize Plot In order to follow the action of the play, you need to understand the events as they happen. Review the summary for each scene. With a partner, draw cartoon-strip characters and have them show the main action for each scene. Use simple stick figures for characters—you might add a skirt for Juliet, a hat for the nurse, a sword for Tybalt, a heart for Romeo, and so on, to distinguish one figure from another. Then add dialogue bubbles for each character. Put their words into modern English. When you finish, compare your cartoon strips with those of your classmates. Use this page to sketch some of your ideas.

The Tragedy of Romeo and Juliet, Act II, by William Shakespeare

Summary

The Prologue provides transition from Act I by confirming that Romeo and Juliet are in love.

Scene i Romeo hides in the Capulets' orchard, hoping to see Juliet.

Scene ii Juliet comes to a window. Unaware that Romeo is hiding, she declares her love for him and wishes he weren't a Montague. Romeo steps out and says that he loves her so much that he will give up his name. They plan to elope.

Scene iii Romeo goes to Friar Lawrence to ask him to marry them. The Friar agrees, hoping to bring peace to the families.

Scene iv Mercutio and Benvolio talk about Tybalt's challenge to duel Romeo. Romeo arrives and jokes with Mercutio. He gives Nurse a message for Juliet to meet him that afternoon at the friar's.

Scene v Nurse delivers the message.

Scene vi Friar leads them away to be married.

Resumen

El Prólogo presenta una transición del Primer acto y nos dice que Romeo y Juliet se han enamorado.

Escena 1 Romeo se esconde en el jardín de los Capulets, esperando ver a Juliet.

Escena 2 Juliet sale a la ventana y, sin saber que Romeo esta escondido declara su amor por él y dice que quisiera que no fuera un Montague. Romeo se hace ver y le dice que la ama tanto que abandonaría su nombre por ella. Los dos deciden huir juntos.

Escena 3 Romeo pide a Friar Lawrence que los case. Friar acepta hacerlo para traer paz a las familias.

Escena 4 Mercutio y Benvolio hablan sobre el desafio a duelo que Tybalt hizo a Romeo. Éste llega y bromea con Mercutio. Luego, Romeo le da a la nana un mensaje para que Juliet se encuentre con él esa tarde en lo de Friar Lawrence.

Escena 5 La nana le da el mensaje a Juliet.

Escena 6 Friar lleva a Romeo y Juliet para casarlos.

Analyze Characters You understand characters by what they say, what they do, and what others say about them. Listen to the audiocassette recording of Act II as you follow along in your text. Listen for what characters do and say. Listen for what others say about them. With a partner, make a character chart like the following for these characters. You may not be able to fill in all the columns for each character.

Character	What They Do	What They Say	What Others Say About Them
Romeo			
Juliet			
Nurse			
Benvolio			
Mercutio			
Friar Lawrence			

The Tragedy of Romeo and Juliet, Act III, by William Shakespeare

Summary	**Resumen**
Scene i Mercutio baits Tybalt. Romeo arrives, knows Tybalt is Juliet's cousin, and ignores Tybalt's insults. Mercutio fights with Tybalt and is killed as Romeo tries to stop them. In turn, Romeo kills Tybalt, then flees. The Prince exiles Romeo. **Scene ii** Nurse tells Juliet that Romeo has killed Tybalt and is hiding at Friar's. Juliet gives Nurse a ring for Romeo and asks that he visit her. **Scene iii** Romeo tries to kill himself, but Friar suggests that Romeo see Juliet and then escape to Mantua. **Scene iv** Capulet arranges for Juliet to marry Paris in three days. **Scene v** Juliet and Romeo spend their wedding night together, parting at dawn. Juliet learns she is to marry Paris. She refuses, but her father vows to disown her if she doesn't comply.	**Escena 1** Mercutio provoca a Tybalt. Romeo sabe que Tybalt es primo de Juliet e ignora el insulto. Mercutio pelea en lugar de Romeo y Tybalt lo mata, cuando Romeo trata de separarlos. A su vez, Romeo mata a Tybalt, y huye. El Príncipe destierra a Romeo. **Escena 2** La nana la cuenta a Juliet que Romeo ha matado a Tybalt y que está escondido en lo de Friar. Juliet le da un anillo para Romeo y pide que vaya a verla. **Escena 3** Romeo trata de matarse, pero Friar le sugiere ir a ver a Juliet y que escapen juntos a Mantua. **Escena 4** Capulet hace arreglos para que Juliet se case con Paris en tres días. **Escena 5** Juliet y Romeo pasan juntos su noche de bodas y se separan al alba. Juliet se entera que deberá casarse con Paris. Juliet se rehusa pero su padre jura repudiarla si no lo hace.

Use a Story Map Organizer Take stock of the events of the play that have unfolded before Act III opens. Use a Story Map to record the events that have built the plot so far. For example, you might include the following events: Romeo and Juliet's meeting; Capulet's arrangement for Paris to marry Juliet; Romeo and Juliet's secret marriage; Romeo's fight with Tybalt. Then add other events as you read Act IV. Decide which event should be considered the climax, or high point, of the plot. Compare your Story Map to those of your classmates and discuss the differences between them.

Setting:
> Place Verona, Italy _____
> Time _____

Problem:

Event 1:   Romeo and Juliet meet
Event 2:   Capulet arranges for Paris to marry Juliet
Event 3:   Romeo and Juliet secretly marry
Event 4:
Event 5:

Climax:
(Turning Point)

Name _____ Date _____

The Tragedy of Romeo and Juliet, Act IV, by William Shakespeare

Summary	Resumen
Scene i Juliet seeks help from the Friar and finds Paris there planning their wedding. When Paris leaves, the Friar makes a plan to save Romeo and Juliet. He gives Juliet a trance-inducing drug to take the night before the wedding. Her parents, thinking she is dead, will put her in the crypt. Romeo will be told. He will be at the crypt to carry her to Mantua when she awakens.	**Escena 1** Juliet visita a Friar y encuentra allí a Paris haciendo planes para su casamiento. Cuando Paris se va, Friar piensa en un plan para salvar a Romeo y Juliet. Friar da a Juliet una droga para tomar la noche antes del casamiento. La droga la dormirá, sus padres pensarán que está muerta y la pondrán en la cripta. Le avisarán a Romeo y él estará en la cripta para llevar a Juliet a Mantua, cuando ella despierte.
Scene ii Juliet pretends to agree to marry Paris, apologizes to her father, and makes Capulet so happy that he moves the wedding up a day.	**Escena 2** Juliet finge aceptar casarse con Paris, pide disculpas a su padre y esto hace tan feliz a Capulet que adelanta la boda un día.
Scene iii Faced with marriage a day early, Juliet takes the drug a day earlier than planned despite her worries about possible mishaps.	**Escena 3** Frente al adelanto de la boda, Juliet toma la droga un día antes, pero se preocupa de que algo salga mal.
Scene iv The Capulets prepare for the wedding.	**Escena 4** Los Capulets se preparan para la boda.
Scene v Nurse finds Juliet, apparently dead. The wedding becomes a funeral.	**Escena 5** La nana halla a Juliet, aparentemente muerta. La boda se convierte en un funeral.

Recognize Dramatic Irony It is important to recognize that Shakespeare's audience knows more than the characters know about what is happening to them. This creates an effect called *dramatic irony*. With a partner, tell the effect on the audience of each of the following situations. The first has been done for you.

1. Juliet speaks with Paris in Friar Lawrence's cell and gives him the impression she intends to marry him.	The audience knows that Juliet does not intend to marry Paris and, therefore, they may feel some pity for Paris while retaining compassion for Juliet.
2. Juliet speaks with her father and mother giving them the impression that she intends to marry Paris.	
3. On Tuesday evening, Juliet tells her mother to "let the nurse this night sit up with you:/ For I am sure you have your hands full all in this so sudden business."	
4. Friar Lawrence consoles Juliet's parents, who believe that their daughter is dead.	

Name _____   Date _____

The Tragedy of Romeo and Juliet, Act V, by William Shakespeare

Summary
Scene i Romeo learns that Juliet is dead. Wanting only to be with her, he buys poison to commit suicide.
Scene ii The friar learns that his message never reached Romeo. Horrified, he sends another message and rushes to the crypt to be with Juliet when she wakes up.
Scene iii Paris comes to mourn; Romeo arrives soon after. They fight, and Paris is killed. Romeo lies next to Juliet, takes the poison, and dies. The friar arrives to find Paris and Romeo dead. Juliet wakes up. He tries to get her to go to a convent, but seeing Romeo dead, she no longer wants to live. Hearing a noise outside, the friar flees. Juliet kills herself with Romeo's dagger. The key characters gather, the whole story comes out, and in their grief, the rival families end their feud.

Resumen
Escena 1 Romeo se entera que Juliet está muerta. Queriendo unírsele, compra veneno para suicidarse.
Escena 2 Friar se entera que Romeo nunca recibió su mensaje. Horrorizado, le envía otro mensaje y va a la cripta para estar con Juliet cuando despierte.
Escena 3 Paris llega a lamentar la muerte de Juliet y Romeo llega poco después. Luchan y Paris es muerto. Romeo se tiende junto a Juliet, toma el veneno y muere. Friar llega y encuentra a Paris y Romeo muertos. Juliet se despierta. Friar trata de llevarla a un convento, pero al ver a Romeo muerto, Juliet ya no quiere vivir. Al escuchar un ruido, Friar huye y Juliet se mata con la daga de Romeo. Los personajes principales se reúnen, se enteran de todo, y, en su dolor, las dos familias terminan su rivalidad.

Recognize Metaphors The drama in Shakespeare is supported by the metaphors, or comparisons, in the language he uses. For example, when Juliet grabs Romeo's dagger, she says, "This is thy sheath; there rust, and let me die." When she stabs herself, her body becomes the sheath for the dagger. She wants the dagger to stay there until it rusts.

With a partner, explain what things are being compared in the following passages. Then find three more metaphors in Act V. Write them on the back of this page, and explain what things are being compared.

1. PARIS (at the graveyard) Sweet flower, with flowers thy bridal bed I strew. . . .

_____

_____

2. ROMEO (at the graveyard) Thou detestable maw, thou womb of death,/Gorged with the dearest morsel of the earth . . .

_____

_____

3. ROMEO (at the graveyard) Thus I enforce thy rotten jaws to open,/And in despite I'll cram thee with more food.

_____

_____

Name _____ Date _____

"I Wandered Lonely as a Cloud" by William Wordsworth

Summary In this poem, the speaker describes a time when, wandering alone, he suddenly came upon a field of yellow daffodils. The flowers, moving in the breeze, were under some trees near a lake. The speaker mentions how many flowers there were, how densely they grew, and how they formed a border around the bay. In the water, the small waves looked as if they were dancing, but the daffodils looked even more joyful; their delight made the speaker happy as well. At the time, he was not even aware of how much the sight affected him. Later, though, at times when he feels bored or thoughtful, he often finds himself picturing the scene again in his mind. Then the remembered vision of those golden daffodils raises his spirits, making him feel as happy as the flowers seem to be.

Resumen En este poema, el que habla, cuenta de una vez que caminaba sin rumbo cuando se encontró con un campo de lirios amarillos. Las flores estaban debajo de unos árboles y se movían en la brisa, cerca de un lago. El que habla dice que había muchas flores y que crecían muy juntas, bordeando la bahía. En el agua, pequeñas olas parecían danzar, pero los lirios se veían aún más felices, y esto hacía al que hablaba también feliz. En ese momento, él no se dio cuenta de cómo todo esto lo había afectado, pero más tarde, en momentos de aburrimiento o meditación, se encontraba volviendo a la imagen de los lirios. Esa visión le levantaba el espíritu y lo hacía tan feliz como las flores parecían serlo.

Infer Feelings In "I Wandered Lonely as a Cloud," the poet describes both what he sees and how he feels about what he sees. Sometimes his feelings are not stated directly. You have to infer his feelings from the tone and rhythms he uses to describe what he sees. In a double-column journal entry, record what the poet sees and how he feels. The first stanza has been modeled for you. Do the same with the other three stanzas of the poem.

Stanzas	Feelings
Stanza 1: I wandered lonely as a cloud That floats on high o'er vales and hills, When all at once I saw a crowd, A host, of golden daffodils; Beside the lake, beneath the trees, Fluttering and dancing in the breeze.	The poet feels as lonesome as a cloud floating high above the landscape. He finds company in a field of daffodils that are blowing in the breeze.
Stanza 2:	
Stanza 3:	
Stanza 4:	

"The Eagle" by Alfred, Lord Tennyson
"'Hope' is the thing with feathers—" by Emily Dickinson
"Dream Deferred" and "Dreams" by Langston Hughes

Summary These four poems use figurative language to express feelings, ideas, and experiences. In "The Eagle," the speaker describes an eagle high on an isolated mountaintop. The bird watches the waves move below and then suddenly drops towards the earth. "'Hope' is the thing with feathers—" describes hope as a feathered creature that lives within the human spirit. Even when life becomes difficult, hope keeps people's spirits up, and it does this anywhere and at no cost. In "Dream Deferred," the speaker wonders what happens to hopes and dreams that are postponed too long. He asks if they dry up, rot, change, lose energy, or explode. The poem "Dreams" expresses the idea that people must hold on to their dreams and goals. Otherwise, life is damaged; a life without dreams is an empty, cold existence.

Resumen Estos cuatro poemas usan un lenguaje figurativo para expresar sentimientos, ideas y experiencias. En *The Eagle,* se describe a un águila en la alto de una montaña. El ave observa las olas abajo y, súbitamente, se lanza hacia la tierra. "'Hope' is the thing with feathers—" describe a la esperanza como un ser emplumado que vive dentro del espíritu humano. Aun cuando la vida se vuelve difícil, la esperanza mantiene el espíritu de la gente, y lo hace en cualquier parte y sin ningún costo. *Dream Deferred,* se pregunta qué pasa con las esperanzas y los sueños pospuestos por mucho tiempo. Se pregunta si se secan, se pudren, cambian, pierden energía o estallan. *Dreams,* expresa la idea que la gente debe mantener sus sueños y anhelos. De otra manera, la vida se daña; una vida sin sueños es una existencia vacía y fría.

Recognize Unusual Comparisons These poems make some unusual comparisons in order to encourage the reader to see things in new and different ways. Look for these comparisons *as you read* the poems. Ask yourself what two things are being compared. Then decide why the poet thinks these two things are alike. Record your responses as shown below.

from "Dreams"
Hold fast to dreams/For if dreams die/Life is a broken-winged bird/
That cannot fly.

The two things being compared:	**How they are alike:**
life without dreams	Both are damaged.
a broken-winged bird	Both are in danger of dying.

Hold fast to dreams/For when dreams go/Life is a barren field/
Frozen with snow.

The two things being compared:	**How they are alike:**
_____	_____
_____	_____
_____	_____

Choose another poem from this section, and practice this strategy.

"Blackberry Eating" by Galway Kinnell
"Memory" by Margaret Walker
"Woman's Work" by Julia Alvarez
"Meciendo" by Gabriela Mistral
"Eulogy for a Hermit Crab" by Pattiann Rogers

Summary These poems use sensory language to share specific experiences. In "Blackberry Eating," the speaker decribes eating plump, cold, fall blackberries. His tongue plays with them just as it plays with certain words. "Memory" paints a picture of unhappy urban people; it uses vivid words to describe their appearance and feelings. In "Woman's Work," the speaker recalls disliking the housework that she did with her mother, who saw it as art. Still, she turned out like her mother, working at home, though now on paper. In "Meciendo," the speaker explains how natural elements cherish each other. She follows their example and cherishes her baby. The speaker in "Eulogy for a Hermit Crab" praises a dead hermit crab for its endurance, courage, and consistency despite all obstacles.

Resumen Estos poemas usan un lenguaje sensorial para compartir ciertas experiencias. En *Blackberry Eating*, alguien come moras jugosas y frías en otoño y su lengua juega con ellas al igual que juega con ciertas palabras. *Memory*, retrata a una pareja que no es feliz y describe su apariencia y sentimientos. En *Women's Work*, una mujer recuerda cuánto le desagradaban las tareas de la casa, y cómo su madre las veía como arte. Al fin, la mujer se vuelve como su madre, trabajando en la casa, pero sobre papel. En *Eulogy for a Hermit Crab*, una mujer elogia a un cangrejo ermitaño muerto por su perseverancia y valentía frente a todos los obstáculos. En *Meciendo*, una mujer explica cómo se cuidan entre sí las cosas en la naturaleza. Siguiendo su ejemplo, ella cuida de su bebé.

Identify Speaker's Attitude A speaker often has an attitude toward the subject of the poem. You can often describe that attitude quite simply in a word or two: *sympathetic, admiring,* or *critical.* The poet's choice of words will usually convey the attitude.

Look at the following underlined phrases. Some show admiration for the subject of the poem, a hermit crab. Others show sympathy—an understanding of the dangers that the crab faces. Decide which attitude each phrase shows. Then practice the strategy by identifying key phrases in another one of the poems.

Key Words and Phrases	Attitude the Words Reveal
You were consistently brave	respectful
On these surf-drenched rocks, in and out of their salty	sympathetic
Slough holes around which the entire expanse	admiring
Of the glinting grey sea and the single spotlight	
Of the sun were spinning and spinning and spinning	
In a tangle of blinding spume and spray	
And pistol-shot collisions your whole life long.	_____
You stayed. Even with the wet icy wind of the moon	_____
Circling your silver case night after night after night	_____
You were here.	_____

"Uphill" by Christina Rossetti
"Summer" by Walter Dean Myers
Ecclesiastes 3:1–8, The King James Bible
"The Bells" by Edgar Allan Poe

Summary These poems are all examples of lyric poetry, a type of musical poetry in which a single speaker expresses personal thoughts and feelings. The poem "Uphill" is a series of questions and answers about a long uphill journey, which will end at a resting place filled with others who have completed the same journey. "Summer" describes many of the things that the speaker likes about summer days, including the heat and the activities. The selection taken from the Bible points out that there is a proper time for every human event—birth, death, silence, speech, love, and hate. In "The Bells," the speaker identifies four kinds of bells (happy sleigh bells, joyful wedding bells, scary alarm bells, and mournful church bells), their sounds and their effects on listeners.

Resumen Éstos son ejemplos de poesía lírica en la que se expresan pensamientos y sentimientos íntimos. *Uphill* es una serie de preguntas y respuestas acerca de un largo y arduo viaje cuesta arriba, que terminará en un lugar para descansar lleno de gente que ha completado el mismo viaje. En *Summer,* alguien describe muchas de las cosas que le gustan de los días de verano, incluyendo el calor y las actividades. La selección es de la Biblia y señala que hay un momento oportuno para cada evento de los seres humanos: nacimiento, muerte, silencio, comunicación, amor y odio. *The Bells,* identifica a cuatro tipos de campanas (alegres campanillas de un trineo, felices campanas de una boda, campanas de alarma que asustan y dolidas campanas de un funeral), sus sonidos y cómo afectan a quienes las escuchan.

Identify Sensory Words Lyric poetry is about someone's personal thoughts and feelings. Often the poet will use sensory language to share his or her feelings. That language helps readers to see, hear, feel, taste, and smell what the poet expresses.

Some of the following sensory words in "Summer" have been identified and classified. Look for additional sensory words, and record them in the proper column. You do not have to write a word in each column. Then choose another poem and practice this strategy.

I like hot days, hot days
Sweat is what you got days
Bugs buzzin from cousin to cousin
Juices dripping
Running and ripping
Catch the one you love days

Birds peeping
Old men sleeping
Lazy days, daisies lay
Beaming and dreaming
of hot days, hot days,
Sweat is what you got days

Sight	Sound	Touch	Taste	Smell
sweat	buzzin	hot days sweat		

Name _____ Date _____

"The Raven" by Edgar Allan Poe
"The Seven Ages of Man" by William Shakespeare

Summary These poems are examples of narrative and dramatic poetry. In "The Raven," a speaker broods about his lost love, Lenore, late one night. He hears a noise at the door, and suddenly, in flies a raven. It speaks just one word: "Nevermore." The speaker asks the raven if he will ever feel better. The bird says only "Nevermore." Growing angry, the speaker tries to drive the raven away. But it stays, and so does the speaker's gloom. In Shakespeare's monologue taken from his play *As You Like It*, the speaker compares the world to a stage. People are just actors who play characters. Over time, the speaker says, a man plays many parts: a crying infant, a complaining schoolboy, a sighing lover, a quick-tempered soldier, a well-fed judge, a foolish aging man, and, finally, a feeble, childlike old man, without anything.

Resumen Éstos son ejemplos de poesía narrativa y dramática. En *The Raven*, un hombre medita de noche sobre Lenore, su amor perdido. Escucha un ruido a la puerta, y, súbitamente entra volando un cuervo que dice sólo una palabra: *Nevermore*. El hombre le pregunta al cuervo si alguna vez él se va a sentir mejor y sólo escucha *Nevermore*. El hombre se enoja y trata de ahuyentarlo pero el ave se queda, junto con la tristeza. En el monólogo tomado de *As You Like It*, de Shakespeare, se compara al mundo con un escenario. La gente son actores que representan papeles. Con el paso del tiempo, un hombre tiene muchos papeles: un bebé que llora, un alumno que se queja, un amante que suspira, un soldado de genio corto, un juez bien comido, un hombre tonto que envejece y, finalmente, un débil anciano, casi un niño, que no dice nada.

Summarize Poetic Narrative In "The Raven," Poe uses sentence patterns that may seem unusual to a modern reader, but the story is not difficult to follow if you think about it part by part. Poe also uses words that repeat certain sounds. In this way he creates the mood or feeling in this poem. Read and think about "The Raven" stanza by stanza, and summarize the story. Then read it again, listening for the words with sounds that seem to create a mood. Follow the example provided to apply this strategy with other stanzas. You may use the back of this paper.

Once upon a midnight dreary, while I pondered
      weak and weary,
Over many a quaint and curious volume of for-
      gotten lore—
While I nodded, nearly napping, suddenly there
      came a tapping,
As of some one gently rapping, rapping at my
      chamber door.
"'Tis some visitor," I muttered, "tapping at my
      chamber door—
         Only this and nothing more."

Summary: Late one night, as I sat thinking about some material I had been reading, I heard a knock on the door.
Words that create a mood: dreary, weary, napping, tapping, rapping
Mood: dark and eerie

"On the Grasshopper and the Cricket" by John Keats
Sonnet 30 by William Shakespeare
Three Haiku by Bashō and Chiyojo
"Hokku Poems" by Richard Wright

Summary These poems all follow strict forms. Two are sonnets and seven are haikus. In Shakespeare's sonnet, the speaker describes how past memories often make him sad as he relives certain experiences. However, if he thinks about his dear friend, his sorrows end. Keats's speaker points out that earth always has poetry. When birds stop singing in summer's heat, the grasshopper sings. In winter, the cricket sings, reminding him of summer's song. The haikus by Basho and Chiyojo create three sharp images: a perfect evening, a wandering dragon-fly catcher, and a wildly swaying tree. In Wright's poems, the speaker comments on a half-exposed snail, a laughing boy changing color in the snow, a peach tree blooming in a city, and a drenching rain that travels from town to town.

Resumen Estos dos sonetos y siete haikus siguen formas estrictas. El soneto de Shakespeare, describe cómo una persona se entristece al revivir ciertas experiencias. Sin embargo, al pensar en sus buenos amigos, sus penas desaparecen. El soneto de Keats, dice que la tierra siempre tiene poesía. Cuando los pájaros dejan de cantar en el calor del verano, canta la cigarra. En invierno, el canto del grillo nos recuerda a la canción del verano. Los haiku de Basho y Chiyojo crean tres nítidas imágenes: un atardecer perfecto, un cazador de libélulas y un árbol que se mece violentamente. En los poemas de Wright, los temas son un caracol casi al descubierto, un niño que ríe y cambia de color en la nieve, un duraznero en flor en la ciudad y una lluvia torrencial que va de pueblo en pueblo.

Restate Poetic Language Sometimes poets use poetic language in place of more familiar language. This is especially true of the poets in Shakespeare's time. Read Shakespeare's Sonnet 30 to identify and list examples of poetic language. Then write more familiar words for the words you list. Create a chart like the one below. A few phrases have been modeled for you. Apply this strategy to one other poem.

Sonnet 30

Poetic Words	Familiar Words
sessions of sweet silent thought	periods of quiet thought
the lack of many a thing I sought	not getting what I want
weep afresh	cry again
The sad account	the unhappy story

The *Odyssey*, Part 1, by Homer

Summary This epic tells the story of the Greek hero Odysseus, who is trying to return home after a long war. In Part 1, Odysseus tells of his many adventures: his visit to the land of the Lotus Eaters; how he blinded, tricked, and escaped from a one-eyed Cyclops; his journey to Hades, the land of the dead; how he escaped from the Sirens, who lure men to their death; and how he avoided destruction by Scylla and Charybdis. He told of his men eating the Sun God's cattle, which resulted in a storm that killed the rest of his crew.

Resumen Esta épica narra la historia de Odysseus, quien vuelve a casa luego de una larga guerra. En la Primera parte, Odysseus habla de sus muchas aventuras: su visita a la tierra de los Lotus Eaters, de cómo enceguece y escapa de un Cyclop, de su viaje a Hades, la tierra de los muertos, de cómo había hecho para no oír el canto de las sirenas y cómo había escapado de Scylla y Charybdis. También narra cuando sus hombres comieron el ganado del Sun God, lo que causó una tormenta que mató al resto de la tripulación.

Identify Story Elements The *Odyssey* is really a series of adventures. It is easier to read and understand if you approach each adventure as you would approach any story—by identifying the setting, the characters, the problem or conflict, the main events, and the conclusion or outcome.

Practice this strategy on the adventure of the Lotus-Eaters, using the following worksheet. Then choose another adventure from the *Odyssey* and identify the same features.

> Upon the tenth
> we came to the coastline of the Lotus-Eaters,
> who live upon that flower. We landed there
> to take on water. All ship's companies
> mustered alongside for the midday meal.
> Then I sent out two picked men and a runner
> to learn what race of men that land sustained.
> They fell in, soon enough, with Lotus-Eaters,
> who showed no will to do us harm, only
> offering the sweet Lotus to our friends—
> but those who ate this honeyed plant, the Lotus,
> never cared to report, nor to return:
> they longed to stay forever, browsing on
> that native bloom, forgetful of their homeland.
> I drove them, all three wailing, to the ships,
> tied them down under their rowing benches,
> and called the rest: "All hands aboard;
> come, clear the beach and no one taste
> the Lotus, or you lose your hope of home."
> Filing in to their places by the rowlocks
> my oarsmen dipped their long oars in the surf,
> and we moved out again on our seafaring.

Setting: land of the Lotus-Eaters _____

Characters: Odysseus, his men, the Lotus Eaters _____

Problem: Those who eat Lotus never want to return home. _____

Main Events: _____

Conclusion: _____

The *Odyssey*, Part 2, by Homer

Summary This epic tells the story of the Greek hero Odysseus, who is trying to return home after a long war. In Part 2, Odysseus returns home disguised as a beggar. His house is filled with men who are courting his wife, Penelope. She and his son, Telemachus, do not recognize him, but his old dog Argus does. Odysseus kills all the suitors, proves who he is, and is finally welcomed home by his wife.	**Resumen** Esta épica narra la historia de Odysseus, quien vuelve a casa luego de una larga guerra. En la Segunda parte, Odysseus llega a casa, disfrazado de mendigo. Su casa está llena de cortejantes de su mujer, Penelope. Ella y su hijo Telemacus, no reconocen a Odysseus, pero su viejo perro sí lo reconoce. Odysseus mata a todos los cortejantes, prueba quién es y finalmente es bienvenido por su esposa.

Paraphrase Conversations The *Odyssey* contains a number of conversations between characters. In order to follow the action of the story, you need to understand what is being said in these conversations. As you read, pause and paraphrase any conversation that may be confusing. See the example below. Use a chart like this one to paraphrase at least five other conversations.

Conversation	Paraphrase
[Odysseus] "I'll tell you now. Suppose Athena's arm is over us, and Zeus her father's, must I rack my brains for more? [Telemachus] "Those two are great defenders, no one doubts it, but throned in the serene clouds overhead; other affairs of men and gods they have to rule over."	If Athena and Zeus help us, isn't that enough? They are powerful but we cannot depend on their help. They may have other things to do.

Name _____ Date _____

"An Ancient Gesture" by Edna St. Vincent Millay
"Siren Song" by Margaret Atwood
"Prologue" and **"Epilogue"** from *The Odyssey* by Derek Walcott
"Ithaca" by Constantine Cavafy

Summary Each of these poems represents a modern interpretation of some part of the *Odyssey*. In "Siren Song," a siren seemingly asks to be set free from her tiresome role, but her flattery and plea for help is in fact the irresistible call that cannot be resisted. The speaker in "An Ancient Gesture" talks of wiping her teary eyes as she waits for a returning husband. She knows that Ulysses also shed tears, but his action was only a false gesture that he copied from his wife, whose tears were genuine. In Walcott's work, a blind blues singer sings of Odysseus, who battled both the sea and despair while his wife waited. He later returned to a happy home and a faithful wife. The speaker in "Ithaca" urges travelers not to fear dangers on a journey to Ithaca, but to enjoy the voyage. Experience gained, not the destination, is the real reward.

Resumen Éstas son reinterpretaciones actuales de partes de la *Odyssey*. En *Siren Song,* una sirena pide ser liberada de su papel, pero su pedido es en realidad su peligroso canto. En *Ancient Gestures,* una mujer habla de cómo secaba sus lágrimas mientras esperaba el regreso de su marido. Ella sabe que Ulysses hizo lo mismo, un gesto falso que él había copiado de su mujer, cuyas lágrimas sí eran genuinas. Walcott escribe de un cantor de *blues* ciego, que canta sobre Odysseus, quien combatió al mar y a la desesperanza, mientras su mujer lo esperaba. Él volvió más tarde a lo que todos realmente valoran: un hoga feliz y una mujer fiel. En *Ithaca,* se alienta a los viajeros no a temer los peligros de un viaje, sino a disfrutarlo. La experiencia ganada, no el destino, es el verdadero premio.

Recognize Allusions Many modern works of literature contain allusions, or references to classical literature like the *Odyssey*. An allusion is a casual or indirect reference. In order to understand the meanings of a piece of literature that contains allusions, you must be familiar with the subject of the allusion. As you read these poems, look for allusions to people or events in the *Odyssey*. Then briefly explain the allusion. An example has been provided.

Allusion	Explanation
Siren Song	The sirens were sea nymphs whose sweet song lured men to their death on the rocks that surrounded their island.